FOR DOCTORS ONLY

A Guide to Working Less & Building More

Fifth Edition

David B. Mandell, JD, MBA
Jason M. O'Dell, MS, CWM
Carole C. Foos, CPA

Guardian
Publishing LLC

2014

FOR DOCTORS ONLY: A GUIDE TO WORKING LESS AND BUILDING MORE, FIFTH EDITION

By David B. Mandell, JD, MBA, Jason M. O'Dell, MS, CWM, Carole C. Foos, CPA.

© 2007 Guardian Publishing, LLC Tel: (877) 656-4362

ISBN: 978-0-9912385-4-5

Manufactured in the United States of America.

To our physician clients—our partners in planning.

About the Authors

David B. Mandell, JD, MBA

David B. Mandell, JD, MBA is a principal of OJM Group. David is an author, former attorney, and renowned authority in the fields of risk management, asset protection and financial planning. David has co-authored the book *Wealth Protection: Build & Preserve Your Financial Fortress* and *Wealth Secrets of the Affluent: Keys to Fortune Building and Asset Protection*, both published by John Wiley & Sons, the oldest book publisher in the U.S. and the largest publisher of business books in the world. For physicians, Mr. Mandell has also written *Wealth Protection, MD, The Doctor's Wealth Protection Guide* and *Risk Management for the Practicing Physician*. His articles regularly appear in over thirty leading national medical publications, including *The American Medical News* and *Physician's Money Digest*, and he has been quoted extensively in *Medical Economics*. He has been interviewed as an expert in such national media as Bloomberg and FOX-TV.

David holds a bachelor's degree from Harvard University, from which he graduated with honors. His law degree is from the University of California Los Angeles' School of Law, where he was awarded the American Jurisprudence Award for achievement in legal ethics. While at UCLA, David also earned a Master's in Business Administration from the Anderson Graduate School of Management.

Jason M. O'Dell, MS, CWM

Jason O'Dell is a principal and managing partner of OJM Group with offices in Arizona, Florida, New York and Ohio. Jason is a co-author of the book *For Ohio Doctors: Shedding Light on Asset Protection, Tax and Estate Planning*, as well as three other state-specific versions in the For Doctors series. Jason has experience as an entrepreneur, financial consultant and investment advisor and has been working with clients for over 20 years.

Jason has conducted financial planning, asset protection and wealth management lectures nationally and has been recognized by Medical Economics as "One of the Best Financial Advisers to Physicians."

Jason graduated with a Bachelor of Arts degree in Economics from The Ohio State University and has earned a Master of Science degree with an emphasis in Financial Planning. Jason serves on the Board of Directors of the Alzheimer's Association of Greater Cincinnati and is a member of the Financial Planning Association, Cincinnati Estate Planning Council and the Advisory Board of Partners Financial.

Carole C. Foos, CPA

Carole Foos is a Certified Public Accountant (CPA) offering tax analysis and tax planning services to OJM clients. She is a contributing author of the book *For Ohio Doctors: Shedding Light on Asset Protection, Tax and Estate Planning.*

Carole has over 20 years of experience in public accounting in the field of taxation. She was formerly a manager in the tax department of a Big 4 firm and spent several years in public accounting at local firms in the Cincinnati metro area. She has been a tax consultant to both individuals and businesses providing compliance and planning services over the course of her career. In addition to her work for OJM, Carole also maintains a tax practice.

Carole graduated with a BSBA from Xavier University in Accounting.

Table of Contents

Lesson #10: Take the Prescribed Medicine 316

Appendices 322

Introduction

At the time this edition of *For Doctors Only* goes to press, the #1 issue on the minds of physicians throughout the country, including most of our clients, is the recently enacted healthcare reform legislation.

Doctors nationwide are concerned that this new law will significantly reduce reimbursement rates and cause increased stress on the healthcare system as a whole. As taxpayers, we are all alarmed by the increases in income, social security and even investment taxes that are either part of the new law or will likely become part of the budget that will need to pass to pay for all of these new changes and expenses.

While no book can solve the dilemmas created by this new path of healthcare "reform," For Doctors Only can help you 'fight back' financially in your own practice and financial life. There has never been a time in the history of the practice of medicine that required doctors to be as focused on the business and financial issues of their practice. These pages can be the start of such a focus for you.

Collectively, we authors have over 50 years of working with doctors throughout the country, and another 30 years of experience practicing medicine. We invite you to begin learning about how you can change your practice and personal finances - to be more efficient, protected, and savvy. We also invite you to contact us directly. Perhaps you can be another of the over 1,000 doctors we have helped over the past 17 years.

Until then, enjoy the reading!

Foreword by Scott Einiger, ESQ.

As risk management counsel to one of the largest malpractice carriers in the US for over 15 years and currently as general counsel to various medical societies, I have heard countless physicians express their fear of litigation and concern about rising verdicts in the malpractice arena. The potential for malpractice liability should be a concern for any licensed medical professionals interested in protecting their practice and personal assets. Doctors of all types are targeted for litigation because they are seen as deep pockets by litigants in actions involving malpractice claims, employment disputes and even motor vehicle accidents. Sometimes having MD plates on your automobile can backfire as it can act as a big neon sign flashing "sue me!"

Most doctors are aware of their professional liability and purchase malpractice insurance for protection. However, traditional malpractice insurance is not nearly enough. Cases brought against doctors each year can result in awards that are above coverage limits or the risks experienced are not being covered by insurance. These "hidden" risks can pose equally as devastating an impact to the financial, physical and mental well-being of physician business owners because they are much more likely to result in large out of pocket expenditures.

Doctors can expend substantial amounts to pay for defense costs related to matters where no insurance coverage has been obtained. Common areas where every practice owner has significant risk include: work related employment disputes, licensure investigations and insurance carrier refund demands, among others. Last year, in New York alone, there were approximately 6,000 licensure investigations brought against physicians—many of whom did not have adequate insurance to cover the cost of the investigation and defense costs. Cumulatively, employment litigations have skyrocketed in this country to the point where 150,000 such suits were filed in this country over the past six years.

In the event you are targeted and go through the full investigatory process, including a licensure hearing or employment investigation, you could literally spend hundreds of thousands of dollars privately funding the legal costs to defend against such charges when adequate insurance is not purchased. If you choose not to defend yourself, this charge could affect your professional license and ability to earn income in the future. What choice do you really have?

Most providers do not have insurance coverage to defend against claims made by commercial insurance carriers who seek refunds relating to coding disputes for medical services rendered. Refunds sought can go back six years in most states and can accrue into hundreds of thousands of dollars as carriers allege the same mistake was made over and over through extrapolation. In both of these areas, clients may expend a significant portion of their savings simply because they didn't anticipate such liability potential and purchase the requisite insurance.

The intent of this book is to raise the level of consciousness of the professional business owner who needs to be cognizant of the risks that can result in financial ruin—and to provide practical solutions to avoid financial setbacks so Doctors can achieve their goals of working less and building more wealth for them and their families to enjoy.

The team of experts that have contributed to the making of this book have cumulatively over a hundred years of focus in servicing the health care community and provide a multi-disciplinary approach to helping physicians accomplish their financial and business goals. As you review the chapters of this book you will gain practical insights and tried-and-true strategies that have been successfully implemented for physicians nationwide.

Before you get into the practical lessons of maximizing wealth, protecting assets from lawsuits and other financial disasters, reducing taxes, investing, and estate planning, there is a simple acronym to help you to help guide you through your PLAN™.

PLAN—P is for Proactive Planning

Being proactive and implementing a PLAN before trouble is on the horizon is the first step to implementing a successful strategy. In the case of asset protection, if you wait until a lawsuit arises to address your concerns, the civil courts have the power to unwind any planning as a fraudulent conveyance. In addition, if you try to rely on additional insurance once an event has taken place, the risk will be excluded as a pre-existing condition. In the cases of premature death or disability, you can't go back in time and secure the necessary insurances. In the cases of taxes, if you wait until April 14th, nearly all of your options will be unavailable. In the case of bad investments, you can't go back in time and undo what you did wrong. Reactive individuals who wait to attempt to implement a planning strategy when the issue has already arisen will likely be frustrated in their attempts. Being Proactive in your planning is the critical first step to proper implementation of an effective comprehensive financial planning strategy.

PLAN—L is for Loss or Liability

Protecting against Losses requires anticipating the most likely liability exposures that an individual or business may have. These can be exposures to lawsuits, taxes, lost income or divorce. The liability can involve business and personal assets. In assessing a person's liability loss potential one must give thought to both the personal as well as the business exposures. Evaluating the individual's totality of assets accrued in personal and business endeavors, as well as how those assets are currently being held is therefore critical. So the L in PLAN™ stands for Liability Loss potential. Once you know how you can lose assets, you are ready to review exactly what you have to lose and PLAN to prevent it from happening to you.

PLAN—A is for Asset Assessment

In your Proactive planning, you first look at all the ways you can lose assets. Then, you analyze all the assets that need to be protected from potential loss or liability. The complete list will include tangible personal assets like real estate, investment accounts, insurance policies and bank accounts. The list will also include tangible business assets like real estate, equipment and accounts receivable. Non-tangible assets include future income, business overhead expense protection, disability protection, among other assets. Once you know what risks you face and what assets you must protect, you are ready to work through *For Doctors Only* and meet with your advisory team to consider practical strategies to help you reach your own personal protection goals.

PLAN—N is for Nothing

If you don't have a plan for success, you should prepare to fail. Doctors typically spend a great deal of time working to make money and acquire assets and very little time planning how to get the most out of their hard work and how to protect these valuable assets. When most doctors finally start to address these important issues, it is usually too late. In order to effectively create a comprehensive financial plan that will help you protect your assets and build greater wealth, you need to be proactive in your attempt to gain a firm understanding of your liability potential and assess your particular assets. With this understanding and motivation to address these issues, you can create and implement a plan that will help you protect and build assets. Otherwise, you are likely to encounter a series of financial and legal losses that could result in your being left with Nothing.

Obviously, your business and personal wealth PLAN is fundamental to attaining your long term financial goals. I encourage you to read this book and to speak with the authors about putting your PLAN in place.

Scott Einiger, Esq.
New York, NY

Work "On" Your Practice, Not "In" Your Practice

In medicine, patients come to physicians when their bodies are unable to heal themselves. Patients who delay seeking medical treatment are missing out on the power of modern medicine and failing to take advantage of an opportunity to dramatically improve their health. Similarly, the financial and legal ailments impacting your medical practice cannot be healed without professional care. Simply working harder and hoping that your practice's problems will solve themselves is just as foolish as the patient who places hope on his body healing itself. In addition, you may not see any "problems" yourself, but you will not be working at maximum efficiency without consulting an expert.

In this Lesson, we will delve further into this concept. We will examine the concept of Leverage in an attempt to help you shift away from "just seeing more patients" as a cure-all for your practice and personal financial challenges. We will also discuss the demographics of the Average American, the demographics of the American Doctor, and compare the planning challenges and financial goals of both groups. We will also discuss how Doctors who look for information in magazines and websites can be dangerously misled. We will conclude with a discussion of how the information in this book is unique for Doctors and can be used to help Doctors meet their asset protection and wealth accumulation goals.

Be Different. Be Rich.
Be Worry-Free.

When you were in medical school, residency, and first starting practice, you relied on a number of mentors to "teach" you valuable lessons about medicine. Undoubtedly, this training was invaluable to your development as a physician. Despite the valuable training you received, you were left inadequately prepared to practice medicine as your profession. While you have learned the "medical" part quite well, do you think you were trained how to "practice?" In other words, did your education and residency prepare you to build a "practice" into an optimal business?

The successful practice of medicine in the 21st century requires so much more than clinical expertise and good bedside manner. The days of simply seeing patients and waiting for substantial income to be deposited into your bank account are long gone. Successfully practicing medicine now requires expertise in disciplines that were never even mentioned, let alone taught, in medical school, residency or even in a fellowship. How are Doctors supposed to learn how to protect themselves from billing and coding errors, employee lawsuits, health insurance fraud, HIPAA violations, Medicare fraud, and OSHA issues? Where will Doctors find the time to learn and understand asset protection, business structuring, estate planning, insurance management, investments, benefits structuring, and tax planning? How can you do all this while continuing to stay abreast of important clinical developments and still find time to see patients and earn a living? This is what Doctors MUST know how to do if they want to successfully practice medicine in the 21st century.

Replicating the actions of the physicians who trained you will not replicate their levels of financial success. The environment has changed dramatically. If you do what most Doctors do and focus only on the clinical issues of medicine, you will expose yourself to unnecessary lawsuits and taxes, and will continue to struggle as reimbursements stagnate or decrease while overhead constantly increases. Do you want to follow this path and be the next helpless victim or do you want to learn how to be different?

The only way to achieve financial success and peace of mind is to break away from the pack—to be different and do things differently than your predecessors. Perhaps this seems counterintuitive. While those who trained you no doubt provided priceless guidance in many areas of your practice, recognizing that today's practices demand new perspectives couldn't be a more valuable lesson. Let's look at a practical example.

How Medicine Has Changed

One of the book's authors, David Mandell, comes from a family of physicians. David's brother is a cardiologist. His father is a radiologist close to retirement age, and his grandfather was a general practitioner from the 1930s to the 1970s. The grandfather worked only for cash—except during the Great Depression, when he accepted food from patients who were unable to pay. He made house calls and knew all of his patients by name. Not once did he utter the words "managed care," "malpractice crisis," or "HCFA audit."

David's father, Charlie, spent nearly 30 years in a lucrative radiology practice. He saw reimbursements *increase* for many years and enjoyed an over-funded pension. He took advantage of numerous tax laws (since legislated away) during his career that swelled his after-tax income beyond what he had ever expected to earn when he began his career in the 1960s. The idea of "going bare" (having no medical malpractice insurance) never occurred to him. Premiums were always reasonable and personal liability was never a major concern.

As you well know, the "business of medicine" has changed dramatically through these three generations. The young cardiologist—David's brother Ken—began his career dealing with a medical malpractice crisis (in his state, many Doctors chose to go without medical malpractice coverage because of its outrageous costs), increased time demands for administration and paperwork, shrinking reimbursements, and increasing regulatory concerns. He thinks about terms like "practice buy-in," "malpractice premiums," and "debt repayment." He wonders if he'll ever reap the financial rewards his father did in medicine or if the landscape has just changed too much for him to ever be able to enjoy the fruits of his labor.

Where do you fit within these generations? Perhaps you are between the radiologist and the cardiologist and are in the prime of your career or you are in its second half. If so, the issues on your mind are likely retirement (not only when, but *if*), asset protection, tax reduction, and even partner buy-out. It is a lot to consider, by any measure.

Treat Your Practice Like A Business

Throughout this book, we will use the term "business of medicine." This is not by accident; rather, it is quite intentional. To use this book as the professionals that helped put it together intended, you must make a paradigmatic shift in your medical career. *You must come to view your practice as a business!*

While we mean no disrespect—medicine is truly a virtuous calling, and your primary motivation to become a physician was likely an altruistic one—the hard reality is that there are myriad business issues that affect your practice and personal finances every day of your career. Unfortunately, the vast majority of physicians are completely unprepared for these issues so they suffer from lower incomes, personal legal liability, shorter and less comfortable retirements, acrimonious practice splits, severe financial stress, bankruptcy and sometimes a premature exit from the practice of medicine.

It is no surprise that 99% of physicians do not properly handle the financial and business issues that affect their careers. Why? Because Doctors have had <u>absolutely no training</u> in these matters. The typical physician may receive over 10 years of clinical training by the time medical school, residency, and fellowship are completed. This is over 3,500 days. How many days of training have you received on topics such as asset protection, compensation arrangements, taxation, investing, and retirement planning? How many days on malpractice insurance options, partner buy-outs, or disability protection? What about employee training, contracts, and practice management?

With this complete lack of non-medical training, it is a wonder that any medical practice survives. Imagine how more economically efficient and less stressful the business of medicine could be if you had been properly trained in all of the above fields. How much better protected would your wealth be from lawsuits? How much more income would you bring home? How much smoother would your practice run? <u>Imagine</u>.

While we cannot attempt to change how the American medical establishment trains its physicians (although we have often been asked to speak to medical schools and residency programs), we can make the following urgent recommendation:

Make today the first day of your self-imposed training program by dedicating time to become educated about the non-medical issues that affect your business and personal financial situation.

As the subheading of this section states, you must treat your practice like a business, learning the operational and financial issues that are crucial to its success. Otherwise, you will never reach your financial goals. By devoting just a fraction of your time on these practice issues—perhaps one day per quarter or one afternoon per month—you will be working ON your practice. For as long as you toil only as the medical worker, you will suffer from the stress and reduced rewards that come to people who handle matters "half-way." Only when you step back and act like the CEO of your practice—and of your career—can you hope to achieve the financial and lifestyle goals that you certainly deserve and that the business of medicine *can* still afford you.

Envision Your Ideal Career In Medicine

When you chose to be a physician, you made a decision to rely on your medical practice to provide you with the things you value in life: control over your time, financial security, reduced stress, a good life for your family, among other things. Think back to before your medical practice, residency, and medical school to your college days. What was your vision of life as a successful physician? What was your vision when you were toiling in medical school or during all-night calls during residency or fellowship? Did you envision your eventual career as a pay-off for all the years of hard work, training and sacrifice?

Now, after considering what the ideal vision of your career looked like to you during different stages of your education and career, take a moment to examine your present practice and personal financial situation. How close are you to your ideal vision? Is there room for improvement? Is it as stress-free, lucrative, and secure as your ideal vision? If not, is it worth devoting a small fraction of your time to working toward this ideal? The answer to these questions for the majority of physicians with whom we speak is obvious.

In the generation of David's radiologist father, the medical business environment was so easy that physicians could almost totally ignore the business and financial issues described above and achieve their life goals rather easily. Even if Doctors made financial mistakes every day, it did not matter. Doctors simply rode the wave of the financial profitability with minimal regulation. It was truly the "golden age" of medicine for U.S. physicians.

Today's physicians, however, operate in a dramatically different environment. Like David's cardiologist brother, you do not have the luxury to make such financial mistakes. It is still possible to enjoy your own "golden age" of benefits, but to do so you must be as effective and efficient as possible. You must be both a skilled physician and an attentive businessperson or you will suffer the consequences of today's more challenging medical business environment.

Avoid the trap of inertia. Be confident enough to envision your ideal situation and use this book and the advisors who contributed to it to help you achieve your goals. You have worked hard *in medicine* to get to where you are today. Now, work *on (the business of) medicine* to take you where you want to go.

Be Practical, Not Political

Many physicians reading this book may get riled up enough to march on Washington and Sacramento and demand malpractice caps, tort reform, lower tax rates, and greater reimbursements. This emotionally charged effort may or may not have any impact on lawmakers' decisions. Whether any legislative changes will have a significant impact on your specific financial situation is uncertain. Though this is not our area or expertise, we do know that changing laws takes time and you need to change your financial situation today.

We are financial and legal advisors to physicians, not policymakers or politicians. In this book, we will not discuss how the laws regarding non-economic damages in malpractice cases should be limited. We will neither opine on the fiscal policies of the malpractice insurers nor comment on Medicare reform. We will not discuss tax policy or medical education. These elements, and any proposed changes to them, are beyond your control as an individual Doctor. While rallying with your fellow physicians as a political group may be effective over the long-term, we will let other voices (like those of your local medical associations) take up that cry.

Our focus here is to show you—in a real, practical way—what you as an individual can do to move your practice and medical career from point A (financially inefficient, high liability exposure, chaotic financial plan) to point B (efficient, asset-protected and organized for maximum financial success). This is the goal of this book, our e-newsletter and our website (www.ojmgroup.com).

The Diagnosis

Like any worthwhile endeavor, education is just the beginning of a process. For you, this means reading this book and digesting the general ideas before determining which of these strategies will make sense for your practice and personal situation. Reading this book is only the beginning—*education without action is fruitless.*

Like a patient who let the pills you prescribed sit in the medicine cabinet, a failure to implement the protocols outlined in this book will result in no improvement in your situation. For your planning, the next step after reading this book will be to discuss your situation with one of the authors to put the knowledge you have gained into action for you. This way, you can ensure that your practice and your life will be as close to your "ideal vision" as possible and that you can enjoy your own "golden age of medicine."

Work Smarter, Not Harder: Don't Just "See More Patients"

In the last chapter, you read how the business of medicine has changed. The implication for you is that you can't keep repeating the same actions time and again and expect to see the results you may have received just a few years ago. But even many of the Doctors who come to this realization still think that the solution is to "see more patients." In this chapter, we will briefly cover the flaws of this strategy and explain the ways in which Doctors can apply the concept of Leverage to address *all* of their financial and legal challenges.

"See More Patients"—A Tragic Flaw

Confronted with any legal, tax, or financial setback, many Doctors follow the business strategy of "seeing more patients." If the practice suffers because of a successful lawsuit, a sudden unforeseen expense, or an unproductive associate, Doctors try to "make up for it" by seeing more patients in hopes of billing more. The same tactic is followed by many Doctors who are behind in their retirement planning, who feel like they are paying too much in taxes, or who are getting divorced. Any financial setback seems to yield the same resulting behavior. Many physicians approach their entire career with the business strategy of working as long and as hard as possible for as long as they can physically endure it. Does this remind you of any of your peers? Do you see someone like this when you look into the mirror?

Certainly, there are many flaws to such a business strategy. Let's examine a few of these flaws so you can understand why other strategies are better:

1. This strategy has diminishing financial returns

Even if you work harder and see more patients, each patient you see will potentially net you fewer dollars. As your marginal expenses for each additional hour of work may be the same and your taxes may increase if you hit new marginal tax levels, your "take home" may actually become less per-dollar as you work harder. Even if this is not the case, the next two limits certainly apply.

2. This strategy has financial limits

Even if you worked as hard as you possibly could and you could make more on each additional dollar earned, you only have 24 hours per day. Regardless of your specialty or sleep requirements, you cannot work 18 or 20 hours per day over an extended period of time. Thus, you are capped in the total income that you can generate by "just seeing more patients." Chapter 1-4 develops this concept further.

3. This strategy will take a great personal toll on you

Extreme stress, physical ailments, divorce, decreased life expectancy—these are all common symptoms for Doctors who choose "seeing more patients" as their business mantra. Are these extreme personal costs worth it? We think not—especially given #4 below.

4. There is a "better way"

If working as hard as you could was the only alternative available to allow you to meet your financial goals, *that* would be one thing. However, the truth is that there is a much better concept upon which you can build your practice and personal finances. This concept will be explained below.

The Concept Of Leverage

Let's consider the following all-too-common scenario. You work a very long day and generate $10,000 of billings. The insurance companies pay your practice $3,000 for your hard work. Your practice overhead is about 50%, so $1,500 of that income is gross profit. However, the $1,500 isn't yours. Of the $1,500 you actually receive, the Federal, state, and local tax authorities will take 40% to 45%, leaving you with only $800 to $900. In other words, less than 10% of the work you do in a given day actually results in money you keep. This means that you have to do $3,000,000 worth of work in order to generate less than $300,000 of money for you to enjoy. Unless you want to continue to work ten times as hard as necessary, you have to learn to work smarter. This is the key to this entire book. We call it **Leverage**.

If you refer to the Merriam-Webster Dictionary and look up the word "Leverage," you will be presented with three definitions:

1. The action of a lever or the mechanical advantage gained by it

2. POWER, EFFECTIVENESS

3. The use of credit to enhance one's speculative capacity

We will offer very simplified interpretations of the three definitions of Leverage stated above. The first definition states that Leverage increases the amount of force exerted. To exemplify this concept, think of Leverage as the act of wedging a stick between two heavy rocks that you could not move with just your hands. In order to efficiently move the rocks, you need to push down on the stick that you wedged between the rocks. In doing so, the rock can be moved. Leverage—the wedging of a stick—allows you to move a rock you would otherwise not be able to move.

The second definition of Leverage simply states that the act of Leverage allows people to be more efficient, effective, and powerful. This can be interpreted to mean that Leverage allows people to get more done in less time. It can also be interpreted to mean that Leverage allows people to get a job done with less effort. In either case, Leverage enables people to be more effective.

The third definition of Leverage applies to credit and loans. In this definition, Leverage allows people to buy things they don't have the money to buy in an effort for them to increase their financial capacity. To illustrate this definition, think of a home loan—the $500,000 home that is purchased by a family with only $100,000 of their own money to use as a down payment. Leverage is the ability to enjoy the use of or participate in the upside potential of an investment you otherwise could not afford.

Quite simply, Leverage is a method by which you can do more with less. Less effort. Less money. Less time. If you are looking for a shortcut to financial success, Leverage is the closest thing to it.

The Importance Of Leverage

Successful physicians know that Leverage is an important tool to increase their wealth. Without Leverage, people would have to do everything themselves, including running their own business, earning money, handling financial affairs, paying for everything with only their own money, micromanaging everything at work and at home, and still finding time to eat and sleep.

If you feel like this is an accurate description of your life, then you are not using Leverage. Leverage makes your life easier. Leverage frees you to do the things that are most important, most profitable, or most enjoyable to you. Leverage is what allows you to achieve greater levels of financial success. No matter what your financial goals, mastering the art of Leverage and incorporating it into your planning will help you reach these goals faster. As we mentioned earlier, Leverage is how physicians can increase the power and effectiveness of their financial planning. You can do the same.

Leverage Limitations

A little Leverage is good. A lot of Leverage is better. Who wouldn't want to get more done with less effort or get more done with less money? Those who understand Leverage have tried to maximize its potential and use for thousands of years.

It may seem like the amount of Leverage one can attain is endless, but there are restrictions on how much Leverage you can achieve. This restriction can be referred to as Capacity. Consider the following:

- You can only exert so much force

- You only have 24 hours in a day

- You only make so much money

- You can only borrow so much money

- You can only manage so many people

The principal goal of Leverage is to maximize efficiency. Efficiency is achieved when Leverage is increased to a point when you have maximized your capacity without going over. When you exceed capacity, problems occur. This causes you to have to address the method of Leverage all over again and possibly repeat certain steps. It is obviously an inefficient process when you have to duplicate any effort. This is why you should be careful not to exceed your capacity and create other, often bigger problems. Examples of problems caused by increasing Leverage beyond your capacity include seeing so many patients that you are: 1) making billing and coding errors (Medicare fraud); 2) working too fast and making mistakes (medical malpractice cases); 3) hiring the wrong employees (employee lawsuits); and others.

You could theoretically increase capacity by working harder, but that is only acceptable if that is the most valuable and profitable use of your time and energy. Leverage is about working smarter, not harder. For this reason, increasing effort is not a viable method of increasing Leverage. The rest of this section will explain ways to increase Leverage and capacity so you can get even more out of your reduced effort. Getting better results from less effort isn't just the subtitle of the book; it is the only way to achieve greater levels of wealth.

The Diagnosis

Leverage makes life easier. Leverage allows you to get more done with less effort or with less money. Once successful investors achieve a measure of Leverage, they use their extra time and money to find better methods of Leverage. This is a never-ending quest to become more efficient and effective in everything they do, so that they can build and maintain their wealth and protect their assets.

The next four chapters will specifically discuss how Leverage applies to financial transactions, effort, employees, and advisors. Lesson #3—Accept Referrals to Specialists—is perhaps the most valuable way to increase the capacity of your Leverage. As such, *For Doctors Only* is filled with practical strategies that can only be enjoyed if you have a team of advisors to help you achieve greater Leverage.

Making Your Money Work for You

Now that you understand the basics of Leverage and its importance in allowing you to get things done more efficiently and effectively, this chapter will apply those concepts to financial and legal planning. Subsequent chapters will demonstrate how physicians can apply these lessons to Leverage assets and people to maximize and maintain wealth.

Financial Leverage: The Foundation Of Wealth

For thousands of years, every great construction project required the use of levers to complete the building process. This was true for moving the large stones to build the pyramids of Egypt and lifting the stones for Stonehenge. Levers were used to build all of the great castles, churches, synagogues, and mosques around the world. Financial projects are very similar to construction projects. They both can seem overwhelming at the beginning—a collection of complex tasks that must be executed with skill and precision. The success of both types of projects begins with significant and detailed planning. After the plans are drawn, they must be implemented accordingly. One person could never accomplish the implementation of such plans. Instead, the plan requires a team of people working together to accomplish the same goal—for us, that goal is building and maintaining wealth.

> **Without exception, every high income earner and wealthy family
> has relied on financial Leverage in one way or another.**

Once you grasp the concept of Leverage and the financial applications of Leverage, it becomes impossible to imagine how affluence could possibly be built without it.

Type Of Financial Leverage

Physicians can use different types of financial Leverage to create and build wealth. These include:

Leverage of Effort

Leverage of effort is a way to get more out of your financial plans and investments. Since the goal of Leverage is to get more done with less effort, all forms of Leverage require that you Leverage your individual effort by including the efforts of others.

Leverage of Assets

Leverage of assets is one way to increase your financial status and get more out of what you currently possess. If you had an unlimited amount of money or land, you wouldn't need to accumulate any more wealth; however, this is not the case for most people. Since we all have limited resources, we want to get the most wealth/asset accumulation and financial protection out of what we have with the least amount of effort and the lowest amount of risk.

Leverage of People

Savvy business owners know that they only have the capacity to do so much and that the Leverage of people is one way to get more than 24 hours out of a day. By leveraging other people's efforts, you can increase the number of tasks you can accomplish in a day. By leveraging people with special skills and expertise you don't possess, you can get things done in much less time than it would take you to do these same tasks—if you could accomplish them at all.

Generally speaking, physicians utilize Leverage to some degree, but they are not thorough in their application. They try to Leverage effort by working hard—we know that. Doctors also may try to Leverage assets in their practice through medical equipment for which they can bill and they may try to Leverage people through technologists, nurses, and physician's assistants, who can generate income to the practice. Still, few physicians apply this concept broadly enough in their practices to result in any real wealth building. Even fewer Doctors effectively Leverage people or assets with respect to their personal finances.

The Diagnosis

Within each of the three categories of Leverage discussed above—Leverage of effort, Leverage of assets, and Leverage of people—there are a number of different applications. In the following chapters, we will review each of these categories, discuss how they can be used to generate wealth and explain which of these types of Leverage are more appropriate for creating wealth and which types of Leverage will best help maintain higher levels of wealth.

How To Work Less

There is no doubt that hard work is a key to success. However, this character trait is not one we can teach. Some people become harder workers as they mature, but seldom does a zebra change its stripes. There are generally hard workers and not-so-hard workers. The goal of this section on Leverage is to help you get the most out of any level of effort. Whether you fancy yourself hard working or laid-back, Leverage can help you get more out of your desired amount of effort. In this chapter, we will discuss the capacity problems of Leverage, how education can increase your ability to Leverage your effort and then suggest ways physicians can overcome the barriers of capacity.

You Can Leverage Hard Work...
But Effort Is A Capacity Problem

The basic and inherent problem with effort is that you only have two hands and two feet, and there are only 24 hours in a day. If we consider the case of two landscapers (Lazy Larry and Manic Mike) with very different work ethics, we can illustrate these physical constraints we all have.

Let's assume that Lazy Larry and Manic Mike earn $50 per house per week. If Lazy Larry works five days per week and landscapes 8 houses per day, he will earn $2,000 per week before paying overhead, staff, equipment, taxes, etc. Manic Mike can work seven days per week and landscape 10 houses per day. This would give him precious little time off for family or personal time, but he would earn $3,500 per week before all of his expenses.

Both of these landscapers might consider themselves successful (depending on their goals and values). But if hard working Manic Mike wants to make more money, there aren't enough hours in the day or days in the week unless he does something that earns him more money per house or he finds a way to Leverage something other than his own effort. The next application of Leverage could help Mike do just that.

Leveraging Education

The idea of leveraging education to create wealth is no secret. In fact, it has become part of the American Dream. For over a century, immigrants have come to America and have taken advantage of the educational system. They have pushed their children to do well in school in hopes that they would get a good job and enjoy a higher standard of living. They have also pushed their children to find careers that pay them more money than a career like Manic Mike chose.

Leveraging education is a key element of building and protecting wealth. To prove this point, consider the following salaries of highly educated professions. When considering the earning potential of these professions, keep in mind that the median U.S. household income for the year 2007 was $48,201, which means that half of all United States households earned less than $48,201 per year. (US Census Bureau's 8/27/07 Current Population Survey (CPS)). According to a USA Today article on 1/18/06, the first year salary plus signing bonus for an MBA (2 years of graduate school) was $106,000.

According to MD Salaries (www.mdsalaries.blogspot.com), the first year salary of a neurosurgeon ranged between $350,000 and $417,000 in each of these cities: Houston, New York, Miami, Los Angeles and Seattle. Neurosurgery requires the completion of four years of medical school, a one-year internship, and a rigorous 5- to 7-year residency. Thus, there is no doubt that leveraging education can help you earn more money per year and increase your wealth faster than if you had a job with a lower level of education. Physicians use this type of Leverage quite well.

Education And Effort Are Not Enough

Would you be surprised to hear that the neurosurgeon mentioned above and Manic Mike have the same problem? While we are not saying that Mike is performing brain surgery, we *are* suggesting that they both have the same fundamental problem—albeit at a different level of income. Mike doesn't have enough hours in the day or days in the week to increase his business. Similarly, a neurosurgeon's income is limited by the number of surgeries he can perform as well as constrained by the number of hours in a day and days in a week. Even if you assume that there is an endless supply of patients who need brain surgery, and there is an endless supply of lawns to be mowed, the surgeon is limited just like Mike. In other words, a landscaper earning $50 per house has the same capacity problem as a neurosurgeon earning $500 per hour because:

1. They are limited in the amount of money they can earn until they figure out how to Leverage what they do

2. They only make money when they are actually working

This is a lesson that savvy business owners and investors figured out long ago. As a result, the most successful business owners:

- Always focus on the Leverage of any business.

- Never consider increasing effort as a legitimate, long term means to increasing income.

- Never enter into a business that requires them to constantly "work" to make money.

For these reasons, we prefer to focus our articles, seminars, books, and personal consulting recommendations on strategies that help **Leverage assets** and **Leverage people.**

The Diagnosis

All teenagers have parents, teachers and coaches who tell them to work harder. We prefer to tell you—and show you—how to work smarter without having to work harder (or having to clean your room or take out the trash). The Lesson applies to anyone—no matter how hard working or lazy you may be. If you want to work less and build more, you can do it. Applications of this "smarter working" lifestyle will be the focus of the next two chapters.

Getting the Most Out of Your Assets

You have undoubtedly heard the phrase, "It takes money to make money." No truer words have ever been spoken. It always takes some investment to generate a return. This chapter will explain how successful investors Leverage assets to create and sustain a high level of wealth. A partial list of assets that can be Leveraged includes:

1. Your own money

2. Other people's money (sometimes shortened to simply "OPM")

3. Intellectual property

Leveraging Your Own Money

Leveraging your own money is the oldest and most basic form of Leverage. It has been documented all the way back to the ancient times of kings and emperors. These wealthy empires had enough money to fund expeditions to discover new lands and acquire even more wealth. A visit to any of the museums of Rome or other ancient cities will bear witness to this Leverage.

Hundreds of years later, you can witness similar Leverage right here in America. Successful investors make their capital work for them in various ways. To illustrate this point, let's take a look at one of the nation's most flamboyant and public billionaires—Donald Trump. If you visit Trump's website, you will see that he has a significant portfolio of real estate which includes properties in New York, New Jersey, Honolulu, Los Angeles, Chicago, Florida, Las Vegas, the Dominican Republic, Seoul, Toronto, Panama, Mexico, and Connecticut. Additionally, he has future plans to develop properties in Soho, Atlanta, New Orleans, and Dubai.

Trump was able to expand his real estate portfolio because he Leveraged his assets. His earnings from real estate generated income for him to support his expansion into golf clubs in six cities, four casino resorts, various television programs and pageants, a university, merchandise, a travel company, restaurants, skating rinks, and other projects. Once Trump started making money from his new ventures, he was able to Leverage those assets into more projects. The profit from those additional projects gave him the capacity to start even more businesses.

You don't have to be a billionaire with a ridiculous haircut to use Leverage. If you have money, you can purchase land or real estate and lease it to others who can't afford to buy the property outright. If you have money you don't need to spend to support your lifestyle, you can invest in long term investments that have higher expected returns than shorter-term investments. These may be investments that otherwise are unavailable to investors who require a short-term return to pay bills. Lastly, when you have money, you can use it as collateral to borrow money and use other's people money to make money, too. This is what Trump and other sophisticated business owners do all the time to maximize wealth. This is the next application of Leverage.

Leveraging Other People's Money

Generally, using other people's money is considered to be the "classic" definition of Leverage. Recall from the first chapter in this section that this is the third definition of Leverage in the Miriam-Webster dictionary list. Using other people's money as Leverage certainly relates to credit, but we will broaden its definition to include all types of Leverage involving OPM.

The most common type of OPM is debt. Many wealthy people throughout history have achieved their wealth by borrowing at lower rates and reinvesting the loan proceeds at higher levels of investment return. Donald Trump's empire was built in a similar fashion—typical of most real estate investors. They put down a small percentage of the total costs to build properties and used OPM to fund the remainder of the costs. By borrowing money from the bank at rates that may be as low as 6% to 8%, and developing properties that may have an overall return of 15% per year, the Leverage gives the investor an amazing return on actual dollars invested. Consider the following:

Investor	Amount Invested	Rate	Amount Earned
Total	$10,000,000	15%	$1,150,000
Bank	$8,000,000	8%	$640,000
Trump	$2,000,000	25%	$510,000

Based on this these numbers, Trump can actually get a 25% return on his investment by using OPM Leverage to fund a project he anticipates will yield a 15% total return. This is a classic example of how Leverage works with real estate.

In other situations, like starting a business or making another speculative investment, people were able to take higher levels of risk because they didn't need the money to pay for living expenses. This allowed them to take chances and realize higher investment returns than less risky investments offered.

The other way to Leverage OPM is called equity—that is, taking someone else's money and giving them a piece of a business or investment in return. In this situation, the investor takes more risk, but also gets a higher expected return than the bank would get with debt. Though this kind of deal ultimately costs the investor a higher piece of their total return, it doesn't have monthly or annual payment requirements (like a loan does). This gives the wealthy more short-term freedom with regard to cash flow since no interest or principal payments are due each month. In fact, even if there is a profit, the wealthy may be able to effectively borrow the investor's share simply by not distributing it and reinvesting in the next project.

Equity is best suited for deals that are more speculative and cannot guarantee regular short-term income. Even well established, publicly traded companies (like AT&T, Disney, Oracle, etc.) do this on occasion. Many wealthy Americans have learned a lesson from these companies and have offered equity positions to investors to help fund the growth of their family wealth while offering participation in the upside.

Leveraging Intellectual Property

Since World War II, the most significant wealth accumulation has resulted from leveraging intellectual property. This intellectual property could be an idea, like McDonald's fast food assembly line concept, or a patent on a technology millions of people use, like Microsoft Windows. Other forms of intellectual property include copyrights like the Star Wars films or Harry Potter books. In each of these cases, an individual or a small group of partners comes up with an idea, proves it can work, legally protects the idea, and then attempts to Leverage it in ways where they can make money as a result of other people's efforts. Let's consider three examples.

Bill Gates and Microsoft created the Windows operating system. He (meaning his firm, Microsoft) didn't create a desktop computer or laptop to run his operating system. He just created a system that other people would run on their computers. Every computer that is built that runs Windows results in a license fee to Microsoft. Gates didn't have to drive the increase in the sale of computers. Rather, he found a way to profit from the efforts of all the other companies who were building and selling computers, and from the efforts of all of the software manufacturers who were designing products to make the use of a computer a more enjoyable—not to mention necessary—part of life.

Another example is George Lucas. Lucas created the Star Wars concept. He made a few movies that became classics. But the interest in the characters and story line didn't end with the movies. It expanded to action figures, lunch boxes, video games, and countless other items that were based on his concept. Lucas could have tried the "do it yourself" technique, but that would have only yielded a fraction of the financial profit the Leveraged approach did. Instead, he licensed his intellectual property to other people. Their efforts made Lucas hundreds of millions, if not billions, of dollars.

The last example is the McDonald's restaurant. One successful restaurant might have generated $100,000—$250,000 of annual profit. An international chain of restaurants whose focus is on fast, consistent food has served 3 billion customers and is worth billions of dollars. One of the authors of this book has actually had a private tour of one of the three facilities that process and package all of McDonald's food worldwide. It is truly an operation designed to create consistency and maximize Leverage.

In less extreme cases, every city has a restaurant, dry cleaner, or other business that isn't particularly profitable on an individual basis. However, the owner may be able to take the unique approach, branding, experience, or know-how and open additional locations to achieve a higher level of financial success.

The Diagnosis

All three categories of leveraging of assets—leveraging your own money, leveraging other people's money, leveraging intellectual property—can be very valuable. Certainly, many people have achieved significant levels of wealth by doing so. The important lesson is that you need to get the most out of your assets if you want to achieve a higher level of wealth and get the most out of your practice. Now that you know how sophisticated investors Leverage assets, you are ready to learn the most powerful Leverage technique—leveraging people!

Using Other People to Make You Money

While leveraging assets and capital are fundamental wealth-building techniques, these techniques cannot succeed without also leveraging people. At the end of the day, every deal, investment or transaction needs people to manage or oversee it. No matter how rich you are, you still only have 168 hours per week. To our knowledge, no one has figured out how to be in two or more places at one time. As a result, the single most powerful type of Leverage is the Leverage of people. By properly leveraging people, you can have multiple levers working at once. This is where greater wealth is created.

This chapter is going to explain why—and how—to get the most out of leveraging people. More specifically, we will focus on:

1. Leveraging employees

2. Leveraging advisors

Leveraging Employees

The most common method of leveraging people is by hiring employees. Those with financial means can afford to hire other people to do jobs for them. The employer has successfully Leveraged people if the collective group of employees helps the owner earn more money than the amount it costs the employer in salaries and benefits.

Simple Leverage: Pay Less Than Productivity

The more employees you have, the more potential Leverage opportunities you have. Sometimes you hire staff to support these employees. That is an investment that you hope increases the productivity of the other employees by more than the cost of the administrative help.

To Leverage your employees successfully and yield a profit, a simple rule is to pay people less than the value they provide your firm. Law firms have followed this lesson for years. For example, law firms may bill out attorneys to their clients at $200 per hour and require the attorneys to bill out 2,000 hours per year. Though the firm collects $400,000 for the services of the particular attorney, they may only spend $300,000 for that particular attorney's salary, benefits, and allocated overhead. The firm earns $100,000 per attorney. If they can afford to hire 10, 20 or 100 less-experienced attorneys and can find enough work to keep them busy, the senior partners of the firm can earn a very nice living—10 to 25 times that of Average Americans and 5 to 10 times that of a less experienced attorney. In doing so, law firms are leveraging their employees' productivity. They are training less expensive attorneys to do the work. This, in turn, enables the senior partners to focus on very profitable activities like landing contacts and building relationships for the firm.

Benefits To Leveraging Employees

In many circumstances, it may not be as easy to quantify the financial return on a Leveraged person as it was in the law firm example above. Often, there may be equally important qualitative benefits in addition to the quantitative ones. For example, consider these benefits:

1. By leveraging someone else, you are able to spend your time performing tasks that create greater profits.

This is a quantifiable benefit. Using the example above, by having associates do the work, the law firm partners can also do what they are best at—bringing in new business. This is likely a "highest and best use" of their time. What is your "highest and best use?" You already have someone to sign in patients, take vitals, file charts, do the scheduling, and other valuable tasks. Is it possible to pay someone to do any more of the less profitable tasks you currently perform? If so, you can take advantage of Leverage!

2. By leveraging an employee, you are able to spend your time doing things you WANT to do.

This is a qualitative benefit. If you could have employees perform more of your work, perhaps you could spend time doing something you prefer to do, such as playing golf or spending time with your family. This is not being lazy—it is using Leverage, not for increased profits, but for a better life. What is more important that that?

3. By leveraging experts, you are able to spend time on your own areas of expertise and save money.

As we will see in Lesson #3, leveraging advisors who have more expertise than you have in certain areas is fundamental to long-term success. While it is possible you could learn to become a CPA, money manager, or an attorney, learning these jobs would not be time well spent. This would take you away from things that are a good use of your time.

Leveraging people who have expertise is very economical. You can pay them less to help you in certain areas than what it would cost you (in time, money, and aggravation) to learn these fields yourself and then try and do the work yourself. Bill Gates didn't learn how to build computers and George Lucas didn't learn how to make action figures, yet they both benefited from someone else's expertise in those areas.

Now that you see how important it is to Leverage employees, let's learn the importance of leveraging advisors.

Leveraging Advisors

Leveraging advisors is one application of Leverage that the wealthy believe is integral to their success, yet many Doctors ignore or undervalue it. Look at any wealthy person's inner circle and you will almost always see key business and financial advisors who are involved in most of their decisions. The advisors' charge is to help develop a plan, analyze how every step fits (or doesn't fit) into their plan, and help them avoid numerous pitfalls that could arise from straying from the course.

Simply put, most successful business owners recognize that it makes more sense to hire advisors to help them handle their planning than it does to try to do it themselves. Doing it themselves is not only a bad idea because the client undoubtedly does not have the experience and expertise in all the areas needed in planning, but it also violates the principles of Leverage.

By "doing it themselves," Doctors would be spending their time sub-optimally, instead of in the desired highest and best use of their time. In other words, does it pay for a neurosurgeon to spend three hours of his time researching a disability policy when a disability expert could do it in one hour? Also, consider that those three hours could have been spent seeing patients and making more money than the disability expert will be paid. And do you think the Doctor would enjoy this research more than he would enjoy playing golf or relaxing on the beach? Probably not.

Finally, what is the likelihood that the Doctor will make the right analysis and decision on the policy? Is he an expert? Has he looked at hundreds or thousands of policies in the past? Why would you think he would do any better job performing this task than would the disability expert in performing a neurological exam?

Despite the obvious pitfalls of fighting the principles of Leverage, some Doctors make the mistake of foregoing advisors and attempting to "do it themselves." They are stuck in the mindset of saving a penny and losing a dollar.

This leads us to a very important statement that may seem crazy at first:

Doctors must realize that time is worth more than money.

Instead of looking for ways to save money by doing things themselves, Doctors must look for highly qualified people to handle as many tasks as possible so they can focus on the best possible use of their valuable time.

Since the right advisory team has expertise that physicians don't have, the right advisors can do the job in much less time than the physician or the wrong advisors could. Since a job done poorly will need to be repeated, doing it right the first time, even at a higher hourly rate, can actually save money in the long run. Additionally, when a Doctor can pay someone to do what they do best, this gives the physician more time to do what he does best—which undoubtedly is what will make the most money (seeing patients, running a practice, investing in real estate, etc.).

Complexity Demands Leveraging Advisors

We have found that, the greater the wealth of the individual or family, the more important the role of the advisor team. As the client's wealth increases, the more complex the comprehensive financial situation becomes. As the situation grows more complex, the client's need to Leverage the advisors' expertise and experience to save time and maximize total benefit increases exponentially.

To illustrate how complexity grows exponentially, let's consider the following two situations. The first chart below shows the relationship between two people. The second chart shows the six different relationships that exist when you have four people in a group.

Situation 1: Relationship Between Two People

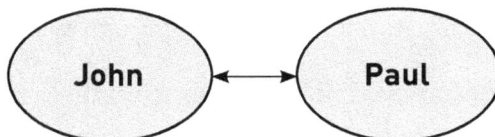

In the chart above, you can see that John and Paul have one relationship. There is only one relationship when you have two people. This seems relatively easy to manage as you have two people and only one relationship. Let us see what happens to the complexity of the interactions when we have four people in a group. This is illustrated in the next chart.

Situation 2: Relationship Between Four People

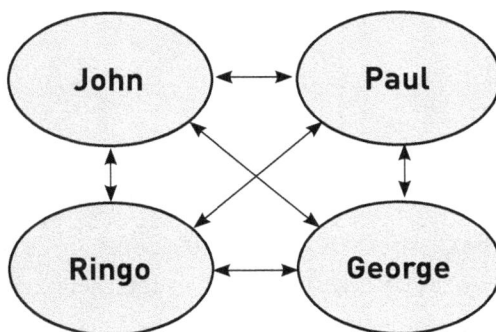

In the chart above, you will see John, Paul, George and Ringo. There are two additional people than we saw in the first chart. Doubling the number of people in the group actually increased the unique interactions by 500% from 1 interaction to 6 interactions (John and Paul, John and Ringo, John and George, Paul and Ringo, Paul and George, George and Ringo). Though it only takes one good relationship for two people to work together, it takes six good relationships for a group of four people to work well together. If one of the six relationships is strained, the entire group may have to be disbanded.

This same analogy can be applied to the elements of your financial plan. All elements of your plan, and all advisors in your plan, must work well together. That means that it is at least 500% more work to manage four businesses or elements of a comprehensive financial plan than it is to manage two businesses or elements of financial plan. If you have eight businesses or elements of a plan, then you have 56 different interactions to monitor. You can see how the complexity of the situation increases quickly!

To see how this general theory of complexity can be practically applied to planning for physicians, we need to understand what the physician's concerns are. Below is a partial list of common financial planning concerns among physicians:

- Managing growth of the assets

- Managing lawsuit risks from employees, patients, and competitors

- Protecting assets from eventual lawsuits

- Managing the investment risk while attempting to grow assets

- Managing tax liabilities to maximize after-tax growth

- Managing business succession and estate planning concerns

- Protecting family members against a premature death or disability

- Protecting family's inheritance against lawsuits, taxes, and divorce

Surprisingly, physicians worry about all of the aforementioned items while continuing to do *everything* they did to help them reach their current level of success. If you think this is impossible, you are correct. It is impossible to do all of these things as a "one man show." Leveraging advisors is essential—it is a fundamental precursor of long-term success.

The Diagnosis

This section explained why Leverage is such an important key to working less and building more. You learned how successful people—whether they are physicians with "medical businesses" or other business owners or investors—Leverage their own assets, other people's money and people. You learned that the biggest limitation to Leverage is one's capacity. This can be limited time or limited money. In either case, the best way to increase your capacity is to build a team of experts to help you efficiently maximize Leverage and increase your capacity for Leverage. This is the focus of Lesson #3—Accept Referrals to Specialists, which could also be titled Building the Right Team of Advisors.

Don't Try to "Fit In" with the Crowd

When it comes to financial and legal planning, the idea that everyone is created equally couldn't be further from the truth. As a Doctor, you are very different. You went to college, then medical school, then residency, then possibly a fellowship. You have much more education and training than the Average American. Though a society needs people to play various roles, you deal with issues of life and death. As a result of your educational and functional differences, you are in a different situation and have very different concerns.

You have a more complicated and demanding profession. You earn more money. You pay more taxes. You have more liability. As a result, you need different advice. Better advice. More appropriate advice.

Before you can understand what advice is right for you, you need to know what advice is wrong for you. To know why most advice is wrong for Doctors, you need to understand the quantifiable and qualitative differences between physicians and Average Americans. Then, you need to understand how the popular media works and how that information can be very detrimental to a Doctor's planning. These are the issues that are discussed in this Lesson. Once you understand and embrace your differences, you will be ready to take advantage of the practical lessons offered in *For Doctors Only*.

Understanding the Average American

Before you can understand the unique challenge facing Doctors and what the more successful ones do to achieve and maintain their wealth, you must first understand the demographics of the Average American. This is crucial because, in order to learn how to act differently in your wealth planning decision-making, you have to compare your financial circumstances to the circumstances of the "norm." It is only through these comparisons that you can truly appreciate the different wealth challenges you have and how you can effectively deal with these challenges.

In this chapter, we will examine the Average American in terms of income level, federal income taxes paid, source of income, retirement needs, asset protection concerns and estate planning challenges.

Important Note: Throughout this book, we will refer to the term "Average Americans." We recognize that, to some, this term may at first seem demeaning or condescending, or imply some sort of value judgment. We do not intend it that way. It is simply a demographic term to describe a particular group defined by income, tax rate and financial circumstances.

Average American Income

The first, and perhaps most important, defining characteristic of the Average American is his or her income level. According to recent US Census Bureau's August 28, 2007 Current Population Survey (CPS), the Average American household earns $48,201. Additional Census data shows that, as of 2005:

20% of American households* earned less than $25,616;

40% of American households* earned less than $45,021;

60% of American households* earned less than $68,304;

80% of American households* earned less than $103,100.

Households may include more than one or two earners.

Another way the Census Bureau analyzes income numbers for households in America is to break down the population into fifths and look at the average income within each grouping (or "quintile"). Consider the following:

Segment of the Population	Average Annual Income
The lowest earning fifth (1/5) of population	$14,767
The second fifth of the population	$35,137
The third fifth of the population	$56,227
The fourth fifth of the population	$84,095
The highest earning fifth of the population	$176,292

If you consider that physician families typically earn well in excess of $250,000 of annual income, then you can see that Doctors earn more than a considerable majority of Americans (who earn less than $176,292). It is likely that many physicians earn more than 95% to 99% of American households.

The significance of the income analysis is fairly simple. Average Americans, as a rule, are earning just enough to pay the bills on a periodic basis, if at all. In many areas of the country, where expenses are relatively high, there may not even be enough income to cover the bills. Long-term uses of funds, such as retirement accounts, insurance and college savings accounts are often luxuries they cannot enjoy.

Federal Income Tax Rates

As you will learn later in the book, Doctors should consider taxes in nearly everything they do because their tax rates can be very high. Contrast that to the situation of Average Americans here.

If you combine the demographics above with the 2007 federal tax rate schedule below for married couples filing jointly, you can make some interesting conclusions.

2007 Federal Income Tax Table—Married Couples Filing Jointly

If taxable income is over:	But not over:	The tax is:
$0	$15,650	10% of the amount over $0
$15,650	$63,700	$1,565 plus 15% of the amount over $15,650
$63,700	$128,500	$8,773 plus 25% of the amount over $63,700
$128,500	$195,850	$24,973 plus 28% of the amount over $128,500
$195,850	$349,700	$43,831 plus 33% of the amount over $195,850
$349,700	no limit	$94,601 plus 35% of the amount over $349,700

After examining this table, you can conclude that about 20% of the population will pay less than 10% of their income to the government in federal income taxes (since the average income for the lowest fifth of the population is less than $15,650).

Further, almost 40% more of the population will pay 10%-15% of their income in federal income taxes. Another 20% of the population will pay less than 18% of their income (average income for the fourth quintile of the population is about $103,000). Only about 5% of the population will earn enough to be subject to the highest marginal federal income tax bracket of 35%.

In other words, Average Americans pay relatively few dollars in income taxes as a percentage of their income. Due to the lower tax rates and the sources of income described below, income tax planning is not a significant concern for the Average American.

Average American Source Of Income

The Average American is almost always an employee who works for someone else. He gets paid as a W-2 employee and may or may not have a modest benefits package. As a taxable employee, taxes are typically withheld from the paycheck each payday and the after tax proceeds are then distributed. Many call this the take home amount. While this eliminates the headaches of calculating and preparing complex quarterly estimated tax payments and saving for these large payments, it also means there is little opportunity for significant tax planning.

The Average American rarely owns his own business. This means that the Average American does not have to manage the complications of a growing or complicated business that may have multiple locations, many employees, and regulatory reporting requirements. This also means that the Average American's income will be determined by someone else. The owner of the company or the management team determines when and if there will be any raises or promotions for the employees. Employees can work hard, but the financial rewards from such efforts are at the discretion of someone else. Because the cost of living increases every year, modest raises may provide relatively modest increased spending and saving potential over a lifetime.

Millions of Americans have made the decision to buy or build a small business. There are countless motivations that drive someone to leave the world of the employed and start or run a business. There are pros and cons of being a W-2 employee instead of running your own business. Let's consider some of the pros and cons of being an employee:

Pros	Cons
Simplified tax reporting	Little opportunity for tax planning
Fixed or predictable income	Little opportunity for significant increases in income
Benefits managed by employer	No control over benefits offered
Job stability	Job stability controlled by employer
Employer Leverages your work	No direct benefit from Leverage
Little lawsuit risk as compared to the employer	
No business succession risk	

There is no doubt that running a business is hard work. The business owner has a lot of responsibility. Owning a business is certainly not for everyone. In fact, most small businesses fail. The point we are trying to make is that there is a trade-off for letting someone else handle all of the responsibility and headaches of running a business. The employees have little say in the planning for the business. This is neither good nor bad. It is just the nature of the situation. This is one of the ways that Average Americans who are employees differ from business owners.

Average American Retirement Planning

For almost a century, a major goal of employment for Average Americans has been to work hard and save enough money to retire. Most Americans would rather be doing something other than working and many look forward to the financial freedom of retirement.

In terms of retirement planning, most Average Americans invest in some type of retirement plan offered through their place of employment, typically a 401(k) plan. Most Average Americans also have a checking and savings account and possibly an IRA or small investment account. However, they do not have substantial or sufficient savings in such accounts. This is the result of a combination of factors, such as:

- People are living longer and have greater financial needs in retirement.

- Employers are focused on quarterly earnings and are forced to cut back on employee benefits, including retirement funding.

- Reduced fringe benefits from employers cause increased spending by the employees' families.

- Average Americans are spending more on consumer purchases than on retirement plans simply because their income doesn't afford them the opportunity to do both.

When companies give less to their employees and employees have to spend more just to pay the bills, the employees simply do not have the discretionary funds after bills are paid to save enough for their desired level of retirement and consequently do not put enough money in these plans. Perhaps, many Americans are relying on Social Security to provide a large portion of their retirement income. You need only read a week's worth of articles in the newspapers listed later in this chapter to get a clear understanding that relying on Social Security is not a wise planning decision. Therefore, most Average Americans do not have many retirement alternatives.

Average American Asset Protection

Next to estate tax planning, this is the area of financial planning where the needs and concerns between Average Americans and Affluent Americans (which Doctors obviously are) differ most. Asset protection—the practice of shielding wealth from potential lawsuits, creditors or other claims—is plainly not of interest to Average Americans for two reasons:

1. They do not have significant assets to protect.

2. They do not face significant liability through their work or investments.

Later in this Lesson, you will see that Doctor's asset protection situations are polar opposites of those of Average Americans. As a result, asset protection becomes a critical factor in planning for Doctors. In fact, this issue is so important that the authors have written four other books on this topic and have dedicated an entire section of this book to it.

Average American Estate Tax Planning

Under current estate tax law (which is set to expire at the end of 2012), only the portion of an individual's estate that totals more than $5 million will be subject to federal estate taxes (i.e. there is a $5 million exemption from estate taxes). This exemption doubles to $10 million for a married couple's estate. The portions of estates that exceed the exemptions are taxed at a 35% tax rate. As mentioned before, estate planning is an area of planning that will more than likely have little impact on the Average American. With pretax income below $150,000 per year, it is unlikely that Average American families will be able to pay their living expenses, raise children, pay educational costs for children, secure retirement, handle unforeseen financial burdens that present themselves from time to time and still have more than $5 million left at the time of their death.

While current estate tax legislation has increased exemptions to levels that will probably not impact the Average American, it is clear to see that there is a very real possibility of such taxes impacting Affluent Americans and such impact may result in the government taking 35% of some portion of your assets at death. Therefore, with current legislation set to expire before 2013, it is important to plan now while favorable exemptions and rates are still on the books.

With pretax income below $150,000 per year, it is unlikely that even Average American families will be able to pay their living expenses, raise children, pay educational costs for children, secure a retirement, handle the unforeseen financial burdens we all encounter during our lifetimes, and *still* have over two million dollars left at the time of death to leave to children as an inheritance. As a result, estate tax planning (focused on reducing estate tax liabilities) is not likely to be a major concern of the Average American family.

The Diagnosis

Average Americans do not have as many opportunities to enhance their financial situation as Doctors do. Average Americans spend most of their income on taxes (albeit at a low rate) and on their living expenses. As an employee, they have neither the opportunity to use many tax saving vehicles nor the flexibility to create their own benefits programs. The Average American family has precious few retirement assets and minimal risk of losing assets to judgment creditors. Upon death, almost all American families can easily pass their family assets to children with little or no estate tax. Average Americans spend the majority of their time trying to manage their financial affairs for the week, month, or year. Few have the time or luxury of preparing for long term needs. Because their needs are so different from those of Doctors and because physicians make up such a small percentage of the population, the popular press has focused on delivering information that applies to the Average American. The illustration of this point and the implication this has on physicians is offered in the next chapter.

The Popular Press Hurts Doctors

Most people believe that there is more financial information available on television, in newspapers and magazines, and on websites than one person could possibly review in a lifetime. They may be right!

Our Google search for "Financial Advice" on August 11, 2007 yielded 112 million results. A search for "investing" yielded 104 million results. We then narrowed our search for sites that had all of the following tags: "investing," "high income," and "financial planning." This narrowed the results down to 133,000.

Obviously, we agree with the sentiment that there are an almost infinite number of places one can look for financial advice. However, who is this advice for? Consider this statement:

> Most financial information available in newspapers or magazines, on television, or within websites is inappropriate and often detrimental to a Doctor's planning.

How can there be so many places to find financial information and so few reliable sources for Doctors? To answer this question, let's start by looking at a list of television stations, newspapers, magazines, and websites. Which of these outlets would you consider to be for Doctors and which would you consider to be directed at Average Americans?

Television: Fox News, MSNBC
Newspapers: *New York Times, USA Today, Wall Street Journal*
Websites: FoxNews.com, CNN.com, CNNMoney.com, USAToday.com, WSJ.com (*Wall St. Journal*), Forbes.com
Magazines: *Smart Money, Money, Business Week, Fortune, Fortune Small Business*

If you are like all of the colleagues and clients we asked informally, you would say that almost all of the aforementioned media would deliver information which would target wealthier Americans, such as Doctors.

To actually compare these media against each other, we went to each of their media kits and compiled a table for you to view. We cannot verify any of the data, but can verify that all of this information was taken from each firm's online media kit as of August 2007. We use the abbreviation HHI to represent household income.

Media	Type	Income Demographic
Fox News	television	$70,929 median HHI
MSNBC	television	$75,588 median HHI (adults 25-54)
New York Times	newspaper	$67,137 median HHI
USA Today	newspaper	$76,929 median HHI, 34% HHI >$70k
The Wall Street Journal	newspaper	$253,100 avg. HHI, $2.5 MM net worth
FoxNews.com	website	$73,000 median HHI
CNN.com	website	$76,419 median HHI
CNNMoney.com	website	$83,431 median HHI, 37% HHI >$100k
USAToday.com	website	$89,263 median HHI, 42% HHI >$70k
The Wall Street Journal*	website	$111,250 mean HHI, mean investor assets $276,373
Forbes.com*	website	$146,263 mean HHI, 17.8% HHI >$150k
Smart Money	magazine	$81,742 median HHI
Money	magazine	$85,336 median HHI
Business Week	magazine	$93,811 median HHI, 18% HHI >$150k
Fortune Small Biz	magazine	$119,986 median HHI
Fortune	magazine	$137,000 median HHI

*By using a mean and not a median to represent that "Average" media consumer, the numbers can be skewed as a result of readers with very high incomes. The mean is a simple average. The median is the HHI associated with the middle person (after all respondents' data are ranked in order). As an example, if three people with HHIs of $50,000, $80,000 and $320,000, the mean HHI would be $150,000 but the median HHI would be $80,000. When analyzing HHI and net worth numbers, you will find that the mean is almost always much higher than the median. In the case of Forbes.com, for example, only 17.8% of visitors have HHI over $150k yet the mean is $146,263. This means that the total combined household income of the 17.8% of its visitors is approximately equal to the total HHI of the other 82.2% of its readers. We are not saying that the average reader doesn't earn $146k, but we are pointing out that fewer than 1 in 5 of the visitors to the site actually earn $150,000. The savvy advertisers understand what this data really means and the content must be focused at the majority of its visitors.

While you might be surprised to see how the media outlets above focused almost exclusively on non-affluent audiences, take a moment to review the popular outlets below. These have an even less-affluent audience.

Media	Type	Income Demographic
ESPN (NFL games)	television	$62,200 median HHI
Los Angeles Times	newspaper	$55,698 median HHI
ESPN.com	website	$77,000 average HHI
Oprah.com	website	$80,000 median HHI
ESPN	magazine	$62,132 median HHI
People	magazine	$63,599 median HHI
Sports Illustrated	magazine	$63,643 median HHI
GQ	magazine	$67,141 median HHI
Newsweek	magazine	$70,995 median HHI

The important point we are trying to illustrate with this data is that almost all of the high-end magazines and websites in the first list have an average audience household income of less than $100,000. Every single one mentioned on that list, except *The Wall Street Journal (TWSJ)*, has an audience with an average household income of less than $150,000.

For the purpose of our next statement, we would like to exclude *TWSJ*. Though *TWSJ* focuses on business and financial markets, its primary goal is to report the news. It does not take a position of encouraging or promoting any particular products, strategies or financial philosophies. Given this caveat, our conclusion from the aforementioned data is:

> Even the highest level media outlets in the United States are not targeting and delivering appropriate content to an audience with an average income above $150,000.

Why is this information important to our discussion of financial planning for Doctors? Let us explain what we learned from the publishing of our last book, *Wealth Protection: Build & Preserve Your Financial Fortress* for John Wiley & Sons.

The Media Business: "Get The Eyeballs"

If you are in the media business, it doesn't matter if you are publishing magazines or websites, or producing television or radio programs. The goal is always the same if there is advertising involved—provide content that will attract a large enough audience to generate ad revenue. You generate ad revenue by proving that you can deliver a significant audience and that you can accurately track the demographics of the audience. All of the sites, magazines and newspapers mentioned earlier are in business to make money. If they don't generate content that maintains an audience large enough to support the necessary ad revenue, the company will go out of business. They must "get the eyeballs." Their business model is really that simple.

To attract a large audience, these outlets have to deliver content that appeals to a large audience. After writing our last book for John Wiley, we appeared on over 120 radio and television programs. Though the book *Wealth Protection* had interesting philosophical lessons and over 62 practical lessons on advanced financial, legal, and tax-saving techniques, almost every producer and interviewer wanted us to discuss topics in the book we thought were the most basic. What we were told by one host was that his goal was to keep as many people as possible interested in the interview. He didn't care if the information was fresh and exciting. He wanted to make sure that "Joe Lunch-Bucket" (his words) wouldn't be put off by the topic. He told us that talking about ways to save $100,000 in taxes or ways to efficiently buy rental properties would alienate most listeners—which, in turn, would cause the show to lose "eyeballs" (or "ears," as is the case in radio). He was not going to allow that to happen.

Until John Wiley asked us to write a book about Affluent Americans (*Wealth Secrets of the Affluent*—publishing date April, 2008), we had received very little interest from the popular press in regard to the education we have regularly offered to high-income clients for the last twelve years.

Consider the following:

- Every information/publishing company is in business to make money.

- The money almost always comes from advertisers.

- Advertisers pay more if the audience is larger.

- A publisher must continuously offer appropriate content to the masses to maintain and grow an audience and attract advertisers.

- Even the high-end distribution channels don't target consumers earning over $100,000.

If you consider these five statements you can clearly conclude that:

It is almost IMPOSSIBLE for Doctors to find useful and appropriate
financial information from popular newspapers, magazines,
websites, or television programs.

This is why most of the information contained in this book may seem foreign to many readers. The tips, tools, and strategies offered here are not the kinds of things that most information outlets would ever deliver because, quite frankly, there is no business reason for doing so. Fewer than 10% of Americans would find much of the information in this book applicable or beneficial. If it is important to "fit in" and do what everyone else does - even if it is not the best course of action - this book is not for you.

Smart Doctors
Don't Want to "Fit In"

We hope that you now understand that there are significant differences between Doctors and Average Americans—at least in terms of basic demographic data. This book will hopefully teach you how you should act when faced with financial and legal issues. These very different attitudes and methods of approaching wealth planning are integral to your success.

We also hope that you have gained some insight into why nearly every newspaper, financial website and financial magazine is forced to focus its content on a group of subscribers or readers that have a very different set of concerns than Doctors. These media outlets need to provide "common sense" advice to the general public (i.e. Average Americans) to fit their business model of attracting the most eyeballs. There are simply far more Average American "eyeballs" than there are wealthy, or more specifically Doctor, "eyeballs."

It stands to reason that, if financial "common sense" has been developed for (and should generally be used by) Average Americans, then this common sense will not apply to physicians. In fact, the only way Doctors can achieve desired levels of wealth and have peace of mind is to follow advice that doesn't make "common sense."

Going against "common sense" is not easy. There are many deeply rooted psychological factors that push someone to go with the crowd, rather than against it. This is certainly true in the financial planning context. As an example, consider this proposition:

> It is a bad financial idea for a Doctor to pay off
> a mortgage and own a home outright.

For many of you reading this now, this may be difficult, if not impossible, to believe. It is exactly the opposite of what your parents told you (and they are the smart people who taught you so many life lessons). It is the polar opposite of what Suze Orman and hundreds of websites, magazine articles, and television programs suggest. Further, it just may not "feel" right, because it goes against what all of your friends are doing. Keep those feelings and thoughts in mind when you read the other Lessons in the book.

Why Ignoring "Common Sense" Is So Difficult

Most children and adolescents try desperately to "fit in." As we get older, we try to find the right groups in college. In our first jobs, we want to toe the company line. All states have laws that govern our behavior. Most religions have commandments, rules, or other codices of condoned and forbidden activities.

Most people avoid actions they fear their friends and relatives would criticize—or at the very least, they refrain from sharing details of their potentially critical activities with their family and friends. We are not implying that Americans are sheep. Rather, we are saying that society typically rewards those who are similar and creates more challenges for those who are not.

This is not a particularly astute observation. It is merely support for the significance of the #1 challenge that must be overcome if you are to truly work less and build more. To do so, you not only have to admit to being different from Average Americans, but you also have to EMBRACE the fact that you are different.

Embrace Affluence And Your Differences: A Key Lesson

If you want to successfully achieve or maintain wealth, you must be comfortable with your unique circumstances and be comfortable doing things differently than your friends. If your only comfort comes from doing something and knowing that "everyone else is doing it," then you are destined to achieve and maintain mediocrity. Wealthy Americans became affluent by being different or by doing something different. If they did what everyone else did, they would be like 80% of Americans who earn less than $80,000 per year and they wouldn't have achieved the wealth they now have.

Savvy physicians don't want to "fit in." They understand that Average Americans work very hard to pay their bills while scratching to save for retirement, occasional vacations, and precious luxury items. Savvy Doctors understand that the two groups have very different financial challenges that require different types of advisors and strategies.

These physicians don't need the financial and legal advisors and firms that cater to 150,000,000 Average Americans. Doctors don't need techniques, strategies, or products that are adequate for the needs of the many. Doctors don't need free checking, higher money market rates, lower online trading costs, do-it-yourself legal documents, or the advisor with the lowest hourly rate. Doctors don't need advisors to tell them how nice their shoes are or how wonderfully decorated their home or office is. They know these things are nice—they bought them. Doctors don't need to be surrounded with "yes" men or women who agree with all of their suggestions. They need advisors to question them, challenge them, and help them consider all alternatives before taking action. Smart physicians shouldn't put much stock in advisors who send calendars, fruit baskets, or sports tickets, or seek out advisors who will take them golfing or out to dinner. You can pay for all of those things yourself.

Doctors need to understand that there are millions of attorneys, accountants, investment advisors, and financial planners who would all like their business. You should know that many of these advisors and their firms regularly give away "special perks" to try to convince people to become new clients or to guilt them into staying with the firm. You should understand that an advisor referred by a friend is a good start, but a referred advisor from a friend who is in a different financial situation is likely a waste of time. There is an entire section on how to build your advisory team in Lesson #3: Accept Referrals to Specialists. The third lesson is a must read for anyone who picks up this book.

Doctors have family and friends just like Average Americans do. You want to spend your valuable and limited free time with your friends (and some of it with family—just like Average Americans). When you spend time with your advisors, you need to make the most of the time by focusing on the important issues you are paying the advisors to help you manage. You should want your advisors to generate a significant return (on the fees you pay them) in value for your family and practice.

Like Average Americans, Doctors can't help but talk business and finance with friends. A common characteristic of successful physicians is that they don't need to brag about their planning or convince their friends to work with the same advisors to generate peace of mind. You need to cherish the novelty of being different. Practically, you should put more effort into choosing your team than you do in the criticism of the solutions and strategies the team recommends and implements. You should not ask friends or other unqualified outsiders for approval of your planning. This would be like one of your patients asking his barber for advice on how you should do your medical procedure. This isn't to say that Doctors shouldn't review and challenge the advisors suggestions and bring in other experts for second opinions. This is a significant and very important part of building and maintaining wealth (Lesson #10).

Average Americans look for bits of cheap advice on websites, in magazines and newspapers, and on television and radio. The Average American relies on mutual fund recommendations that come in a $5 magazine or on a free website that could possibly reach millions of different people per day. Smart Doctors never give a second thought to any financial or legal suggestion that isn't offered by someone who is intimately familiar with their situation and goals. Doctors don't *want* to spend the time and money for customized planning—they *MUST* spend the time and money on a specially trained and experienced team of advisors to customize a plan that will help them most efficiently and effectively reach their specific, personal goals.

The Diagnosis

Whether you are a young Doctor trying to pay off some student loans and save for retirement or a successful physician trying to save what you've earned from taxes, lawsuits, or a divorce, you have important challenges in your financial life. As we hope you have gleaned from our discussions above, there is an abundance of financial information and advice to be found. However, if you are a physician who wants to learn the lessons that will help you build and protect wealth, this book is for you. Much of the information presented in the 10 Lessons may be financial lessons and advice that you literally cannot get anywhere else. This book contains only some of the important lessons that you can learn when you accept referrals to specialists who are experts at helping Doctors with their unique challenges. To learn more about how these specialists can help you and why you need them, you should read the next section, Lesson #3—Accept Referrals to Specialists.

Accept Referrals to Specialists

In Lesson #1, you learned that the only real way to build and maintain wealth is by leveraging effort, assets, and people. You learned that leveraging people is the most powerful method of Leverage and that leveraging advisors is the most powerful way to Leverage people. It wouldn't be a stretch to say that once you figure out how to use Leverage to achieve even a modest level of wealth, learning how to Leverage advisors is the single most important thing you can do if you want to save time and money and get the most out of your medical career.

To help you better understand this lesson, you need only look at the practice of medicine. A primary care physician is generally the first line of contact for a patient. Though the Doctor has a very wide range of general knowledge, he or she will have to refer patients to a number of specialists. In some instances, the Doctor may request the help of radiologists to review tests. In other instances, there may be a referral to surgeons who will undoubtedly need to work with anesthesiologists. The Doctor will encounter cases in which patients will need referrals to obstetricians, gynecologists, urologists, cardiologists, orthopedists, oncologists, and other specialists. The situation with respect to your finances is very similar.

In this Lesson—Accept Referrals to Specialists—we will examine the types of advisors who can help you Leverage your time and money, review the benefits and limitations of each specialist, point out some common pitfalls, and ultimately recommend how to assemble the right team of advisors.

The Value of Financial Specialists

The best way to maximize your benefit from leveraging people is to work with experts in many financial and legal fields. As you learned in Lesson #2, you have very different needs than Average Americans do. As a result, the right specialists for most people are not likely to be the right advisors to help you.

As you become more successful, you need advisors even more. Adding employees, making additional investments, purchasing equipment and real estate, and creating new businesses add complexity to your plan. This increased Leverage exponentially increases the complexity of your comprehensive financial plan. This complexity necessitates the need for a team of advisors. Without a very strong team, you will struggle to find the time to focus on the important things that make you money, let alone enjoy any free time. To illustrate the value of advisors, refer to the equation below:

Wealth can only be achieved through Leverage.

+

Leverage can only be managed with a team of Advisors

=

Wealth can only be achieved with a team of advisors managing the Leverage

In this chapter, we will discuss the reason *why* Doctors need a team of knowledgeable advisors with diverse areas of expertise. Then we will discuss *how* to maximize the value of your advisors and suggest tips for working with your team.

Managing Complexity: The Need For Advisors

Most people realize that wealth creates complexity. What Doctors need to realize is that the management of complexity and Leverage is not the job of a traffic cop. As wealth grows, the number of complicated, technical risks that the Doctor faces also grows exponentially.

As an example, the transition from running a sole proprietorship to having a single employee may not seem to be major, but that couldn't be further from the truth. The addition of just one employee creates a need for:

- Payroll creation, funding, and payments

- Regular payroll tax payments (or you can go to jail)

- Withholding tax filings and payments

- Workers compensation insurance or fund payments

- Occupation Safety Hazard Association (OSHA) compliance

- Separate retirement plan (ERISA) regulations and contribution requirements

- A host of other state and federal reporting requirements.

In addition to all of the aforementioned specific issues, the Leverage of assets also increases the need for more general categories of planning, like asset protection, banking (private and commercial), business planning, financial planning, healthcare law, HIPAA, Medicare, income tax management, investing, life insurance analysis, disability insurance analysis, property and casualty insurance analysis, long-term care insurance analysis, educational funding, retirement planning, family law, gift and estate tax planning, charitable planning, Medicaid planning, and a host of other areas.

Each category of planning has its own technical areas that can be competently handled by an advisor who has expertise in that area. Although it is common to find an advisor who has expertise in several areas, there are categories in which the input of two advisors may be necessary. For example, tax issues are typically handled by a both a tax attorney and a CPA. As a result, there is no way that a small team of two or three advisors could possibly handle the needs of a Doctor. This means that a Doctor may need to Leverage the services of six or more advisors over their career.

While the concept of such a large team may seem overwhelming, consider your profession of medicine. Adult patients do not continue to see the obstetrician who delivered them or the pediatrician who treated them in childhood. Patients need to see a number of specialists as they mature and as their needs change, often consulting with a number of Doctors at once.

If you are like your patients, you may want to be able to keep the same financial "primary care" advisors for as long as possible. Having someone you know and trust as your primary contact is very comforting. This "primary advisor" can help explain situations to you, find the right specialists if a need for one arises, and help communicate with you as complicated procedures take place. Keep this in mind. In Lesson #10, there will be discussion of your team of advisors. One of your advisors on this team is going to be the primary contact to help you through it all.

Working With Your Team

Having the right team of advisors is another step in the right direction, but there is still more to do. Having a team that is run poorly is like having an alarm installed in your house but never turning it on. You have to "work" with the team for the team to provide any value. In our discussion with the partners of The Founders Group in San Diego, we learned some valuable lessons about successful business owners (and Doctors need to consider themselves business owners). The Founders Group only deals with families with businesses or net worth above $25,000,000. They have found that the most successful clients and families arranged annual or semi-annual all-day or multi-day meetings with all of their advisors, business partners, and key family members. Sometimes, the costs of flying in advisors to perform these meetings and paying them their hourly wages can cost thousands of dollars per year.

According to Joe Strazzeri of The Founders Group:

> "Professionals and business owners who make the effort to spend time with the experts on their team generally see these meetings as the most productive use of time and money."

Tips For Working Within A Team

As with any collaborative endeavor, the collection of people into a coordinated team is not enough to ensure success. Every conference call and meeting must have an agenda and someone to manage the meeting to make sure that all-important items are handled within the allotted time. It is common to put one of the advisors in charge of organizing and facilitating information between the other advisors. This is usually a financial planner and not an accountant or attorney—though the "quarterback" could be any one of the advisors on the team. Within the group, you need to identify roles and responsibilities and make one person accountable for the completion of each task.

When considering different options, it is wonderful when there is a unanimous decision on whether to go in a particular direction. However, many decisions will not be unanimous. You need to set the rules (51%, 66%, 80%) on how decisions are to be made within the group and share them with the group. If they know how you are going to make decisions, it will make it easier for them to participate in the group and allow them to continue to participate even when the rest of the group disagrees with a particular decision.

The Diagnosis

You can't possibly expect to achieve and protect wealth while holding on to your sanity unless you assemble the right team of advisors. Trying to achieve financial success without a team of advisors is like a patient trying to get 100% of his or her healthcare from one Doctor. Without the help of orthopedists, dermatologists, neurologists, obstetricians, oncologists, and dozens of other specialists, patients' life expectancies would certainly suffer. Society has benefited from the development of expertise in specialized medicine. Similarly, Doctors need to look to specialized legal and financial advisors to provide the greatest financial benefits.

You must realize that the process of building and maintaining wealth in today's world brings with it potential challenges from all areas of law, accounting, finance, insurance, and business. When you accept this reality and embrace the need to Leverage the expertise of advisors in all of the areas mentioned above, you will be one step closer to reaching your goals.

What types of advisors do Doctors need to utilize? How do you divide the responsibilities within the team? How do you choose the actual advisors? In the next two chapters, we will answer all of these questions.

The Specialists Doctors Need

Before you can choose your advisors, delegate responsibilities to team members or begin to benefit from the Leverage of advisors, you need to understand the types of advisors you need. In this chapter, we provide a list that covers the team members that 90% of situations require. Some advisors, like mortgage brokers, are not discussed because they typically play a transactional role at different points in the client's lifetime. The other advisors may review mortgages, but the mortgage broker typically is looking for the lowest price and isn't changing loan offers based on the other pieces of the comprehensive financial plan. In addition, unique circumstances may call for some teams to require additional advisors with very unique skills. Below is the list of the most common advisors:

- Accountants

- Asset Protection Attorneys

- Estate Planning Attorneys

- Tax Attorneys

- Insurance Professionals

- Investment Advisors

- Financial Planners

Accountants

The term *accountant* will be used to generically describe an accountant, Certified Public Accountant (CPA), or Enrolled Agent (EA).

What They Do: Accountants (and CPAs and EAs) are trained and licensed to prepare tax returns for submission to the Internal Revenue Service. Each state has its own licensing and accreditation procedures for accountants and CPAs. The CPA has a multi-part exam that is required to earn the CPA accreditation. Enrolled Agents complete a federal licensing process. In all situations, these advisors primarily prepare tax returns. In the most desirable client-advisor relationship, the accountants also provide clients with advice on tax matters.

Limitations of an Accountant:

1. The U.S. tax law is potentially the most complex set of rules created by human-kind, and significant changes are made to these rules every year. Therefore, **it is impossible for any accountant to be well versed in all areas of tax policy.** More likely, the accountant may only know one or two areas (of 20 or more potential areas) intimately. Tax planning is like medicine—each area has become so complex that one can't possibly expect to become an expert in many disciplines. In the medical arena, most patients and physicians realize that one Doctor can't do everything. They both readily accept being referred to, or referring patients to, other physicians. A gastroenterologist would no sooner make diagnoses for skin conditions than a dermatologist would try and diagnose and treat an intestinal issue. Unfortunately, this is what happens all the time in the tax arena.

2. **Some accountants are comfortable acknowledging what they know and don't know.** Some accountants feel responsible for answering all tax questions and resist referring clients to other accountants for specific needs for fear of losing the client altogether. This is more of a limitation of an individual than it is a limitation of the profession as a whole, but it should be recognized.

3. **Conflicts of interest may arise.** Many accountants are beginning to look for additional revenue opportunities by getting licensed in life insurance and securities. They will then recommend their clients particular investment and insurance products. This can create significant conflicts of interest with clients who are looking for tax advice, but who are getting financial suggestions. Clients should be concerned how accountants who deal with very complex tax issues find time to become experts in insurance and investments. In revisiting our Doctor analogy—how could a practicing dermatologist find the time to learn oncology on the side and offer high-quality consultation to the dermatology clients who develop cancer? Savvy patients would prefer a full-time oncologist in that situation. Despite the conflict and impracticality, many CPAs with years of accounting experience are now trying to increase revenue by advising clients on investments and insurance, despite having little or no practical experience in these areas.

Asset Protection Attorneys

The term *asset protection attorney* describes an attorney who has a strong working knowledge of and experience in the area of creditor protection. There is no state-specific accreditation for asset protection. All attorneys must be admitted to the Bar Association in the state(s) in which they wish to practice.

What They Do: Asset protection attorneys specialize in the field of asset protection. They help clients arrange their personal and business affairs in a manner that protects their wealth from potential future lawsuits and other creditor risks. Because many of the tools used in asset protection are the same tools used in estate planning and business planning, it is common for asset protection attorneys to also have a strong working knowledge in those areas as well.

Limitations of Asset Protection Attorneys:

1. Because asset protection is a relatively new field of law and most attorneys are overwhelmed in their primary fields of interest (litigation, business law, estate planning, etc.), **few attorneys have found the time or had the interest to study this important field of law.** As a result, there are very few attorneys who are experts in this area. Though one of the co-authors (Mr. Mandell) specializes in this area, he is one of fewer than 50 attorneys in the country whose focus is exclusively in this area.

2. **Asset protection attorneys are NOT estate planning or tax attorneys—or any other type of attorney, for that matter.** Do not expect that you will get estate planning or tax advice from these attorneys unless they also have specific training in these areas. However, your asset protection attorney should be willing to interact with attorneys from the other fields who will be necessary to help you complete your planning.

Estate Planning Attorneys

The term *estate planning attorney* describes an attorney who has a strong working knowledge of and experience in the area of trusts, probate, and estate planning. There is a state-specific accreditation for estate planning in many states. All attorneys must be admitted to the Bar Association in the state(s) they wish to practice.

What they do: Estate planning attorneys focus on helping families address the financial needs that arise at death or as death approaches. Estate planning attorneys are required to draft estate planning documents such as wills, limited partnerships, and various types of trusts. They have a strong working knowledge of gift, estate, and generation-skipping tax issues. Though many estate planning issues are federal issues, there are some state-specific issues that require a local attorney. For very complex issues, the most savvy affluent families will often use the best estate planning attorney they can find (anywhere in the US) and have a local attorney co-counsel the case so state specific issues can be addressed.

Limitations:

1. **We have seen many estate planning attorneys who almost exclusively create estate plans using legal tools they can be paid to create.** They have little experience or

knowledge of important financial vehicles that can play a significant role in the estate planning of wealthy families. By excluding entire categories of planning tools (most often cash value life insurance), these attorneys often fail to help their clients create the liquidity necessary to handle the financial obligations that arise at death. Sometimes attorneys shy away from recommending financial and insurance tools because they do not properly understand these tools and they fear the potential liability of recommending things they don't understand. The proper solution to this limitation is to do what the savvy affluent do—make sure there are attorneys and insurance experts on the financial planning team, so that the clients can get the best combination of planning tools to most efficiently meet their needs.

2. **Estate planning attorneys generally are not asset protection or (income) tax attorneys either.** While attorneys in these different fields may use similar legal tools from time to time, that is not enough. A scalpel in the hands of a surgeon can be an important tool to help save a life. A scalpel in the hands of a mugger is a knife that can kill someone. We are not suggesting that one type of attorney is an angel and one is a devil (readers are encouraged to insert their own joke here). We are merely saying that tools used differently can have very different outcomes and can offer varying benefits. For this reason, it is best to involve specialists in asset protection and income tax to work with the estate planning attorney, if needed.

Tax Attorneys

The term *tax attorney* describes an attorney who has a strong working knowledge of and experience in the area of income tax and possibly estate tax. There is a state-specific accreditation for tax attorneys in many states. Most tax attorneys have added another year of education beyond law school to earn a degree in taxation, called an LLM (short for Master of Laws). All attorneys must be admitted to the Bar Association in the state(s) in which they wish to practice.

What they do: Tax planning attorneys are required to give advice on the tax ramifications of certain transactions (i.e., selling an appreciated asset) or strategies, and to assist with the creation of the legal documents used in these transactions. These specialized attorneys have a strong working knowledge of income and capital gains tax issues, as well as taxation of corporations, partnerships, and other entities. All attorneys must be admitted to the Bar Association in the state(s) in which they wish to practice. Since most states' tax laws are built upon federal tax code, many national tax attorneys can handle all of a client's tax issues.

Limitations:

1. **Tax attorneys do not generally prepare tax returns.** Though they have a very strong working knowledge of tax, the preparation is a specialty that is generally left to the accountant (as mentioned earlier).

2. **Though some of these attorneys are also experts in estate planning, most do not work in this area regularly.** This results in two limitations:

   a. Tax attorneys may not be as aware of potential estate planning solutions that are more appropriate for very affluent clients

   b. They are likely to have very limited knowledge of financial and insurance vehicles and their place within an estate plan, because they are tax attorneys first and estate planning attorneys second. If full-time estate planning attorneys don't have time to fully understand financial vehicles, how could you expect part-time estate planning attorneys with another full-time focus to have time?

3. In addition, **tax planning attorneys generally are not asset protection attorneys.** While they may know a bit about this area, the same comparison of the surgeon and the mugger needs to be revisited here—a little knowledge can be dangerous. It is best to involve specialists in asset protection and estate planning to work with the tax planning attorney.

Insurance Professionals

Insurance Professional is a term used to describe life and health (life) or property and casualty (P&C) insurance agents. Life and P&C agents must have a resident agent license in the state in which they reside. In some states, a weeklong course and a state-sponsored exam are required to earn a license. They can apply for non-resident licenses in the other states to provide insurance to clients in those states as well. Certified Financial Planners, accountants, investment advisors and attorneys can all secure life insurance licenses. Many of their regulatory agencies require those advisors to disclose the potential conflict of interest to clients in instances where the advisor could benefit from multiple income sources (e.g., professional fees and insurance commissions).

What They Do: At the most basic level, insurance professionals provide various types of insurance policies to clients. Some insurance professionals also offer financial planning or investment solutions. The life insurance professional works closely with the estate planning attorney to help clients meet their estate planning needs. If you are interested in purchasing any type of insurance, it is imperative that you consult with a licensed insurance professional experienced in the insurance area at issue. Typically, one person can only be an expert in one area of insurance. If you look at the list of types of insurance below, you can see why it is so important to work with a financial firm like O'Dell Jarvis Mandell (www.ojmgroup.com)– that has a number of insurance and investment experts on staff to help clients with their various insurance and investment needs.

Life Insurance

In Lesson #8, you will learn why cash value life insurance is a fundamental building block of wealth planning for Doctors. By offering tax benefits, wealth accumulation, liquidity, and protection against financial disasters, life insurance should play a role in every Doctor's financial plan.

Disability Income Insurance

In Lesson #4, you will learn how to protect your family and practice from financial disasters. For Doctors, the single greatest asset may be your earning potential. Disability income insurance is required for every Doctor whose income is needed for the family to pay bills or meet other financial needs. Disability income insurance should be handled by a life and health insurance agent who specializes in disability insurance.

Long-Term Care Insurance

Also in Lesson #4, you will learn that long-term care insurance (LTCI) is an important tool for Doctors who want to avoid losing their hard-earned wealth to a Medicaid spend-down to pay for nursing home, home care, hospice, and a host of other services most of us will need in our final years. Long-term care insurance covers health related expenses that will not be covered by social or private insurance in retirement. In addition, some families use long-term care insurance to protect retirement savings for their heirs (as an inheritance). LTCI can be handled by life insurance agents who have completed the additional LTCI-specific training (that some states require).

Property and Casualty Insurance

Property and Casualty (P&C) insurance is a separate set of insurances that require a different training course and license than the license needed for the aforementioned types of insurance. P&C insurances are quite common, even though you may not have previously run across the acronym "P&C." These coverages include homeowners, personal auto, commercial auto, professional liability insurance, worker's compensation, umbrella, premises, product liability, flood, hurricane, and many other policies. To protect wealth, Doctors need to address P&C concerns by adding an insurance agent who is an expert in these areas.

Limitations of Insurance Professionals:

1. **Some are working for the insurance company or themselves, rather than working for you.** Some insurance agents have "career agent" contracts with certain insurance companies. These agents are highly motivated to sell a specific company's products, because they must hit their sales goals or risk losing their health and financial benefits. Other insurance companies, like Northwestern Mutual, have "captive" agents who, due to contract terms, can only offer you products from a single company. They can't shop for the best policy, realistically provide an unbiased position, or ultimately have your best interest in mind. Many insurance agents are neither career nor captive agents. Even independent agents will have a personal preference toward certain companies or products. Doctors should always work with independent insurance professionals who have a range of op-

tions they can offer and can display a track record of using different companies for their clients' best interest. Doctors should also look for agents of the highest moral character, who are experienced and successful enough not to be influenced by slightly higher commissions or other incentives that competing insurance companies may offer. One client said about his choice of an agent, "I wanted an agent who wanted my business, but not one who needed my business." Another client said, "I feel comfortable knowing that my agent is interested in a long term relationship and doesn't need to sell me anything to pay the bills."

2. **Many agents work only for commissions.** Doctors should realize that insurance professionals, like all of us, need to make a living. They do not begrudge the insurance professional for earning a commission that is inherent in the insurance product (or the real estate agent or any other commission-compensated person). However, when asking for advice and recommendations on how to address a financial need, you have to expect a commission-based advisor to suggest only commission-based products. You may get the best commission-based solution, but are not likely to receive a recommendation of the best possible solution if that solution doesn't involve a commission. This is the converse limitation to the estate planning attorney that only recommends legal solutions. Doctors should want independence. This is much more important for certain products like life insurance, than for less expensive products such as homeowner's, or even disability, insurance.

Unfortunately, it is true that many advisors in the financial planning and insurance industries allow commissions to bias their view of insurance products. The authors insist that they be compensated on a fee basis for any advising, planning or product consultation that they provide. If an insurance professional works like this, he or she is much less likely to be biased towards lucrative commissions or to "sell" a product at all. Insurance agents who are "commission only" need the sale or commission to stay in business and their business model is shaped accordingly. Therefore, Doctors should work with fee-based advisors when evaluating insurance products and wealth planning involving insurance.

3. **Few have significant training in other areas.** To obtain a license in most states for any of these types of insurance, an individual typically only needs to attend a weeklong class and then pass an exam. Contrast this to earning an MBA (2 years), law license (3 years law school, plus bar exam), or medical license (4 years medical school, 4-8 years internship/residency, plus board exams).

Because of this limited training, many insurance "professionals" are simply salespeople without the sophistication or training to do more than sell. Doctors would be wise to look for more from their insurance advisors. This "more" they seek should be education, training, years of experience and the professional's "team." Again, as an example, our firm has 3 MBAs, 2 attorneys, and a CPA among its team's designations. Our firm is certainly not the only firm with very highly qualified professionals. We just believe it is a good example of what you should seek out in a firm if you are looking for well-educated professionals who can help you with many facets of your planning.

Investment Advisors

We use the term *investment advisor* to include money managers and stockbrokers. These advisors have to study and pass a 3-hour securities exam and a 90-minute ethics exam or file as an independent Registered Investment Advisor directly with the SEC.

What They Do: Investment advisors essentially handle investments for clients. They typically charge a fee based on the amount of assets they manage. Stockbrokers may also be paid based on the number and size of the trades they make.

Limitations:

1. **Most fail to adequately manage taxes.** The overwhelming majority of money managers primarily handle pension or corporate (institutional) assets, which are not as sensitive to taxes as are the non-pension assets of Doctors. As a result, these advisors focus on their gross, pre-tax investment returns. This gross number is what they publish in their marketing material, how they are measured against their peers and how they are compensated. This is obviously what they care about most. This is understandable, except that this is exactly what Doctors should be trying to avoid. Doctors should be interested in the <u>post-tax</u> return of the investment. We will discuss this in greater detail in Lessons #7 and #8.

2. **Most have very little knowledge or interest in any kind of "planning."** Like most specialists, investment managers have to focus on their craft. Since the world markets are now integrated, investment management is practically a 24-hour per day job. When Japan is closing, London is opening. When London is winding down, New York is ramping up. It isn't easy for investment advisors to be well versed in other planning areas and it is basically impossible for these advisors to act as the team's quarterback because of their limited knowledge of the areas outside of the markets.

Financial Planners

We use the term *financial planner* to describe someone who charges a fee to create a financial plan for a client. Sometimes, this is a Certified Financial Planner who has taken six courses and passed an exam. Other times, this person is an accountant who has financial training and may have passed an exam in addition to the training as an accountant and possibly passing the CPA exam. Still other times, this could be someone with an MBA, with a concentration in Finance, who has professional experience and has spent two years learning about business, business law, economics and finance.

What They Do: Ideally, a financial planner is someone who uses a planning process to help the client Leverage the other planning areas above. The planner integrates all of the focused planning efforts of the other advisors into one comprehensive plan to help the client's family meet its objectives. They should have a strong working knowledge of many of the disciplines. Their level of proficiency should be enough to allow them to interact at a high level with the various specialists and add some value in each area from time to time. More often than not, this advisor will also act as the "coordinator" or "quarterback" for all of the specialists (like the primary care Doctor analogy used earlier). The financial planner provides motivation, understanding and a disciplined periodic review to make sure all of the various planning areas stay "on track." We will develop the discussion of a quarterback for your financial plan at the end of this Lesson and in Lesson #10.

Limitations:

1. **Can be a Disguised Salesperson.** It can hard to decipher between the true planner and the disguised salesperson that is, in actuality, focused on selling something. It is okay for a planner to be used in the implementation of a plan, but you must focus on the plan itself first. Be wary of financial plans offered for free. You should know that anything you get for free is not worth much. Further, the business model of such a "planner" is simply to use the "plan" just to sell you something—how else could they recoup whatever little time they spent on creating such a plan?

2. **Weak Knowledge of Disciplines.** This could be the biggest potential problem. If your financial planner is supposed to be acting as the quarterback of your planning team, they have to understand what the other advisors can and will do and be able to spot important issues within each of the disciplines. In working with hundreds of insurance agents and financial planners, we have only encountered a handful that have a strong working knowledge of asset protection and tax planning. Bringing only insurance and investment knowledge (the products that they typically sell) is insufficient to make a good financial planner. The top four planners at O'Dell Jarvis Mandell have 3 MBAs, a law degree, and a CPA between them.

Other Advisors

In addition to the list of advisors already provided, there are other advisors who may be valuable to help increase your Leverage. These include business or corporate attorneys, real estate attorneys, private bankers, charitable planners, Medicaid attorneys, and family law attorneys. Each of these experts may have a specific role to play in your planning at some point.

The Diagnosis

You now have an understanding of what types of advisors you could add to your financial planning team. You may even foresee some of the benefits you and your family may achieve from working with the specialists on your team. Before you jump into hiring team members, it is important to learn from the mistakes of thousands of people before you. Read the next chapter on the seven mistakes to avoid when building and working with your team. Avoiding these mistakes can save you a lot of time, money and aggravation in the long run.

Seven Outdated Procedures to Avoid

In our many years as financial planning professionals, we have seen many clients make mistakes when selecting and working with their advisors. These mistakes are common among Doctors and non-Doctors alike. However, these mistakes can all be avoided. We know this because many of our clients have effectively built their fortune and protected their assets by building the right team of advisors. There are seven pitfalls of choosing and working with advisors on your financial plans. The seven pitfalls to avoid are:

1. Friends or Family as Advisors

2. Choosing Only Local Team Members

3. "If It Ain't Broke, Don't Fix It"

4. Never Getting a Second Opinion

5. Hiring Yes Men and Women

6. Not Accepting that Complexity Requires Outside Experts

7. Failing to Insist on Advisor Coordination

In this chapter, we will examine these seven pitfalls and explain how each can be avoided.

Pitfall #1: Friends Or Family As Advisors

One of the biggest mistakes we see is the inclusion of friends and family in the planning team. We can't fault people for thinking that trust is important when choosing people to help manage money. Trust is very important. However, unless you are willing to lose the friendship to achieve the financial goals, this should probably be avoided. It is perfectly acceptable to become friendly with your advisors. This is appropriate because the friendship will have grown out of a business relationship. However, when the relationship instead begins as a friendship, problems may later arise when you disagree on a course of action or when the advisor makes a mistake.

Pitfall #2: Choosing Only Local Team Members

The best available team members need not be the best available advisors in your neighborhood. We have helped clients who built their team with advisors from all four corners of the country. In today's age of technology, information is easily shared through email, fax, and, more recently, online data sharing applications. Unlike the surgeon who needs to be in the room to do surgery, a financial or legal professional doesn't need to be in the room to do what he or she does well. Don't be afraid to enlist the best advisors you can find—even if they are not in your backyard.

Pitfall #3: "If It Ain't Broke, Don't Fix It"

Having worked with someone for 10 or 20 years is not a reason to continue with the same advisor. If you applied that logic to medicine, patients would still be seeing their pediatricians long after turning 18 years old. There is a high likelihood that, as you accumulated wealth, your financial needs changed. Though your advisor was there for you when you had simpler needs, you are not required to stay with that advisor when you have outgrown the advisor's, or firm's, capabilities and expertise.

The first mistake that the overwhelming majority of Doctors make in the financial, legal or tax aspects of their careers is the method they use to initially choose their professional advisors. Whether it was their CPA, investment professional or attorney, many business owners made a poor choice because their method of evaluating the potential advisors was flawed.

When you consider the typical pattern, this is not surprising. Most Doctors chose their advisors when they were starting out in residency or fellowship. They may have needed some life or disability insurance, a will and someone to prepare and file tax returns. Working long hours, and without the means to evaluate an advisor, young Doctors typically do what other busy people do and take the path of least resistance. They use the advisor their parents or friends use, or hire a friend or family member.

Though this un-scientific approach is obviously flawed, it serves its purpose when there are bigger challenges at hand (like 20-hour work days). Your life was so hectic that you just needed to "get it done fast." The advisor you chose at that point simply had to be competent and inexpensive—and that was good enough. Like a triage nurse in an emergency room, the advisors do not have to be top-trained specialist when all you need are some basic stitches. This approach is quite understandable.

What is so alarming to us is not this initial choice of advisor, but *the fact that so many Doctors stay with the same advisors who handled their "triage planning" for the rest of their careers!* The justification for this is rarely anything concrete or, in our opinion, sufficient to explain why the Doctor would choose an advisor over his or her own financial security. Answers like "we've been together so long, I'd hate to change now," or "if it ain't broke, don't fix it" are unpersuasive. Further, this begs the question: "How do you know 'it ain't broke' if you don't get a second opinion?"

Most alarming to us—despite the fact that we see it every day –is when a physician stays with an advisor when the Doctor has clearly outgrown the expertise of the advisor. Consider the case study of Ned the Neurosurgeon:

Case Study: Ned the Neurosurgeon

Ned, a neurosurgeon in Florida, contacted our firm after reading our last book. While his income was over $1 million per year and he was part of an extremely successful practice, he used the same local lawyer who created his wills 20 years ago when he was just starting out. When we were Florida, we had a meeting with this attorney.

Not only was this attorney not a tax specialist (despite the fact that he was advising on tax issues), but he also continued to advise the Doctor in other areas that were clearly beyond his expertise. While he was certainly a nice gentleman, and perhaps was competent at doing basic planning for someone with minimal tax or estate planning concerns, he had no understanding of the advanced techniques that a Doctor making over $1 million per year should be considering. He had no knowledge of asset protection planning or other fairly routine planning that we implement for high-income Doctors. While this gentleman may have been an acceptable choice for the Doctor when he was starting out, continuing to use this attorney as his primary advisor was a total disservice to this client.

Self Test: How did you choose the professional advisors you work with today? How many other professionals did you interview prior to choosing one? Have you periodically interviewed others as your needs have changed?

Pitfall #4: Never Getting a Second Opinion

A good way to grade your existing advisors and test the competencies of potential team members is to get a second opinion. Good advisors are busy helping clients like you. They are professionals and will expect to be paid for the analysis. Sure, there are plenty of advisors who will analyze your situation for free, hoping to dazzle you with their recommendations to earn your investment, insurance or legal business. However, the goal of these people is to sell you something. As mentioned previously, your planning team should consist of talented advisors who want your business—but don't *need* your business. Treat them fairly by paying them for their time and advice. Stepping through this short-term engagement exercise will provide insight into how organized their firm is and how well they communicate.

Of the flaws discussed here, never getting a second opinion is the most damaging. Unfortunately, it is also the most common. It is most damaging because a second opinion is the primary way of identifying planning mistakes or noticeable omissions from your planning.

Just as good physicians encourage patients to get a second opinion, good advisors should encourage their clients to do the same. This is the only way for you to adequately judge an advisor's performance. You are no more qualified to look at a trust document or tax return and see flaws, as we are to examine a report on a chest CT and see a misdiagnosis! With your entire financial future banking on the success of your professional advisors, it amazes us how few of you have paid another professional to review your existing advisor's work. If your life were in jeopardy, wouldn't you get a second opinion? Isn't your financial life important as well?

Case Study: The Value of a Second Opinion

In 2000, co-author David Mandell's prior law firm was retained to perform a self-audit by a long-term client. The client, an extremely successful businessman, was concerned that he might become an IRS target. He hired the firm to do an audit of his personal and various businesses' income tax returns for the prior five years. What the firm found was shocking.

Even though this client had used four different accounting firms for his various returns (including a well-known 500-plus person firm), the taxes he had paid were far from what he owed. Luckily for him, it was an <u>overpayment</u>—in millions of dollars.

That is a true story. Because of the self-imposed audit that David's firm oversaw, the client was able to file for a huge refund from the IRS and state tax agency. Luckily for him, he was concerned about poor tax advice and spent the money to hire the firm to perform the audit.

Self Test: Have you ever paid an outside advisor to review your attorney's work? Your CPA's work? Your investment advisor's work? If not, why not?

Pitfall #5: Hiring "Yes" Men and Women

When we asked numerous successful clients what advice they would give, we received many suggestions. The suggestions included: "find experts," "don't look for 'Yes Men'," and "hire people smarter than you are." We put them all in the same category because the end result is the same. The wealthy have wealth because they did something very well. The very successful ones realize that they can't be experts at everything. Some rightfully believe that they could focus on finance or law and probably be just as smart as some advisors. They also realize that it would take many years to reach an adequate level of expertise. To Leverage their time, they instead choose to hire experts in different disciplines to work for them. The wealthy are likely paying someone less per hour than they could earn running their businesses. An additional benefit is that the advisors are getting the work done *in less time* than it would take the Doctors to do it themselves.

Our most successful clients have told us that they have enough "Yes Men" in their lives. Interestingly, they cherish the moments when advisors stand up to them to challenge their positions or question their decisions. They see this as an opportunity to improve their position. Some even enjoy the challenge.

Pitfall #6: Not Accepting That Complexity Requires Outside Experts

If your medical condition necessitated a stent, you would not go to a general practitioner to have it done. Moreover, you would not consult with any specialists outside of cardiology. In fact, you would not even settle with seeing the standard cardiologist. You would only seek the help of an interventional cardiologist to handle this procedure. The point is that medicine is highly specialized. If you have a specific issue, you want a physician properly trained and experienced with this particular issue.

The notion of seeking out a specialist to help you with your health concerns may be obvious. However, we can attest that in the areas of law, taxation and finance, Doctors fail to see the parallels to the world of medicine. To illustrate this, we should consider the area of taxation. The ever-changing United States tax law is perhaps the most complex set of rules ever created by one society. The lengthy and confusing Internal Revenue Code is only the beginning. IRS revenue rulings, private letter rulings, tax memoranda, announcements, circulars, and tax court and federal court cases only serve to add additional complexity to the field. If you step foot into any law library, you are likely to see an entire floor dedicated to tax documentation. Suffice to say, no single person can possibly be an expert in all areas of tax law.

Nevertheless, a physician will typically rely on one CPA to serve as a "tax advisor" in all areas of tax. The taxation issues that require guidance typically include retirement planning, income structuring (salary vs. bonus), payroll tax, whether to be an "S" or "C" corporation, whether to implement a deferred compensation plan, estate tax planning, taxation on sales of real estate, individual tax returns, corporate tax returns and buying or selling a practice. All of these areas are actually particular sub-specialties that require a unique knowledge base. As if this wasn't bad enough, we have seen many Doctors ask their tax advisor to guide them in areas that are far outside of tax planning altogether—such as asset protection or investing.

We cannot tell you how many times we have attempted to work with a Doctor's CPA or attorney to implement a particular strategy and run into the same problem. It was obvious that this advisor had little experience in the Doctor's area of concern. Ninety-nine percent of the time when situation occurs, the client suffers needlessly.

Because the primary advisor is so fearful of bringing in a specialized advisor who may "steal" the client, the attorney or CPA will take an over-protective stance, failing to admit his or her shortcomings to the Doctor and recommend another specialist. One reasonable alternative would be for the advisor to admit his or her lack of experience in the area and agree to review the area in question, and then charge the client for the time needed to "get up to speed." Most advisors are afraid to do this. Possibly, they are afraid that the client will see them as "inadequate." Instead, the advisor will tell the client the idea "doesn't work" without giving any substantial reason (see the "warning signs" below). In the end, the Doctor is clueless as to what is really going on—and the problem is not solved.

Self Test: Ask your CPA or attorney which tax areas noted above are his or her **expertise**. Ask the advisor how they would handle an issue for you that occurred outside of this area.

Self Test: Ask your tax advisor if he or she does **asset protection planning**. If the answer is yes, ask a follow up question: "Have you ever created a domestic asset protection trust or self-settled foreign asset protection trust?"

Pitfall #7: Failing to Insist on Advisor Coordination

Even if you have a team of highly-experienced advisors in the fields of tax, law, insurance and investments working for you, your plan can still be in complete disarray. If the advisors are not collaborating to utilize their collective expertise to implement a comprehensive, multi-disciplinary plan for your benefit, your planning will suffer significantly.

All too often, we see the symptoms of such a lack of coordination. Clients who come to our offices often have paid a technically sound attorney to create a very comprehensive living trust, but the family's assets have not yet been titled to the trust (potentially making the document useless). We frequently see life insurance policies and life insurance trusts that, because the proper steps were not taken to combine the two vehicles, do not work as they should. As a result the death benefit of the insurance may be unnecessarily taxed at rates as high as 50%. We notice investment accounts that are managed like they are in a pension, with no regard for taxation—and the end result is often a 24% to 45% reduction in the gain of the investments. Conflicting advice from professionals in different areas OR a lack of respect for what the other professionals do often leads to planning inertia or just plain bad planning.

Like the radiologist, surgeon, and anesthesiologist who must work together to make sure a patient has a successful surgery, your CPA, attorney and financial advisors MUST work together to help you successfully achieve your financial goals. If the surgeon never saw the films or charts, or the anesthesiologist and surgeon didn't speak, it would be pretty difficult to successfully treat a surgical patient.

Self Test: How often do your CPA, attorney, financial, and insurance advisors sit down to discuss and coordinate your planning? Once per quarter? Once per year? Ever?

Warning Signs That You Are Ill-Advised

Do any of these "warning signs" that you are ill-advised seem familiar? If so, you are likely suffering from flawed professional advisory relationships:

- You have had the same advisors for years—and never interviewed prospective competitors

- Your advisors don't bring you detailed analyses of your practice and personal situation, complete with helpful suggestions, annually

- You have no idea what the true sub-specialties of your advisors' professions are

- Your present advisors reject ideas you bring to them without providing detailed written explanations of why they don't make sense for you

- Your present advisors have never told you that a certain idea required further research for which they would need to charge you

- You rarely, if ever, have paid for second opinions from other professionals

- You have trusts, partnerships or other legal entities which may not be funded

- Your CPA, attorney, and financial advisors do not meet periodically to coordinate your planning

- You stay with your present advisor(s) out of lethargy, guilt, or an "if it ain't broke, don't fix it" mentality

The Diagnosis

In the first three Lessons, you have learned very valuable philosophical lessons. The misunderstanding and misuse of these lessons have been the major roadblocks to financial success for most people. Now that you are in the proper mind frame—keeping an open-mind, recognizing the importance of Leverage, and understanding why you need advisors to help you—you are ready to learn the practical lessons and applications that *For Doctors Only* offers.

The next seven Lessons to working less and building more are valuable guides that are built upon the experiences we have had in working with our most successful clients. Inside of each Lesson, there are many chapters with specific suggestions, strategies or tools that may or may not be applicable to helping you achieve your goals. A mentioned strategy might be perfect for one family but detrimental to another. Only by collaborating with your team of advisors can you properly determine the techniques and tools appropriate for your needs. Together, you can identify your needs, analyze all available options, make a decision and implement the chosen strategies.

You are now ready to continue. There is no use in focusing on accumulating more wealth if you will only lose it. This is why we want to start by teaching you how to protect your existing and future wealth. The next part—Lesson #4—will teach you how to avoid financial catastrophes. Once you know how to avoid mistakes, you can work on implementing strategies to help you build and protect wealth. This is what Lessons 5 through 10 will do.

First, Do No Harm

Many people believe the roadmap to financial success includes focusing on a goal, putting your head down and relentlessly pushing ahead until you reach it. Though hard work and perseverance are common personality traits of most physicians, another key ingredient to long-term financial success existed among all of our most successful Doctor clients. Every single successful medical family we encountered was able to avoid, or at least mitigate, catastrophic financial losses through a combination of luck and risk management planning. Since we do not espouse luck as a prudent strategy, we will focus on managing financial risk by planning to protect your family from financial disasters.

One common financial disaster that can result in a significant loss of assets is a civil lawsuit. Lessons #5 and #6 will offer almost two dozen specific solutions to help mitigate litigation risks. Though malpractice lawsuits are a significant risk for physicians in today's society, they do not pose the most significant risk to one's wealth if proper insurance is in place.

This Lesson will explore those additional—and more devastating—financial disasters that must be addressed if you wish to achieve and maintain wealth. These risks include both health-related and financial events. More specifically, this section of the book will teach you how to:

- Protect your family from an unexpected death

- Keep paying your bills even if you can't work due to disability

- Handle long-term care expenses before they arise

- Make sure you don't run out of money in retirement

- Avoid healthcare and insurance threats

- Avoid employment threats

- Obtain insurance to protect against business and personal risks

Protecting Your Family from an Unexpected Death

The emotional distress caused by the premature death of a loved one cannot be exaggerated. Long before the psychological scars begin to heal, financial devastation for surviving family members may begin. If proper planning is not undertaken, the value of the medical practice, which could be a saleable asset to help the family, may be lost.

There are various obstacles to successful financial planning in the case of unforeseen death simply because none of us knows when our time will come. The 2003 National Safety Council's study on deaths (http://www.nsc.org/lrs/statinfo/odds.htm) and the 1999 US Census Bureau's Statistical Abstract of the United States, which surveyed the year 1997, reported the following statistics in regard to unforeseen death types:

- There is a 1 in 24 chance (4.17%) that you will ultimately die from a stroke

- There is a 4% chance you will die from an accident or the adverse effects of one

When you add these two risks together, you can see that approximately 1 in 12 people will die from an unforeseen risk. In addition, a number of people will find out they are terminally ill and their families will not be able to purchase personal life insurance to help them manage the financial burden created when they pass away.

Another obstacle to successful financial planning in the case of unforeseen death is that most people don't enjoy contemplating, let alone discussing, the death of a family member. As a result, few families are financially or emotionally prepared for this traumatic event.

In this chapter, we will discuss two financial losses that can occur at the time of death:

- Loss of income

- Loss of an estate (via estate taxes and probate costs)

Physicians and their families can use particular insurance planning strategies to efficiently manage the risks that often result from the premature death of a family member. In addition, proper legal documentation must be created to allow for efficient handling of financial matters at death—including offering the executor of the estate the legal power to effectuate a transfer prior to the estate going through probate. If there are unnecessary delays in this process, the patients will seek another practitioner, thus diminishing the value of the practice further. This chapter aims to teach you how to protect wealth from the death of a patriarch or matriarch. Let's explore how this can be done.

Income Protection

A key to successful planning is an ability to put one's fear of death aside and focus on the financial impact a death may have on a family. The first financial impact of death, especially for younger families, is the lost income. Once a father or mother has passed away, they obviously will not earn any more income. If the family hasn't met all of its saving goals (most don't until they are well into their fifties), there will be a significant financial strain from the death. The key to maintaining wealth is making sure that no financial catastrophe wipes out the family. To show you how significant this loss of income can be, consider the following.

The present value of twenty years of lost income for the Average American family (with $45,000 of annual income) is approximately $636,000. That means that, at the time of death, the family would be in the same financial situation if they had 20 years of income OR had a lump sum of $636,000.

For the family of a physician who earns $300,000 per year, the present value of twenty years of lost income is over $4,200,000. For the family of a very successful specialist who earns $1,000,000 per year, the present value of 20 years of lost income is $14 million. The simple estimate implies that a family needs approximately 14 times the annual income of the breadwinner to replace twenty years of lost income. If you have a younger breadwinner or a breadwinner who just intends to work 30 more years, the multiple used to approximate the present value of future income is 18 times one year's income.

What these examples illustrate is that a family needs life insurance in the amount of at least 14 times the annual income of each wage earner just to keep them on track to meet their financial goals (assuming that their current earnings were keeping them on track before the death). Also, this estimate assumes no adjustment for inflation. Over twenty to twenty five years, the value of a dollar is reduced by 50%. For that reason, you could estimate that a family needs between 14 and 28 times one year's after-tax salary to replace twenty years of income. Do you have enough life insurance to protect your family and leave them in a position to meet their goals if you were to die?

In addition to lost income, the practice asset will be lost if proper estate planning doesn't allow the executor or administrator of the estate to promptly sell the assets through a power of attorney pre-probate, or depending upon the state laws, establish a trustee with a power of sale. It is very important to know which method is applicable, because in some states power of attorney expires upon death, therefore the agent or executor would have no authority to sell after death . The asset value (of the practice) will be significantly diminished or lost altogether if the sale needs approval from the court. Proper estate planning and a well-crafted and documented exit strategy (like a buy-sell agreement, see Chapter 5-5) to sell the medical practice are key elements to have in place long before an unexpected death occurs.

Estate Preservation

Although Lesson #9 focuses on the most common estate planning tools Doctors should utilize, it is important for us to mention the impact an unforeseen death can have on an estate in this chapter. In particular, the second most significant financial disaster that may occur after a premature death can be the decimation of the estate through taxes and fees.

For example, if the sudden death involves the loss of a husband and a wife (or the second of the two of them passes on), there could be significant estate tax liabilities. You will learn in Lesson #9 that the death of the second spouse in a family with a net worth over $1,000,000 could result in estate taxes of approximately 50% (and taxes of up to 75% on pensions and IRAs). Estate taxes and unnecessary probate costs can throw a wrench into a family business or real estate portfolio. If there is valuable family real estate or a family business, these assets may have to be sold to generate liquidity to pay the tax bill. The most financially astute Doctors never let taxes or laws dictate when they sell their assets. They make sure that they have adequate liquidity so they can wait out poor sellers' markets and never are forced to have a fire sale. This is a philosophy you have to adopt as well if you want to protect your family.

Many clients use life insurance to preserve their estates. The intelligent use of life insurance has helped astute families avoid financial disasters and maintain their level of affluence from generation to generation. Conversely, many Average Americans with less savvy financial planning strategies have lost valuable assets through the combination of poor planning, unlucky timing of deaths, and unexpected taxes. Because we don't know when we are going to die, and certainly don't know whether it will be a good time to sell assets when we do die, we have to rely on insurance policies to give our families the financial flexibility to withstand poor markets that may exist when we may unexpectedly pass away. This, and many other points, will be discussed in greater detail in Lesson #9.

The Diagnosis

Since our surviving family members are unlikely to be able (and possibly unwilling) to support themselves in the event of our premature deaths, we have to consider ways to protect our families. The easier way to do this is by purchasing the right life insurance policy. Since life insurance is cheaper when the applicant is younger and healthier, and is often unavailable once the applicant develops serious health issues, we strongly suggest you secure life insurance at as early an age as possible. Before you get upset at the idea of purchasing life insurance, you need to understand how this can benefit you and your family.

You will learn in Lesson #5 that many states offer complete asset protection of the cash values of life insurance policies. You will learn in Lesson #9 how life insurance is an important piece of the estate planning puzzle. In Lesson # 8, you will learn why the wealthiest Americans invest as much as they can into life insurance policies and how this strategy increases their after-tax investment returns significantly over those returns of mutual funds or most managed investment accounts. From this chapter, you need only understand that life insurance is the only way to protect your family from the financial disaster of a premature death. For those of you who have partners in your medical practice or outside businesses, the next Lesson will explain how devastating a death can be to a business, the partners, and the partners' families. We provide you efficient strategies for dealing with this risk.

Paying Bills Even if You Can't Work

If you are like most of our other clients with high incomes, the single greatest asset your family has is your earning power. This reality motivates most people to buy life insurance as protection against a premature death. For most people, purchasing life insurance is "common sense." While most people with whom we speak are underinsured, they do have at least some protection against a premature death. However, most Average American professionals, entrepreneurs, business owners, and executives often overlook a more dangerous threat to their long-term financial stability—their own disability. What is the risk that the average individual will suffer a disability? According to marketing materials of more than one life insurance company:

> **"Probability of at least one long-term disability (90 days or longer) occurring before age 65 is: 50% for someone age 25; 45% for someone age 35; 38% for someone age 45; and 26% for someone age 55."**

Inadequate disability income insurance coverage can be more costly than death, divorce, or a lawsuit. Responsible financial planning includes planning for the best possible future while protecting against the worst possible events. No one ever plans on becoming disabled—though **half** of those aged 25 will have a disability of three months or longer at least once. This chapter explains not only why you need disability insurance, but also what to look for in a disability policy.

The Need For Disability Insurance

In our opinion, the disability of the family breadwinner can be more financially devastating to a family than premature death. In both cases, the breadwinner will be unable to provide any income for the family; however, in the case of death, the deceased earner is no longer an expense to the family. Yet, if the breadwinner suddenly becomes disabled, he or she still needs to be fed, clothed, and cared for by medical professionals or family members. In many cases, the medical care alone can cost hundreds of dollars per day. Thus, with a disability, income is reduced or eliminated *and* expenses increase. This can be a devastating turn of events and can lead to creditor problems and even bankruptcy.

If you are older (near retirement) and have saved a large enough sum of money to immediately fund a comfortable retirement, then you probably don't need disability income protection. Of course, you may have some long-term care concerns, but that is covered in the next chapter. On the other hand, if you are under 50 years old, or if you are older than 50 and have several pre-college age children, you should consider *the right* disability insurance a necessity. The challenge is determining what type of disability income policy is "right" for you.

Employer Provided Coverage Often Inadequate

If you are an employee of a university, HMO, or other large corporation, your employer may provide long-term disability coverage. The premiums are probably discounted from what you would pay for a private policy. We advise you take a good look at what the employer-offered policy covers, and buy a private policy if you and the insurance professional on your advisory team decide you need it. For many people, this makes a lot of sense because employer-provided group policies are often inadequate. They may limit either the term of the coverage or the amount of benefits paid. For instance, benefits may last only a few years or benefit payments may represent only a small part of your annual compensation. Since this is most commonly an employer-paid benefit, the money received during your disability will be income taxable to you. For most, this arrangement would result in your taking home less than half of the original amount in your paycheck after taxes are paid!

Give Yourself A Check-Up

Most people with employer-provided disability insurance coverage will find the benefits inadequate. To help you determine where your existing coverage may be lacking, we have provided some questions for you to ask when you are giving yourself an insurance check-up. When you are ultimately working with the insurance professional on your advisory team, you should keep some of these questions in mind as well. They will help you better compare coverage options from different companies so that you can find the best policy for your specific circumstances and goals. Below are a list of some questions you should ask yourself as well as short explanations of the appropriate answers:

- How long does the disability coverage last?

- How much is the benefit? (Some plans may cap the benefits at $5,000 per month)

- What percentage of your income is covered? (Generally, you cannot receive more than 60% of income and the benefit is capped at $7,500 or $10,000, depending on your age). Though most group LTD plans are good for the purpose that they serve, they are only a partial cure. Because of the limitations or 'cap,' they have a built-in discrimination against higher income employees—like you!

- Who pays the premiums? (TIP: If you pay the premiums yourself, and not as a deductible expense through your business or practice, your benefits will be tax-free.) You may be seduced by the income tax deduction of the premiums, but the extra tax burden today is much easier to swallow than the tax burden will be if you suffer a disability and have a significantly reduced income *and* increased expenses. When you and your family need the money the most, you will have more.

- Is the policy portable, or convertible, to an individual policy if you leave the group? If so, do you maintain your reduced group rate?

- If your business distributes all earnings from the corporation at year-end in the way of bonuses to all owners/partners (typical of C-corps as a way to avoid double taxation), you should see whether these amounts are covered by the group policy. If not, and if bonuses or commissions make up a substantial part of your income (which we have seen to be the case with many people), you'll probably need supplemental coverage.

- What is the definition of disability in the group policy? Own-occupation, any occupation, or income-replacement? (Please see the discussion of these three terms below.)

- Are your overhead expenses covered if you are disabled? If you can't perform your duties at work, will the business keep paying you? If you can't generate income for the business, many of your expenses will keep on piling up, won't they? For professionals, a business overhead expense policy also covers hiring an outside professional to replace the insured during disability for up to two years.

Getting The Best Insurance Coverage For The Money

Now that you have given yourself a check-up and realize that you may need a new or supplemental insurance policy, you need to know what to look for in order to get the best coverage available at a reasonable rate. The following questions are important for you to ask when considering a disability policy.

What is the benefit amount? Most policies are capped at a benefit amount that equals 60% of income. Some states and insurance companies have monthly maximums as well. You have to ask yourself how much money your family would need if you were to become disabled. Generally, you want to find companies that offer at least 60% of pre-disability after-tax income with maximums of at least $7,500 or $10,000 monthly. There are additional monthly benefits of $5,000 to $25,000 per month available through more specialized channels for those high earners who want more monthly income than the traditional limits.

What is the waiting period? This is the period of time that you must be disabled before the insurance company will pay you disability benefits. The longer the waiting period before benefits kick in, the less your premium will be. Essentially, the waiting period serves as a deductible relative to time—you cover your expenses for the waiting period, then the insurance company steps in from that point forward. This is not unlike the deductible you have on your car, except that auto insurance deductibles are in the form of amounts paid ($100, $250, $500, etc.), not relative to a period of time. If you have adequate sick leave, short-term disability, and an emergency fund, and can support a longer waiting period, choose a policy with a longer waiting period to save money. Though waiting periods can last as long as 730 days, a 90-day waiting period may give you the best coverage for your money.

How long will coverage last? It's a good idea to get a benefit period of coverage that lasts until age 65, at which point Social Security payments will begin. Be aware that many policies cover you for only two to five years. Unless you are 62 to 65 years old, this would be an inadequate period because most people want coverage that pays them until age 65. Unless you are so young that you haven't yet had time to qualify for Social Security, a policy that provides lifetime benefits, at costly premiums, is generally not worth the added expense.

What is the definition of disability in your policy? Definitions vary from insurance company to insurance company, and even from policy to policy within the same company. The definition of disability used for a particular policy is of the utmost importance. The main categories are Own-occupation, Any-occupation, and Loss of Income. The Own-occupation policies, which pay a benefit if you can't continue your own occupation (even if you can and do work another occupation after the disability), are the most comprehensive and, of course, the most expensive. Two important elements to look for in an Own-occupation policy are:

1. Are you forced to go back to work in another occupation?

2. Will you receive a partial benefit if you go back to work slowly after the disability and still make less than you did before the disability?

Does the policy offer partial benefits? If you are able to work only part-time instead of your previous full-time hours, will you receive benefits? Unless your policy states that you are entitled to partial benefits, you won't receive anything unless you are totally unable to work. Also, are Extended Partial Benefits paid if you go back to work and suffer a reduction in income because you cannot keep up the same rigorous schedule you had before you became disabled? For example, this would be an important benefit for anesthesiologists, as they often work ridiculous hours in their younger years and most likely will work less after any disability.

Important Note: Partial benefits may be added on as a rider in some policies and should be seriously considered, as only 3% of all disabilities are total disabilities. Some policies even have a recovery benefit that, in the event that a business has lost clients during the disability due to the insured not being able to service them and the insured has suffered a loss of income because of this, there may be a benefit payable. The insured does not have to be disabled at all—there can be just loss of income due to disability-related attrition.

Is business overhead expense (BOE) covered? When you go out on your own, the last thing you think about is how you *won't* be able to pay your bills. Whether you have $10,000 or $20,000 of monthly disability benefit, you likely don't have enough to cover your lost income PLUS the costs of running the business. Though most companies have limited how much an individual can get in monthly benefit (often 60% of after-tax monthly income—capped at $10,000 per month), many carriers still offer up to $25,000 or more per month to cover business overhead expense. Many business owners who contact us have failed to implement this important defensive policy.

Is it non-cancelable or guaranteed renewable? The difference between these two terms—non-cancelable and guaranteed renewable—is very important. If a policy is "non-cancelable," you will pay a fixed premium throughout the contract term. Your premium will not go up for the term of the contract. If it is "guaranteed renewable," it means you cannot be cancelled, but your premiums could go up. As long as non-cancelable is in the description of the policy, you are in good shape.

How financially stable is the insurance company? Before buying a policy, check the financial soundness of your insurer. If your insurer goes bankrupt, you may have to shop for a policy later in life, when premiums are more expensive. Standard & Poor's top rating for financial stability is AAA. A.M. Best Co. uses A++ as its top rating for financial strength. Duff and Phelps rates companies on their ability to pay claims and uses AAA as its highest rating. Moody's uses Aa1 to rate Excellent companies. There are no guarantees in life, but buying a policy from a highly rated company is the safest bet you can make and we would not recommend gambling on your disability insurance to save a few dollars.

Other issues to consider when determining if you are getting the best disability insurance coverage for your money so that you can avoid financial disasters caused by the disability of the breadwinner in your family include:

- Increased Coverage

- Cost-of-Living Increases

- Waiver-of-Premium

- Return-of-Premium Waiver

- Unisex Pricing

- HIV Rider

- Multi-Life Pricing Discounts

- Protection of Future Pension Contributions

Disability Of A Business Partner

The disability of a business partner has the potential to be just as financially crippling as the disability of the family breadwinner. There is a strong financial tie between business partners. The financial dependence between business partners can be even stronger than that between spouses. When a partner becomes disabled, the business will undoubtedly lose significant revenue, while possibly facing increased costs in an attempt to replace the disabled partner. This will put a significant strain on the remaining partner who now needs to run the business without the help of the deceased partner and replace the income of the disabled partner. Absent a buy-sell agreement tied to disability income insurance with a lump sum payout to generate funds to buy out the disabled partner and have sufficient funds to pay for a replacement physician, the end result could be financial devastation for the remaining partner and the business.

The Diagnosis

The likelihood of a disability is greater than the probabilities of a premature death, a lawsuit, and a bankruptcy combined. Doctors see patients every day who are hurt and can't go back to work. Most Doctors know this is a risk, but fail to adequately address it in their own planning. A disability income insurance policy is the best way to protect your future income. We cannot overstate the importance of having a comprehensive disability policy as part of any personal financial plan and a policy as a funding mechanism for a buy-sell agreement in the case of the disability of a business partner. This is handled in Lesson #5, where you will learn how to turn your practice into a financial fortress. For now, let's move on to the next chapter, where we will show you how to manage health risks that may arise after you retire.

Handling Long-Term Care Needs Before They Arise

Some people are lucky to accumulate wealth because they are in the right place at the right time. Others are unfortunate and lose assets because they are in the wrong place at the wrong time. Doctors obviously don't believe in relying on luck to build wealth. If they did, they wouldn't spend so many years in training. Would it surprise you to learn that, after all that hard work to build careers in medicine, most Doctors ultimately leave their wealth accumulation and asset protection to chance?

We are not saying that Doctors don't work hard after they get into practice. To the contrary, the opposite is true. Doctors work too hard when they need to be working smarter. This chapter explains how Doctors can efficiently protect themselves from long-term care risks, get a valuable tax deduction, and preserve their valuable retirement assets. This is a key to working less, as it allows a retiring Doctor to quit practice with a smaller, yet more effective, safety net!

Before we discuss long-term care insurance and how to most efficiently purchase the right policy for you, we need to first see how big a risk the expenses associated with long-term care really are.

Why Is Long-Term Care A Big Risk?

According to the AARP Research Report on Long-Term Care (Ari N. Houser, AARP Public Policy Institute, October 2007 (http://www.aarp.org/research/longtermcare/ternds/fs27r_ltc.html)), on average, two-thirds (69%) of people over age 65 today will need some long-term care. The average duration of need, over a lifetime, is about three years. Women live longer and have higher rates of disability than men, so older women are more likely to need care (79% v. 58%), and, on average, need care for longer (3.7 years v. 2.2 years).

In the U.S., the average stay in a nursing home is between two to three years. In some areas of the country, the cost of nursing home care or quality around-the-clock in-home care may be $200-$300 per day. This means that the average home healthcare stay costs between $150,000 and $320,000. Additionally, the U.S. Health Care Administration reports that costs are increasing 5.8% per year and are expected to more than triple in the next 20 years. At these projected rates, the costs may be between $500,000 and $1,000,000 by the time you or your spouse need long-term care. Are you sure that you, your parents, and your in-laws all have hundreds of thousands of dollars in "extra" funds within your retirement and estate plans to cover this highly plausible expense?

Long-Term Care Insurance (LTCI) covers health insurance costs for those people who cannot take care of themselves. These costs may include nursing home care, in-home care, and many other expenses. This chapter will explain why and how the most financially astute Doctors make long-term care planning a high priority in their planning. More specifically, this chapter will discuss the need for LTCI, why is often overlooked, why the government won't help you, what types of coverage exist, and how they can help you.

The Need For Long-Term Care Insurance (LTCI)

There are two basic reasons why many Americans may need to obtain long-term care insurance. First, modern advancements in medicine, science, and technology have helped to increase the average life expectancy of people. Predictably, with this increased life expectancy, there is a greater chance that people may suffer a debilitating illness that will require them to seek significant long-term care. Even though medicine keeps people alive longer, there are still incurable diseases that don't kill you, but will leave you requiring assistance. Neurological disorders like Alzheimer's are perfect examples. An Alzheimer's patient could need significant care for 15 or 20 years before dying. These advances in medicine can come with a hefty price tag for some people.

With the trends of increasing life expectancies, in conjunction with the increasing costs of medical expenses, long-term care will impact an increasing percentage of the population and can be very expensive. Doctors are aware of the increased life expectancies and rising medical costs, but need to be consciously aware that long-term care costs can easily wipe out retirement savings and eliminate any inheritance you would have otherwise left for children or grandchildren (or would have received from your parents or in-laws). When armed with the right information, Doctors can make the decision to include LTCI in their comprehensive plans and work with their advisors to do so as cheaply and efficiently as possible.

In addition, having a plan for long-term care demonstrates a desire to have quality care in the event it is needed and represents a financial prioritization of that desire. Having a system in place will make it more likely that necessary care and assistance is provided *earlier*. Children of aging parents often delay getting help because they are concerned about how it will be afforded. According to the National Census Bureau (2006), the average national income is $48,201 and adult children may be ill-prepared to spend from their own income for supplemental care and reluctant to request spending from their parents' funds to obtain the needed help.

An AARP Study, *Valuing the Invaluable: A New Look at the Economic Value of Family Caregiving* (June 2007), found that the contributions of family caregivers often go unnoticed, but in fact their contributions are the backbone of the nation's long-term care system with an estimated economic value of **$350 billion** in 2006. The study concludes that, "the unpaid services family caregivers provide are not without costs to the caregivers and society. Lost time at work, lost benefits and declining health can add to the emotional and physical strain of actually caring for a loved one. The study underscores the need to better support family caregivers through programs that provide respite (a break from caring), tax credits, information and other supports." Having a plan in place makes it easier to get needed care earlier, without creating additional stress and financial strain on family members or other loved ones.

Why Most People Fail To Secure LTCI

Before we discuss the various types of LTCI policies, it is important that we address some reasons as to why LTCI is not often a part of people's financial plans. In this section, we will answer the following questions:

- Why won't the government cover these long-term care costs?

- Why don't most people have LTCI?

Why Won't The Government Cover These Long-Term Care Costs?

To many people's surprise, the government will not cover long-term care costs the way people would like them to. Did you know that in California, an individual does not qualify for LTCI coverage unless his net worth is LESS THAN $3,000? In addition, once that individual begins receiving LTCI benefits, the state takes all but $30 per week of income from the patient. Many Average Americans and all Doctors would have to spend every last dollar of their savings before they could receive any health care help. Even if you may have more than enough saved to pay for these types of expenses, your potential health problem could wipe out your entire inheritance, which you had hoped would go to your children or grandchildren.

Incidentally, many of our clients buy LTCI policies on their parents, because they know they will have to take care of their parents if the need arises and they want to make sure that it does not affect their financial status. After all, such unplanned expenses could result in a major financial disaster and emotional problem. Imagine if you are getting ready to retire and suddenly one of your parents or in-laws gets sick and needs $75,000 to $150,000 per year of medical expenses. Unfortunately, this will most likely be paid with after-tax dollars if you do not plan accordingly and have LTCI.

Why Don't Most People Have LTCI?

You may also be surprised to learn that many people do not have LTCI. However, many people do not want to bear the risk of self-insuring their long-term care costs. So why haven't more people purchased LTCI? In one word: ignorance. We see clients insure their lives, homes, cars, and income, but not events (like long-term care and disability) that have the next highest probability of occurring in one's lifetime (behind only death). Why? It could be an "it's not going to happen to me" mentality. It could be a false sense of security that Social Security will take care of things. It could also be frugality—that is, some Average Americans may not want to pay LTCI premiums for the next 20 to 40 years with only a 50% chance of getting a benefit from the insurance.

Types of LTCI Policies

Now that you know why you need an LTCI policy, you need to know what you should look for in such a policy. Common types of policies include:

Traditional LTCI Policies: Traditional LTCI policies feature benefits, options, and riders that vary in availability and scope among carriers. These traditional policies do not have cash value, nor do they have a death benefit. Once a person becomes eligible for LTCI benefits, (inability to perform two of six Activities of Daily Living), the traditional policy pays a daily reimbursement for approved expenses up to the maximum daily benefit chosen by the insured. Upper and lower limits vary among carriers but are in the $20-$300 per day range. Benefits can be received for life or for a period of time, as determined by a total insurance dollar value of the policy, often referred to as "the pool of benefits." "Facility-only" or "facility and in-home care policies" are also available. Elimination periods (deductibles) apply and can range from 0 days to 90 days.

Other features, options and riders that vary among carriers are inflation protection, bed reservations, alternative plan of care, restoration of benefits, personal care advisor, respite care, joint policy discounts, premium waver, rate classes, non-forfeiture benefits, indemnity benefits, caregiver indemnity benefits, and 10 year paid-up, 20 year paid-up, and non-level payment options.

A major resistance to purchasing traditional LTCI is the possibility of paying long-lasting premiums, in conjunction with the fact that a person may never actually use the policy's benefits. If this is the reason you do not have LTCI, one should seek a carrier that offers paid-up policies and/or non-forfeiture riders. Paid-up policies will require yearly premiums for a specified number of years, usually 10 years or 20 years. After this time, premium payments stop and the insured owns the policy for life. Nonforfeiture riders allow the policy owner to name a beneficiary and, upon death, all premiums that have been paid are then paid to the named beneficiary, even if benefits have been received. However, the policy must be in force at the time of death for the beneficiary to receive the paid premiums.

Universal Life Insurance Policies: A different method of addressing long-term care needs is to purchase a Universal Life Insurance policy with an attached rider that can accelerate all or a portion of the death benefit to be used for approved long-term care costs should the need arise. Benefits are received in much the same way as a traditional long-term care policy. This requires a single premium payment and purchase of a paid up policy. In most cases, an existing cash value policy can be exchanged with no tax consequence (consult your tax professional regarding your particular situation). The larger the single premium paid, the larger the death benefit that can be converted to daily benefit maximums for approved long-term care costs divided over a two-year, four-year or lifetime period at a decreasing daily maximum amount. The policy can be purchased to provide benefits for an individual or couple.

Asset-based LTCI Policies: Some companies offer LTCI policies that allow people with assets to invest those assets and secure leveraged LTC coverage (about 4:1). These policies are unique in that they pay regardless of outcome: If you need coverage, it's there; if you cancel your coverage, you get your assets back; if you never make a claim and pass away without needing they policy, your children will inherit the assets you invested. When wealthier individuals have the funds to invest in this sort of policy, it can be a no-lose proposition.

Overall, the most important feature of a good LTCI policy is a financially sound insurance carrier. Do not consider purchasing the cheapest LTCI policy that you can find. LTCI carriers must have the financial strength to sustain their ability to pay claims well into the future, when the millions of baby boomers will begin needing LTC benefits. In a nutshell, don't be pennywise and pound foolish.

Using LTCI To Protect Your Retirement Income

Would you consider paying for your LTCI premiums if you could do so in a tax-deductible manner and do so over a finite period, like five or ten years? Would you consider paying for LTCI if you knew that your heirs would receive every dollar of that premium at a later date?

Most baby boomers are saddled with the problem of having to take care of their children, themselves, and possibly their parents. The biggest financial disaster that can effect your retirement is that you, your spouse, your parents, or your in-laws suffer significant health problems and do not have a sound financial plan. The omission of a LTCI policy for family members would certainly destroy your retirement and any inheritances that might exist before the illness arose.

As established earlier in this chapter, the cost of long-term care for one person can be hundreds of dollars per day. For this reason, many physician clients don't just purchase long-term care insurance on themselves and their spouses, but they also buy long-term care insurance on their parents and in-laws. This is a growing trend we are noticing with our younger clients. They are buying LTCI policies on their parents and in-laws as a way to take care of their parents and protect their own retirements. There are many different bells and whistles to consider and a variety of LTCI payment options, which range from single payment to 10-payment, 20-payment and life-pay programs. Regardless of the payment option you choose, remember it is essential that you buy a LTCI policy so that you can avoid financial disasters and protect you and your family's assets and retirement income.

The Diagnosis

Increasing medical costs and increasing life expectancies have led to ballooning spending on medical-related expenses. The reduced benefits of social insurance leave this increased burden to individuals and families. The impact of this expense can be devastating. Hundreds of thousands of dollars per year can be spent on long-term care. With a mental illness that could last ten or more years, the cost to a family could be millions of dollars. For retirees on a fixed budget, this could bankrupt them. For physician families, long-term care expenses could unnecessarily decimate the bulk of an estate. Luckily, LTCI is available and can be purchased through a corporation to make it more tax efficient. To learn another way to make sure that you, your parents, and your in-laws don't run out of money in retirement, you should read the next chapter as well.

Making Sure You Don't Run Out of Money in Retirement

The last, and one of the most important, financial disasters that we will discuss in this Lesson is the threat of running out of money during retirement. In this chapter, we will focus on the type of investments you can make to ensure that you avoid financial disaster and don't run out of retirement savings.

This may sound odd, but the reason this chapter is so important is because we don't know when we will die. Because you cannot predict that day you will die, you can't possibly know how much in retirement savings you need or know how much retirement income you can afford to take out each year. Many retirees operate in such fear of running out of assets that they make the mistake of never touching their principal. This leads to a lower quality of life in retirement and to unnecessary estate taxes at death.

One of two things will certainly happen. You will be like many retirees and either die with money leftover for your heirs (and for the government via estate taxes) or live longer than expected (or spend too much) and run out of money in retirement. If you die with money leftover, we assume you would rather leave it to your heirs than to the federal government (this is where this chapter overlaps with the estate planning topics discussed in Lesson #9). We also assume that you don't want to have to rely on your children, your children's spouses, or your grandchildren to support you.

In this chapter, we will explain how certain Doctors get the most out of their retirement plan assets without risking running out of money in retirement. These savvy physicians get the most out of all of their assets. They also make sure that they don't have to experience financial and emotional disasters like running out of money in retirement and having to ask children or grandchildren to support them. A very valuable tool to help avoid this financial catastrophe is the Life Annuity.

Life Annuities

Retirement is a time for you to worry less, not more. You have already worked for thirty or more years, raised children, dealt with weddings (and maybe divorces), and handled thousands of day-to-day crises with your kids, among many other troubles. The last thing you want to do in retirement is worry about how you're going to support yourself and still leave something for your children, grandchildren, or your favorite charity. The Annuity and Insurance strategy eliminates the risk, "guarantees" you an adequate income in retirement, and leaves as much as money as possible to your heirs and/or charities, if there is anything left. In our best-case scenario, we can do all of this while reducing, if not eliminating, the income and estate taxes in the process. The first part of that strategy mentioned above includes a life annuity.

The life annuity (not to be confused with the variable annuity) is designed by actuaries to pay interest and principal back to you over your lifetime. The amount the insurance company pays you is "fixed" and will not decrease if the stock market crashes or if interest rates fall. Moreover, if you outlive your life expectancy, the insurance company continues to pay you or your spouse for as long as you are alive. This is a good way to remove the investment risk of your retirement plan assets and "lock in" a fixed income in retirement.

You may be wondering how much income one can expect from a life annuity policy. To answer this question, simply look at the table below, which shows some numbers for clients of ours (some individuals, some couples) at varying ages. Of course, these numbers are only examples and may differ based on a variety of economic and medical factors. However, once a life annuity is purchased, the monthly or annual income amount cannot change (unless a cost of living rider that increases the annual payout 1% to 3% annually is also purchased).

If you are afraid of running out of money or are just uncomfortable with investment risk and how it may impact your retirement, you may want to consider what sophisticated clients have utilized for years—Life Annuities. Your multidisciplinary planning team can help you integrate life annuities into your planning to minimize risk, maximize after-tax retirement income, and maximize your estate. How life annuities can be part of an estate plan will be discussed next.

Client's Income from Life Annuity*		
Client	**Cost of Life Annuity**	**Monthly Income for Life**
Dr. B—age 82	$433,000	$6,243
Dr. F—age 65	$1,000,000	$7,900
Dr. and Mrs. G—ages 67 & 63	$1,500,000	$9,200*

*Pays this amount as long as either Dr. or Mrs. G is alive.

Using A Life Annuity To Leave Money For Heirs

Life Annuities also are a valuable tool in helping you give retirement funds to your children and grandchildren, without enduring financial burdens. In most cases, the life annuity policy pays you more than you need to cover your cost of living. We recommend you gift the "excess" to an irrevocable life insurance trust (more in Lesson #9, which focuses on estate planning) and buy life insurance to replace the value of the pension assets. Because pension assets are only worth 25%+ to your heirs after income and estate taxes (also discussed in the estate planning Lesson), this solution almost always gives more to the heirs, reduces income taxes paid on withdrawals, AND provides a fixed income stream in retirement. If you're not sure how this solution would work in your situation, please feel free to call us and we will run an illustration for you.

The Exclusion Ratio Can Save Taxes

Interestingly, there is a way to get tax-free income with a life annuity. If you purchase a life annuity with non-retirement plan assets, you will receive a significant tax benefit. Savvy Doctors know this and consequently implement a life annuity policy into their financial plans so that they can save even more in retirement and avoid financial disasters.

Each life annuity of this type has what is called an "exclusion ratio." This is the amount of the monthly or annual payment that is NOT income taxable. The older you are, the greater the tax-free percentage of the life annuity payment. For an 80-year old retiree, 70% of the annuity payment may be tax-free. As an example, if you received annual annuity payments of $100,000 that were 70% tax-free, you would pay tax on only $30,000 of that payment per year. Assuming a cumulative tax rate of 25%, you would pay only $7,500 in taxes on $100,000 of income. For this reason, many retirees like to purchase life annuities rather than live off of the interest of their savings and subject themselves to the risk of outliving their funds.

In the context of retirement plans, should you decide against utilizing the life annuity and take your chances with the stock market, it is possible that you could end up with a sizeable retirement plan balance at the time of your death. While you think this is desirable because it will benefit your children or grandchildren, you would be gravely mistaken. Many of your retirement plans will be subject to taxes of 80% when you die. Avoiding this hidden tax trap is a concern that warrants its own chapter within Lesson #9.

The Diagnosis

One of the biggest fears most Americans share is running out of money in retirement. Not only would this create a financial challenge, but it would also bring about a number of emotional issues. Most Doctors are "independent," responsible people who don't want to have to ask children for money or be forced into a nursing home. By addressing protection of your income in retirement with your advisory team, you can avoid this important financial challenge that is becoming more serious as people live longer while relying on retirement vehicles that were designed in a completely different environment.

Before we proceed to strategies for structuring your practice, there are two more specific issues that every Doctor must understand—Healthcare/Insurance issues and Employment issues. These are growing risks that threaten Doctors' livelihoods more than medical malpractice and cannot be ignored.

Avoiding Healthcare & Insurance Issues

Before we can show you how to turn your practice into a Fortress and an Engine in the next Lesson, we have to show you what to avoid in your practice so that you don't cause any insurmountable financial damage to yourself or your practice. In addition to personal lawsuits, Doctors need to worry about business issues as well. This is consistent with our previous discussions about the "business of medicine."

Many physicians have a false sense of security and believe that malpractice insurance will protect them from lawsuits. We agree with you that a medical malpractice claim is not "likely" to result in a significant depletion of your estate. However, if you go to trial and lose, you could be in serious financial trouble. According to *Current Award Trends in Personal Injury* (Copyright 2007), half of all jury awards for medical malpractice claims in 2005 exceeded $1,184,000. The average medical malpractice jury award in 2005 was $3,830,000. If you consider that most doctors carry $1 million of per occurrence medical malpractice liability insurance, half the doctors who lose a judgment will be out at least $200,000 and the average personal loss from a judgment will exceed $2.8 million of the doctor's own money (after insurance has paid its limits).

In addition to medical malpractice threats, there are unexpected risks that carry an even higher likelihood of causing asset depletion. As a Doctor, business issues include liability for your business as well as liability that may result from regulatory issues and administrative investigations (i.e., OPMC, HCFA, Stark, HIPAA, OIG, etc.) and contract issues (i.e., Medicare Medicaid Fraud investigations, over-billing claims, and refund audits from insurance companies). These types of claims are increasingly overshadowing the threat of medical malpractice because, unlike malpractice risks, they are usually not covered by insurance, leaving the physician to privately fund the defense costs out of pocket. In addition, mistakes in regulatory issues can even land a Doctor in jail. No other risks in this book carry such a serious threat.

In this chapter, we will discuss some of the specific healthcare and insurance related risks, explain how they can be avoided, and offer suggestions on how to protect yourself from mistakes that may occur even when you do your best to avoid them.

HIPAA

The Health Insurance Portability and Accountability Act (HIPAA) of 1996 was originally enacted to enhance (not guarantee) certain health care insurance coverage for Americans. HIPAA also creates a national, standardized set of rules for maintaining (security) and protecting (confidential) patient medical information known as PHI (Protected Health Information). The failure to institute a good faith and reasonable office compliance program, to provide privacy notice to patients concerning their rights, to protect against the unauthorized release of confidential records and implement security safeguards for data in transit and maintained in the office could potentially place physician owners, their employees (including administrative office staff) and even business associates at grave risk for monetary fines and even criminal penalties for the unauthorized disclosure of PHI which is enforced by the OCR. Such penalties and sanctions could include civil penalties and fines for each violation ($100 per violation with a maximum penalty of $25,000/year for identical penalties) and for intentional violations of the law could even include criminal penalties (i.e. fines between $50,000—$250,000 and imprisonment terms from 1 to 10 years).

Over-Billing Issues

A key operational element in the business of medicine is the process of billing, coding and collecting professional fees from insurance companies. In some cases the payers are insurance companies and in other cases, the payers may be Medicare or Medicaid. Aside from the United States tax code (which we will call the most complex system of rules in the history of mankind in Lesson #7), the Medicare coding system may be the most complex system of rules ever created.

Despite best efforts to train administrative staff, medical offices are regularly audited by insurance companies, Medicare and Medicaid. These audits routinely result in claims of overbilling. Many Doctors fight a losing battle against the large insurance companies (and their teams of attorneys) and ultimately have to surrender funds they previously collected for services rendered. Unfortunately, when the audit comes from Medicare or Medicaid, Doctors have more to lose than just money. A Doctor found guilty of Medicare fraud can actually go to jail. Because of the significant costs resulting from both Medicare fraud and commercial insurance carrier audits, we will examine them both separately.

Medicare Fraud

Anyone who provides, or receives, healthcare services, could commit Medicare fraud. Fraud is defined as an intentional deception or misrepresentation that someone makes, knowing it is false, that could result in the payment of some unauthorized benefit. Abuse, on the other hand, involves actions that are inconsistent with sound medical, business, or fiscal practices. Abuse directly or indirectly results in higher costs to the Medicare program through improper payments that are not medically necessary. In the eyes of investigators, fraud and abuse both have the same effect. They steal valuable resources from the Medicare Trust Fund that would otherwise be used to provide benefits to Medicare recipients.

Fraud Investigations

The federal law enforcement agency responsible for investigating Medicare fraud is the Department of Health and Human Services, Office of Inspector General (HHS-OIG). In some cases, HHS-OIG may involve other agencies, such as the Federal Bureau of Investigation (FBI), the Internal Revenue Service (IRS), or the Postal Inspection Service.

Many complaints are simply misunderstandings or billing errors and can be resolved fairly easily. Some complaints help identify abusive billing practices. The Medicare contractor will educate the health care provider, collect any overpayment, and then follow up to make sure the provider does not make the same mistake again. Other complaints involve Medicare fraud. These cases often require long, complex investigations by federal law enforcement agencies.

Penalties

The U.S. Attorney General's office targets health care providers for civil and/or criminal prosecution. Some of the penalties for someone convicted of Medicare fraud are listed below.

- The False Claims Act provides fines up to $10,000, treble damages, and up to five years in prison.

- The Anti-Kickback provisions of the Social Security Act provide for fines of up to $25,000, and up to five years in prison.

- Civil monetary penalties provide for fines up to $50,000 and treble damages.

- RICO—the Racketeering Influenced and Corrupt Organization Act—has recently been used in Medicare fraud cases. Those convicted criminally can get prison terms of up to 20 years. Civil conviction under RICO provides for asset forfeiture.

- The Health Insurance Portability and Accountability Act, often called Kassebaum-Kennedy, created a new crime called Health Care Fraud. This crime allows up to 10 years in prison, or up to 20 years if serious bodily injury results, or up to life in prison if death occurs.

In addition to these penalties, the Department of Health Services can also exclude a health care provider from the Medicare system.

Commercial Carrier Audits

The practice of medicine has undergone a transformation with the advent of managed care healthcare delivery. Physicians need to be cognizant of the coding and billing requirements set forth by third party insurers for services rendered to ensure that their documentation satisfies the level of services provided. Managed Care organizations have recouped millions of dollars in refunds from providers who are unable to justify the level of services provided.

What physicians should realize is that a health insurer's fundamental existence and financial success require detailed analyses of each provider's practice patterns using information management systems that cost millions of dollars. Insurance companies make huge financial and personnel commitments to information technology over-utilization within the medical services industry.

As a result, carriers have extensive data banks that report the frequency with which each participating physician bills a particular CPT code and how that compares on a percentage basis with CPT codes billed by providers serving a similar patient population. The third party payers generate practice profiles by gathering data indicating how often a physician performs specific procedures (e.g., colonoscopy), where (s)he performs those procedures (e.g., in or out of a hospital setting), and what CPT code the physician assigns to that procedure.

All the while, insurers are comparing each physician's practice profile to other providers. Additionally, insurers maintain data banks that compare how often a provider orders laboratory tests and which tests they order and, similarly, generate provider profiles based on this information.

Once the insurer determines that a physician or a group of physicians has billing/coding patterns that deviate from a calculated norm, the insurer will, in all likelihood, commence an expanded investigation. Unfortunately, physicians usually are unaware that their billing patterns deviate from such a norm until the insurer initiates an expanded investigation. As a result, physicians have little opportunity to amend their coding and billing practices and often are completely surprised when learning they are the subject of an insurance audit.

Licensure Investigations

Each state has set up, through its Department of Health, a licensure division that has jurisdiction to investigate and prosecute matters that are perceived to be indicative of professional misconduct. This prosecution can result in sanction to a professional's medical license. Unlike a civil proceeding where a physician can be sued for monetary damages and would be normally insured to cover damages and defense costs, most physicians don't have insurance to protect against the cost of this potentially costly administrative proceeding.

Office Of Professional Medical Conduct (OPMC)

As and example, the Office of Professional Medical Conduct (OPMC) is the arm of the New York State Department of Health responsible for investigating all complaints of professional misconduct brought against a physician or physician's assistant and, when warranted, prosecuting those cases. Its employees are made up of investigators and medical coordinators, who investigate and evaluate the complaints, attorneys who oversee and prosecute the cases, administrative law judges who preside over hearings and support staff. In recent years, OPMC received a budget increase of 67% in conjunction with the Physician Discipline Reform Legislation, which was used to hire approximately 100 new staff employees including investigators, attorneys, administrative law judges and medical coordinators.

OPMC investigators are primarily persons with health care (i.e., nurses) or investigatory background (i.e., former police officers or insurance investigators). In investigating complaints involving issues of clinical practice, they consult with medical coordinators (N.Y.S. licensed physicians) who assist in determining whether the complaint warrants further investigation and ultimately whether the case merits submission to BPMC's investigation committee.

Investigators have a number of tools at their disposal to obtain information after a complaint is received. These include obtaining medical records, obtaining other documents pursuant to subpoena issued by the Board (such as hospital quality assurance or personnel files of the physician under investigation), interviewing witnesses, colleagues, and the physician under investigation (if he/she consents), reviewing a database of the malpractice history of the physician under investigation, and surveillance in limited instances.

When clinical issues are the basis of the complaint, the physician's office records and hospital records will be reviewed to determine whether there is any basis to conclude that professional misconduct has occurred. Investigators will routinely review a physician's hospital quality assurance files to determine whether the physician under investigation has other cases that might create a pattern of deficient conduct.

Stark, Stark II and Stark III

On March 26, 2004, the government released the latest version of that hydra-headed monster known as Stark II in an effort to clarify the original vaguely worded language. But the new, more precisely worded language may be more troubling for Doctors who now find it harder to meet the tougher updated standards. In addition, most states also have laws prohibiting self-referral. Typically, these laws apply to Medicaid, state health and workers' compensation plans, and to private health plans.

For something as complex and sprawling as Stark, its basic message is fairly simple: You can't refer Medicare or Medicaid patients for certain services that you—or an immediate family member—have a financial relationship to unless an exception applies. If you ignore the basic Stark prohibition, and then bill CMS for those designated health services, you may be subject to civil monetary penalties of up to $15,000 for each service plus twice the reimbursement claimed, and may be excluded from participating in Medicare and Medicaid.

Protecting Yourself

As a professional, you certainly want to do everything possible to avoid these various threats.

This will require you to become more educated on the issues at hand, consult an expert, and possibly change your behavior to reduce risk. Even after taking all of those steps, you will still need to prepare for inevitable mistakes. We will examine each of these steps now.

Step 1: Educate Yourself

More often than not, mistakes are unintentional. Doctors often make mistakes because they were unaware of the issues and how to manage them. It is important for you to continue to read your professional journals, attend the seminars offered by your association, and send your administrative staff to the appropriate programs. In addition, you should consider reading our other recent book for physicians.

Risk Management for the Practicing Physician©, from Guardian Publishing, is accredited for four hours of Category I CME Credit in Risk Management for all specialties in all 50 states. Co-written by a practicing physician, an attorney and a financial advisor, this 99-page monograph includes chapters on: providing care in today's malpractice environment, liability and the doctor-patient relationship, managing diagnosis-related liability, minimizing risks of miscommunication, managing high risk communication areas, managing the dangers of drug therapy, non-medical liability risks for the practicing physician, and liability in the new health care delivery system.

You can purchase this book by using the tear away discounted order form in the Appendix of this book or you can go to www.ojmgroup.com and order the book online.

Step 2: Find An Expert To Help You

No matter how much effort you make to understand the rules, it is unlikely you will be able to stay abreast of all of the developments and changes while trying to practice medicine and run a busy practice. There are law firms who have teams of people studying the latest legislative changes. In some cases, these firms are involved in lobbying for and drafting legislation. It is in every Doctor's best interest to have a healthcare attorney on retainer. When you understand that any mistake you may make could result in civil and/or criminal penalties, you will recognize the importance of having an expert on your team to give you advice on every element of your practice's operations.

Step 3: Change Your Behavior

After reading *Risk Management for the Practicing Physician*©, attending all of the appropriate seminars, and consulting with your healthcare attorney, you are likely to identify a number of areas where you should make changes to reduce your risk. These changes may include creating an effective confidentiality and security compliance program to help avoid the penalties and sanctions that apply for noncompliant programs (with respect to HIPAA). You may need to change your referral process to comply with Stark. You may have to hire additional staff or a specialty consulting firm to make sure you are properly billing and coding so that you avoid claims of over-billing. This may help protect you from having to pay to defend yourself in Medicare fraud or insurance company audits.

Step 4: Prepare For Inevitable Mistakes

Once you have made all the changes to your operations that were suggested by **Risk Management for the Practicing Physician©**, your healthcare attorney, and your practice consultants, you will be much less likely to be sued. However, accidents and mistakes happen. When they do, you need to be protected.

The first step to protecting assets is structuring your practice properly. If your practice is not structured properly, mistakes by you or anyone working at your practice could lead to losses of personal and practice assets. Lesson #5 will explain the core strategies that you should adopt at the practice level.

The second step is to employ all of the personal asset protection techniques offered in Lesson #6. In many healthcare law claims, the Doctors can be found personally liable for the judgments even if they have a corporation. For this reason, you need to protect personal assets—most effectively by using exempt assets (see Chapter 5-6).

The third step to protect assets from healthcare lawsuits is to consult with a healthcare attorney. Any significant change to the structure or operation of your practice—like creating an agreement between Doctors, opening a new practice location, or making structural changes to your business—you should begin by consulting a healthcare attorney. It is also a wise strategy to execute a practice audit every 12 to 24 months. This review will help save you unnecessary fines and fees and keep you out of jail. Can you think of any better goals than those?

The Diagnosis

In medical school, you learned about anatomy and about practicing the clinical side of medicine. When you got into private practice, you had to figure out that you were also a business owner and learn to negotiate what can often be a dangerous business landscape. As a successful Doctor, you have all of the clinical risks of being a Doctor, all of the risks of being an employer AND the specific risks of Healthcare law that only apply to medical practices. Compounded and navigated without proper consultation, these risks can cost you a great deal of money or even time served in jail.

Unless you don't care about money and you don't mind going to jail, you must take these risks very seriously. By educating yourself and by hiring specialists (see Lesson #3) to assist you, you can effectively manage these risks so that you can worry less and enjoy your practice more. In the next Chapter, we will discuss the other employment issues that weren't taught to you in medical school or residency.

Avoiding Employment Threats

After over a decade of educating Doctors on the importance of asset protection, we are seeing a noticeable increase in awareness. Unfortunately, the majority of Doctors who fail to employ asset protection planning give the same excuse: "Doctors never lose malpractice lawsuits with awards above coverage limits." This is wrong for two reasons. First, half of jury awards against physicians are over $1,000,000. Second, malpractice suits are only a small percentage of the awards against Doctors. A less visible but arguably larger concern is that an employee will file a suit against the Doctor. In this Chapter, we will discuss the challenges of employment liability, which may result in very expensive defense costs—even in the event of fraudulent cases that you win. We will give some examples of cases that may be of interest, explain increased risks in the information age and offer some solutions.

The Risk Of Employment Lawsuits

Over the past 20 years, there have been monumental changes in the employment arena. There are a host of Federal Laws that have been put in place to protect employees' rights and open the possibility for lawsuits against employers. Many argue that these laws are appropriate to protect the rights of workers while employers often argue that these laws place undue restrictions on their ability to manage their firms.

Regardless of which side of the issue you sit, the reality is that there are numerous "Laws of the Land" which employers must follow. Inclusive of these are the FLSA [Fair Labor Standards Act]; the ADA [Americans with Disabilities Act]; FMLA [Family Medical Leave Act]; Title VII of the Civil Rights Act of 1964; The Civil Rights Act of 1991; and many more. In addition to the federal law, each individual state's laws add another layer to these regulations. So what does it all mean? It means that you have to learn how to protect yourself against one of the fastest growing areas of liability.

What many employers—including Doctors—face today is the challenge of working in an ever increasingly complex world of employment regulations and guidelines. Most small business owners may have few resources with which to address human resources concerns and little or no training. This can result in the owner being held financially responsible for any mistakes they may make. It means that age-old established practices may plot a course for a company to end up in ruin. It means that business owners—including Doctors—must pay greater attention to how they hire employees; how they supervise them; and how they terminate them.

This environment has fueled the growth of Human Resources ("HR") outsourcing. Many firms have established themselves as specialized providers of these functions for businesses, with the intent of alleviating the business owner's HR headaches. While these firms do provide reliable HR services, they typically do not provide liability coverage for the companies they serve, especially in the realm of employee suits claiming sexual harassment, unlawful termination or discrimination. So, while business owners may benefit from outsourcing some HR tasks, they cannot outsource the risk and their companies are still responsible for their own actions. Insurance policies that address these risks are available to protect against catastrophic liability—one example is EPLI [Employment Practices Liability Insurance], also known as HIRE insurance (see www.hireins.com for more information). If the risk is real, and protective insurance is available, why are the vast majority of small business owners, including Doctors, operating without such coverage?

To small business owners, this type of coverage has historically been out of reach due to cost restrictions. Thankfully, this is now beginning the change. More affordable coverage solutions are making their way into the market. In fact, low deductible policies with coverage amounts as high as one million dollars can now be found. These more accessible policies, coupled with employment risk management services, provide a shield that can protect small business owners—including Doctors—from these potentially devastating claims.

Examples Of Employee Lawsuits

In June, 2007, the 1st U.S. Circuit Court of Appeals ruled that a hotel president was personally liable for multiple wage-hour violations. The court found that he "was not just any employee with some supervisory control," but that he "had ultimate control over the business's day-to-day operations," and was "instrumental in 'causing' the corporation to violate the FSLA [Fair Standards and Labor Act]." Chao v. Hotel Oasis Inc., 493 F.3d 26 (1st Cir. 2007).

In September, 2006, the 5th Circuit established a new law by holding that a public supervisor can be held personally liable for retaliation against an employee. This Texas case involved a woman who claimed that her boss retaliated against her, refused to grant her leave under the Family Medical Leave Act and fired her. Modica v. Taylor, 465 F.3d 174 (5th Cir. 2006).

And, in 2006, a federal judge allowed a suit to proceed against ex-Environmental Protection Agency chief Christine Todd Whitman personally for allegedly misleading New York residents and workers by stating that the air quality was safe enough for people to return after the attacks of Sept. 11, 2001. The case is presently on appeal. Benzman v. Whitman, No. 04-CV-1888 (S.D.N.Y.).

Protecting Your Practice

There are two ways to protect your practice assets from risks. First, you can insure against the risk, effectively sharing the risk and passing it along to someone else. Second, you can assume the risk yourself and use asset protection and risk management strategies to protect assets from the threats. The second strategy is covered in Lesson 6. Here we will focus on passing off all of that risk to other people through insurance.

Fewer than 5% of small businesses (and, we imagine, even fewer medical practices) have any insurance coverage providing protection from employment-related lawsuit risks. This is despite government statistics clearly indicating that this threat is a growing problem. Additionally, recent federal court rulings have begun finding owners and management "personally liable." This means that just incorporating a business will NOT, by itself, protect a business owner from being found personally and financially liable in employment-related suits. Thus, insurance coverage is key to protecting a business owner's interests.

A solid EPLI policy coupled with a comprehensive risk management course can be obtained today for under $2,500 (sample for businesses of 10 employees or less). Retaining these services provides small business owners with the tools necessary to enforce the protections of the insurance coverage. By coordinating an insurance policy and consulting services, the small business owner/Doctor can expect to see a significant reduction in the threat posed by an employment lawsuit. Contact the authors at 877-656-4362 for more information.

Risks In The Information Age

Information is the currency of modern America. The role of the Internet—and its ability to locate and distribute information—has exploded in recent years. It has become the source of much of our information—our *de facto* provider of answers, so much so that the first thing a person will do when faced with a potentially life-changing issue is often to "Google it."

What else, then, would you expect of an employee that feels they were treated unfairly? Most likely, they will explore the information available online and learn that they may have options available to them. In the past, individuals seeking to file a complaint would have to first take the step of consulting an attorney. But in the spirit of today's "instant information" culture, the EEOC's website now features a simple form for initiating a federal claim without requiring any legal consultation.

The wealth of information and ease with which claims can be filed may partly explain why the number of claims filed with the EEOC jumped from 77,990 in 1997 to over 84,400 in 2003, following a period of decline from 1995, when the number had exceeded 91,000. Coincidentally, this appears to correlate to the number of Americans that consider themselves "web-centric," which has consistently grown since the late 1990s.

Federal courts are also getting into the act and ruling more consistently to hold the individual business owner liable in employment cases.

The Diagnosis

The solution for small business owners today is to be educated about the risks and take reasonable steps to lower their overall risk of complaints in the employment field. However there is no substitute for obtaining proper insurance coverage to protect one's assets. This can be accomplished by instituting a Risk Management course and appropriate EPLI coverage. When a small business can get both at the same time in a cost effective manner then he or she is truly protected.

The bottom line is that the potential exposure to small business owners, including Doctors, is increasing and the federal courts are more consistently holding owners personally liable. Therefore, it is more important than ever for small business owners to protect their assets and get serious about the HR world like their big business counterparts.

Life insurance can protect a family from a premature death. Disability income insurance can protect a family from an injury that reduces a breadwinner's ability to earn a living. Long-term care insurance can protect a retiree from losing retirement funds and can help protect a family's estate. Various annuities can help protect a retiree from running out of money. If you want to avoid the financial disasters that have stopped many families from achieving their desired levels of wealth, you must consider all of these tools in your planning with your advisory team. Once you have protected your family so you can "do no financial harm," you will be ready to learn more advanced lessons in asset protection and wealth accumulation.

The next Lesson discusses how to turn your practice into a financial Fortress and wealth-building Engine. Since a Doctor's income and liability almost always start at the practice level, this is a very valuable lesson you need to understand and embrace before you begin protecting personal assets or learning how to build greater wealth.

Turn Your Practice into a Financial Fortress and Wealth-Building Engine

Do you run your own practice or hope to run your own practice in the near future? If your answer is "yes," then you will want to pay close attention to the information within this Lesson. The purpose of this section of the book is to help you get the most—financially speaking—out of your practice. You will have to do more than the typical cookie-cutter planning that many CPAs and attorneys will suggest. As you learned in Lesson #3, an advisor who doesn't specialize in the unique issues that Doctors face is likely to miss a number of key elements in their planning.

If your goal is to efficiently get the most out of your practice, you may find this Lesson to be the most valuable in this book. While intelligent planning can improve all aspects of your life, it is the impact on your practice that can be the most significant. You need to begin thinking about your practice not only as a treatment facility for patients, but also as a financial Fortress and a wealth-building Engine for you.

The Fortress analogy is important because we want to make sure that the practice is fortified. As the vehicle through which you will make most of your earnings in your career, the practice needs to be protected against all financial and legal threats. As you learned in the previous sections of the book, these threats are not just medical malpractice lawsuits. They include healthcare issues, employment risks, and other financial threats that can impact your ability to work and make money.

The Engine analogy is crucial because we want your practice to be an engine for wealth accumulation. You will want to apply the important concepts explained earlier in this book (e.g., Leverage and Efficiency) to your practice structure and operations. By doing so, you will finally be able to derive as much financial benefit as possible out of your practice—both during your working years and through your retirement.

In this Lesson, we will discuss ways to structure and operate your practice so it will act both as a Fortress and as an Engine. Specific chapters will cover other risks to the practice not yet discussed, including the premature death or disability of a partner. This Lesson will also explain how to turn the practice into a Fortress by protecting your accounts receivable, real estate, and equipment. You will also be introduced to tools that can be used to transform your practice into a smooth-running Engine—including the use of qualified and nonqualified plans, friendly lease-back arrangements, and captive insurance companies. Finally, we will explain the ultimate wealth-building Engine—the million-dollar retirement buy-out.

How NOT to Structure Your Practice

Every year, we meet many Doctors who are practicing within a structure that offers very little, if any, protection for the assets of the practice. Even worse, we encounter Doctors who have put absolutely no barrier between the potential risks of their practice and all of their personal assets. In some cases, this is due to ignorance on the part of the Doctor. Other times, this is the result of poor advice. Many accountants have suggested that Doctors might not see enough benefit from incorporation to warrant the added time and expense corporations require. Other advisors still recommend general partnerships, although this practice form is all but extinct. In this chapter, we will discuss the pitfalls to avoid when structuring your medical practice.

It may be difficult to believe, but most Doctors who call us have practices that are structured with two things in common:

- Maximum lawsuit exposure

- Minimum tax-saving potential

In this chapter, we will discuss the common medical practice structural and operational mistakes that can cause these two highly undesirable outcomes. After you learn how *not* to structure your practice, you can continue reading the rest of this Lesson and learn how you can structure your practice for maximum flexibility and efficiency, enabling you to create the Fortress and Engine you desire.

The Worst Way To Structure A Practice: As A General Partnership

Fortunately, it is far less common for Doctors and their advisors to structure new medical practices as general partnerships today. Though new practices are rarely configured as general partnerships, we still come across dozens of mature (and profitable) practices every year that continue to be operated as general partnerships. There are rarely absolutes in medicine, finance, or the law. However, here is one simple rule: *You should never operate any medical practice or other busi-*

ness practice as a general partnership. Why do we say this? The general (pun intended) reason is because a general partnership is a creditor's or plaintiff attorney's dream and a partner's liability nightmare. More specifically, let's consider the three hidden dangers of a general partnership:

1. Partners Have Unlimited Liability for Partnership Debts

This tragic fact goes unrealized by many Doctors who are involved in general partnerships. Without signing personal guarantees on every debt, the Doctors who are involved in a general partnership are, by default, personally guaranteeing every partnership debt and personally assuming the risk for malpractice, accidents, and other liability sources of the entire partnership. These Doctors fail to consider that their liability as a partner is joint and several with all other partners. A plaintiff who successfully sues the partnership can collect the full judgment from any one partner. Let's look at an example to see how dangerous this arrangement can be:

Case Study: Jane and Ted's Real Estate Venture

Jane and Ted were physician colleagues who wanted to increase their income by buying "fixer upper" houses, renovating them and then selling them. Events went well for a while, but the real estate market went sour and they defaulted on a $650,000 loan to the bank. Jane was much wealthier than Ted, so the bank pursued Jane for the full amount, ignoring Ted, under the theory of joint and several liability. To collect Ted's share of the liability, Jane had to file suit against him, thereby destroying a long-term friendship.

2. Partners Have Unlimited Liability for Their Partners' Acts

When your business is structured as a general partnership, you assume all risks that any partner in the partnership could cause. When a lawsuit arises from one partner's acts or omissions in the ordinary course of practice, every other partner is personally liable. The dreaded joint and several liability then applies. This means that each partner can be 100% liable for the actions of any of the other partners. If you operate within a general partnership and one of your partners gets into trouble, you can be personally liable for the entire amount, even if you were neither involved in the alleged incident or even aware of it.

Think of the many ways a partner could get you into trouble: He commits (or is convicted of) malpractice, gets into a car accident while on partnership business/ time, defrauds someone through the practice, sexually harasses an employee, wrongfully fires an employee, directs an employee to improperly bill an insurance company or Medicare, etc. Multiply this risk times the number of partners in your partnership. You have a lawsuit liability nightmare! Here is a real-world example that should help illustrate the point further:

Case Study: Michael Gets Burned By His Partner

Michael was the founding partner in a successful three-owner surgery center. One of the firm's employees sued the firm for sexual harassment. Settlement negotiations were unsuccessful and the trial jury awarded an extremely large verdict against the partnership. Of course, this was not covered by any malpractice policy. Since Michael was the wealthiest of the partners and his assets were unprotected, the plaintiff's lawyer pursued him first. This was the plaintiff's quickest way to receive cash. Michael was forced to pay the entire $250,000 judgment from his personal savings. Although Michael had much less contact with this employee than his partners, he was stuck with the bill. Now, Michael has to begin his own costly legal battle against his partners to prove that they owe more than he does because they were more involved with this former employee. This is a no-win situation for Michael—who now understands the risks of a general partnership.

3. You May be an "Unaware" General Partner

A general partnership does not require a formal written agreement like a limited partnership does. You can verbally agree to start a venture with another person and, by default, create a general partnership, with all of its liability problems. Think about this whenever you start a new practice (or any other business) venture with someone.

Even if you make no agreement to partner with another person, the law may impose general partnership liability on you if the general public reasonably perceives the two of you as partners. You may already be part of a liability-ridden general partnership and not even know it.

Case Study: Roger Inadvertently Has Partners

Roger was one of four physicians who used a common office arrangement. They each had their own patients, which they did not share. They did, however, share a common waiting area, some support staff, and used the same in-house bookkeeper/accountant to help them manage the costs of their practices. Each professional had his own practice methods, set his own hours, and was not otherwise accountable to the other Doctors.

When one of the Doctors was sued by a patient for professional misconduct, Roger and the two others had a rude awakening. Although only the patient's physician was negligent, all four were defendants in the lawsuit. The court found that the patient could reasonably conclude the four professionals were partners together because of their office set-up and common support staff. Therefore, the court allowed the plaintiff to proceed with the suit against all four as a general partnership, with each jointly and severally liable for the plaintiff's losses.

If your practice still operates as a general partnership or may be considered one as above, you should review the situation and alternative structures with experienced counsel as soon as possible.

The Second Worst Way To Structure A Practice: A Sole Proprietorship

While relatively few general partnership medical practices exist these days, we cannot say the same thing about practices that operate as sole proprietorships. Every week or two we speak to Doctors who have been operating their practice as a sole proprietorship. In other words, these practices have no legal entity and all income and expenses are recorded on the Doctor's Schedule C of the personal tax return. These Doctors simply operate the practice in their own name, with their own social security number, often with a "DBA" in the name of a medical practice (i.e., "Smith Medical Practice"). At its most basic level, the flaw of a sole proprietorship is that it provides absolutely no barrier between the Doctor's professional and personal life. As a result, any risks and liability from the medical practice threatens all of the Doctor's personal assets and any personal lawsuit against the Doctor or the Doctor's family (including teenage children) threatens the assets of the medical practice (including accounts receivable, real estate, and equipment). Let's examine these problems more closely.

Drawbacks of Sole Proprietorships

The two significant drawbacks of sole proprietorships are the following:

1. There is no shield between practice liability and all of the Doctor's personal assets.
This is a crucial asset protection failure. Because there is no legal entity, there is no fortress at all. While no legal entity will protect the Doctor from personal liability for professional malpractice, medical malpractice is not the only risk from the practice. As you read earlier in this Lesson, employment liability can be significant. Healthcare-related lawsuits are increasingly common and judgments can be huge. Add to these premises liability and other non-medical claims and one would wonder why any Doctor would choose to expose all of his or her personal wealth to such risks!

2. Without a legal entity, the practice's options for tax reduction are limited.
In addition to the asset protection drawbacks above, using a sole proprietorship also limits a Doctor's tax planning options in the practice. A number of benefits plans and tax planning options are available to corporations and not to sole proprietorships. Every Doctor we have spoken to over the years wants to get more retirement dollars out of their practice and wants to legally reduce income taxes. Since you can't accomplish these goals as efficiently with a sole proprietorship as you can with

a corporation, you have to wonder why Doctors would ever continue to operate as sole proprietorships once they learn of these opportunities.

Why Doctors Get Stuck in Sole Proprietorships

Given the significant drawbacks of using a proprietorship to operate a medical practice, it does seem strange that thousands of Doctors would do so. In our combined experience, this cannot typically be blamed on the Doctor. <u>In fact, what we have seen over the years is that Doctors who use proprietorships almost always have been told to do so by an accountant</u>.

Unfortunately for their Doctor clients, there are a large number of accountants across the U.S. whose view of this issue is extremely limited. For these accountants, the costs and headaches of using any kind of legal entity for a single Doctor medical practice is not "worth the trouble." Thus, they advise their client to simply operate the medical practice as a proprietorship. Let's examine their logic.

If the simple alternative to a proprietorship is to use a professional corporation (PC), a savvy businessperson would look at the costs and benefits of each strategy, weigh them, and make a choice. To do so here, you need to first understand the costs and headaches of such an entity (we will use PC throughout this chapter to also mean Professional Association or Professional Limited Liability Company).

You can expect the legal fees (drafting Articles of Incorporation if a corporation or Organization if an LLC, Bylaws if a corporation or Operating Agreement if an LLC and Organizational Minutes for either) and filing costs (Name Reservation for either a corporation or LLC, Articles of Incorporation or Organization and Filing Fees for either) of creating a PC to be between $3,000 and $5,000, depending on the state of formation, and annual state fees and legal and accounting costs to be roughly another $2,000 to $3,000.

If you pay such costs to a competent advisor, the only "headache" should be signing a few documents and making sure you use business checks for business expenses and personal checks and debit cards for personal expenses. Thus, the question becomes: Are the significant asset protection and tax drawbacks of the proprietorship worth saving about $2,000 per year... especially when those dollars are tax-deductible?

The key factor that many accountants seem to miss is the asset protection concern. Accountants typically focus on the fact that a PC cannot protect a Doctor from his or her own malpractice. While this is true, the PC can protect that Doctor from the following: patients or vendors who may slip and fall when they visit the practice, claims from acts of employees and many other risks we referenced in the first two chapters of this Lesson. Attorneys know about these tradeoffs and have a very similar issue. How many attorneys forego the "cost" and "hassle" of a PC and run their law practices as proprietorships? We rarely see one. If knowledgeable attorneys who understand legal risks never use proprietorships, why should Doctors be any different? It is unfortunate that some accountants have not learned the same lesson and continue to give bad advice to the Doctors who are relying on them.

If your practice still operates as a proprietorship, you should engage experienced counsel to remedy this as soon as possible!

The Protections Of Professional Corporations

If you are not in the minority of Doctors who are stuck in a general partnership or proprietorship, you are using some form of professional entity. This could be a professional corporation (PC), professional association (PA), or professional limited liability companies (PLLC). For simplicity, we will use "PC" for all of these. The most important benefits of a PC are.

- **PCs can protect the Doctor from the acts or omissions of subordinates and associates.** For instance, a Doctor can protect him or herself from the acts or omissions of nurses or other Doctors, if the Doctor at issue was not involved in the act of liability.

- **PCs may protect Doctors from non-malpractice lawsuits.** As we outlined earlier in this Lesson, there are many non-medical malpractice liability risks facing Doctors today. The PC may provide a shield for the Doctor's personal assets in many situations.

- **The PC may allow the Doctor to take advantage of certain tax-saving options not available for proprietorships.** Deducting long-term care insurance premiums, plans authorized under Section 79 of the tax code, non-qualified deferred compensation plans—all of these options, as well as several others, are only available to practices that operate as PCs.

The Bare Minimum Way to Structure a Practice: Lone PC

You may be surprised, given the discussion above, that we would call the use of a PC as a "bare minimum" technique. Certainly, when compared to a general partnership or a proprietorship, the PC is much better. However, it is still far from ideal. The following diagram illustrates how nearly all medical practices are arranged in the United States. Perhaps yours is organized this way.

In this arrangement, there is one legal entity that operates the practice and hires all the employees. This same entity also owns all of the key assets of the practice—the accounts receivable (AR), the real estate (RE), and any valuable equipment. In addition, this same entity is the one that bills insurance companies, Medicare, and patients. Finally, this same entity offers the benefit plans to the Doctors and other employees. What is wrong with this picture below?

"All Eggs in One Basket" Practice Structure

```
                    "Practice"
                  P.C., P.A., PLLC

   Owned by        Paid for        Offers         Owns AR,
   Doctors. Has    medical         retirement &   Real Estate &
   employees       services        benefit plans  Equipment
```

The problem with this diagram, and the legal structure it represents, is fairly simple—all of the practice's "eggs" are in one basket. In fact, not only are the "eggs" (assets) in the one basket, but so are all of the threats to those assets. Employees, partners, and all of the services provided by the practice are within the entity. As you will learn in Lesson #6 (personal asset protection), it is never a good idea to mix assets with liabilities. The crux of the problem is that all of the assets are exposed to all of the liability threats of the one legal entity. This means that one mistake from any of the risks could threaten all of the assets of the practice. This is obviously not a desirable condition. Also, with only one corporation, you only get the tax benefits of one type of taxed entity. With multiple entities, you might be able to benefit from two types of tax environments. In the next 2 chapters, we will examine ways to solve this problem.

The Diagnosis

In this chapter, we pointed out that many Doctors are still operating their medical practices in the worst ways possible—as general partnerships or sole proprietorships. We explained why these are terrible ways to run any business, not just a medical practice. We also explained that a Professional Corporation, Professional Association, or Professional Limited Liability Company are steps in the right direction, but still have serious problems. If the structure of your practice resembles any of these examples, you are subjecting yourself to unnecessary lawsuit risk and are sacrificing valuable tax deductions you may be able to receive from a more appropriate business structure. The good news is that, even if you have operated with a general partnership or sole proprietorship for fifty years, it is neither too late nor too difficult, to change your structure and start taking advantage of the benefits that alternative structures offer. If you truly want your practice to operate as a Fortress and a wealth-building Engine, you should first make sure that you are using the right type of entity for tax purposes.

S Corporation, C Corporation or Both?

Choosing the form and structure of one's medical practice is an important decision. Most advisors to medical practices believe that the avoidance of potential double taxation makes the S Corporation the logical choice. This "conventional wisdom" overlooks the potential benefits a C Corporation can offer. If you want to truly have your practice be an engine and explore ways to reduce unnecessary taxes *and* would like to see how you can do this without having to change any of your insurance provider or Medicare provider numbers, understanding this chapter is crucial.

The Tax Basics of Corporations

Per the last chapter, there is no reason to practice as a sole proprietorship or general partnership. This results in unnecessary lawsuit risk, in addition to the inability to take advantage of many valuable tax-deductible business expenses mentioned in this chapter.

In our analysis, we need to compare and contrast C Corporations and S Corporations (remember that PLLCs and PAs that are used in some states are also taxed as either an S or C corporation). All businesses that incorporate are automatically C Corporations, absent an election to become an S Corporation. Both S and C Corporations have separate tax ID numbers and are required to file tax returns with the federal and appropriate state tax agencies. Both entities have shareholders. Both entities can be created in any state in the country.

When a C Corporation earns profit, it must pay tax at the corporate level. Profit is the difference between income and expenses. Compensation paid to physicians, as long as it is reasonable, is deductible by the corporation on its tax return (and is therefore not taxable to the corporation). The salary received by the owner is taxable to the owner as wages. After the C Corporation pays taxes, distributions of earnings already taxed at the corporate level can be paid to the physician-owners in the form of dividends. These would generally be taxed to the physician-owners as qualified dividends, thus leading to the "double taxation" of such earnings. As you will see below, this drawback is often overrated.

An S Corporation is also a separate entity that must file its own tax return. However, the S Corporation is often referred to as a "pass through" entity. Rather than paying tax at the corporate level, all income and deductions pass through to the shareholders and the shareholders must pay tax on any S Corp income at their individual rates. Whether the income to an S Corp is paid to the physician-owners as salary or as a distribution will not impact the federal or state income tax rates that will be applied to that income for the physician. There is never any tax to the corporation, therefore there is no "double taxation" in an S Corporation.

Double Taxation—Much Ado About Nothing

Mistakenly, most physicians think of S and C Corporations as having exactly the same benefits. Since the C Corporation has a potential double taxation, most doctors and their advisors elect to form an S Corporation to avoid one more potential problem. First, the double taxation problem can be easily avoided by reducing practice profits to zero, or close to zero, at the end of the year. This is done by the thousands of medical practice C Corporations that exist today. Second, after you review the next sections you will see the increased benefits C Corporations offer medical practices, including the cost (in time, not money) of using and zeroing out a C Corporation far outweighing the benefits of an S Corporation.

Additional Deductible Benefits of a C Corporation

Contrary to much "conventional wisdom," a C Corporation can be the right choice for many small entities because of the deductions it allows. The corporate deduction for fringe benefits paid to employees is generally limited for shareholders owning more than 2% of an S Corporation. However, a C Corporation enjoys a full deduction for the cost of employees' (including owner employees) health insurance, group term life insurance of up to $50,000 per employee, and even long term care premiums without regard to age-based limitations. The C Corporation can also deduct the costs of a medical reimbursement plan. If one has a small corporation and a lot of medical expenses that aren't covered by insurance, the corporation can establish a plan that results in all of those expenses being tax deductible. Fringe benefits such as employer provided vehicles and public transportation passes are also deductible.

In contrast, health insurance paid by an S Corporation for a more than 2% shareholder is not deductible by the corporation. The shareholder must generally take a self-employed health insurance deduction on his personal return. Long term care premiums paid through an S Corporation are also not deductible with regard to these shareholders. The shareholders, in deducting them personally, are subject to the age based limitations.

Digging Deeper on the Potential Benefits of a C Corporation (over an S)

Before some of the authors were educated on the potential benefits allowed for C corporations, we too often advised doctors to use S Corporations. However, when we realized that the potential tax benefits to many doctors can be hundreds of thousands of dollars over a career by using a C Corporation rather than an S, we changed our minds.

The two most financially significant benefits allowed for C corporations are the following:

1. **Only C Corporations can offer Section 79 plans**

   As you will read in chapter 5-5, there are different types of benefit plans authorized in the tax code. One type of plan, authorized under Section 79 of the tax code, is only available to C Corporations. These plans can be utilized <u>in addition</u> to a qualified plan like pension, profit-sharing plan/401(k) or IRA. While the specifics of Section 79 plans are beyond the scope of this section, feel free to contact us to learn more. It is important to note a few of the following important benefits:

   - These plans can be utilized <u>in addition</u> to a qualified plan like a pension, profit-sharing plan/401(k) or IRA.

   - The funds in these plans can grow in the top (+5) asset protection environment in most states and in a (+1) to (+3) environment in other states.

   - Maximum contribution levels are $100,000 per doctor in practices with 10 employees or less. In larger practices, these levels can be even higher.

   - In a group practice, not every doctor need contribute the same amounts—this is extremely beneficial for group practices with doctors who want to "put away" differing amounts.

2. **Only C Corporations Can Offer Doctors Full Deductibility for Long-term Care Insurance**

   As you will see in chapter 7-4, long-term care insurance—a coverage vital to preventing your family's forced "spend down" and loss of assets—can be deductible to a corporation. However, it is not deductible for an S corporation as to the 2%+ owners. This means that for 99% of medical practices, the insurance would not be deductible to the S corporation practice. Using the C corporation, however, such policies would be 100% deductible. As the total premiums on this type of insurance can be over $100,000 over ten years, the total tax saving could be $40,000 or more per doctor—typically, well worth the time of creating year-end bonuses.

Changing from an S to a C Corporation

If you are already operating as an S corporation and are interested in converting to a C, the good news is that it is extremely easy. A simple revocation of the S election can be made instantly for an S corporation. This can be done until March 15th for that calendar year and any time for the next calendar year.

Get the Best of Both Worlds—Why Not Use Both an S and a C?

If you are already using an S corporation and it is after March 15th and you do not want to wait until the following year for these benefits, you could consider what many practices have done—

for this, and general asset protection reasons—that is, to create a 2nd entity as a non-medical management company.

In fact, many practices can take advantage of both the C Corporation and the S Corporation by setting up two distinct entities to operate different aspects of their practice. Perhaps the S Corporation will be used for the operating side of the practice (professional practice of medicine) while the C Corporation will be used for management functions (billing and administration). In this way, the practice as a whole can take advantage of both the tax deductions and benefits afforded a C Corporation and the "flow through" advantages of an S Corporation. See the diagram below. This may also provide some additional asset protection. As long as all formalities of incorporation are followed, as well as compliance with rules for employee participation in all benefit plans, medical practices can benefit from this "dual" corporate structure.

Medical Practice: Multiple Entities

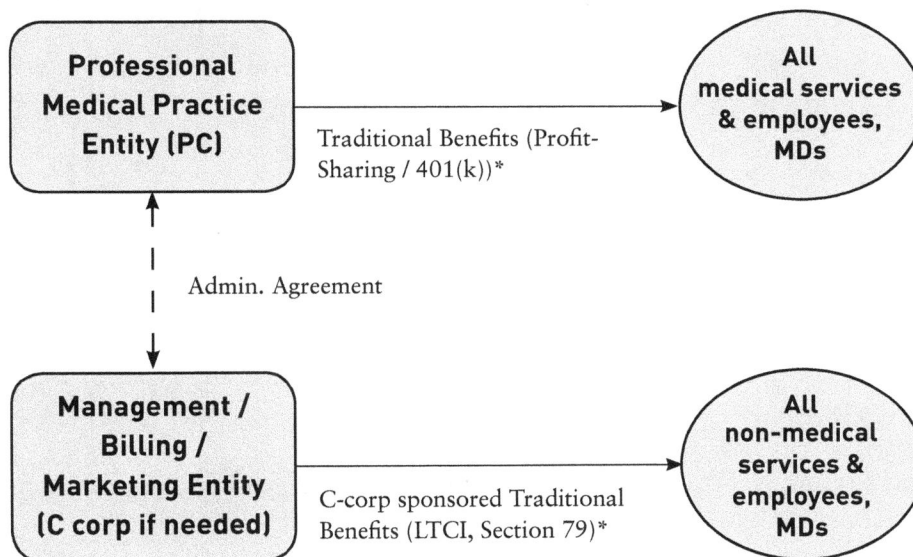

Professional Medical Practice Entity (PC) — Traditional Benefits (Profit-Sharing / 401(k))* → **All medical services & employees, MDs**

Admin. Agreement

Management / Billing / Marketing Entity (C corp if needed) — C-corp sponsored Traditional Benefits (LTCI, Section 79)* → **All non-medical services & employees, MDs**

Affiliated Service Rules Apply

The Diagnosis

In this chapter, we pointed out that many Doctors may be using the wrong type of legal entity for their practice. If wealth creation and asset protection are priorities in the practice, a C corporation should be strongly considered—and the special benefits C corporations allow should be closely examined. For doctors using S corporations, it is easy to convert to a C Corporation, and to use a 2-entity structure as well. In the next chapter, we will explain other ways to use multiple entities for medical practice asset protection.

Using Multiple Entities For Asset Protection

In the last chapter, you learned how a C corporation can make more financial sense for a medical practice than a S corporation. You also learned that, if you have an S corporation now, you can easily convert to a C corporation—or use both an S and C corporation in a multi-entity structure. The strategy of using multiple entities goes beyond the tax and financial benefits of S and C corporations, as you will see here. In this chapter, we will explain additional multiple entity asset protection concepts that can help you better shield practice assets from lawsuits (Fortress) and earn more without seeing more patients (Engine).

Protecting Practice Assets By Using Multiple Entities

We understand that it is a tremendous risk to put all of a practice's "eggs" into one basket, but what's the solution? For your practice, it may be as simple as using multiple baskets. In fact, using multiple entities to run a practice is quite common in many types of business outside of medicine. Consider:

- Most restaurant businesses use different entities if they expand beyond one location.

- Most real estate developers or investors use multiple entities for different pieces of property.

- Many owners of taxicabs use one entity to own each taxicab.

Why do these business owners use multiple entities in this way? They do so primarily because they want their businesses to be Fortresses—shielding different business units or assets from claims against other businesses or assets. If one restaurant location performs poorly or there is a lawsuit at one property, the restaurateur does not want the other locations to be held responsible. If one taxicab is in a terrible accident, the owner of the taxicab business does not want the income from the other taxicabs to be exposed to the lawsuit creditor. Doctors can use the same tactic for the exact same reason.

How should a Doctor use multiple entities to protect a medical practice? The most common way is to separate the practice's assets into various entities. Typically, the practice's accounts receivable (AR) is its greatest asset. We will deal with this asset in its own chapter later in this Lesson. After AR, many practices own the real estate where the practice operates, as well as some valuable equipment.

There are three asset protection goals of separating the ownership of the real estate and equipment (RE) from the operating practice.

1. First, the RE is a valuable asset that should be isolated from any liability created by the practice. By isolating the practice from the real estate, you may have isolated malpractice or employment liability created by the practice from the valuable RE.

2. Second, the RE itself may cause liability, such as slip-and-fall claims from those coming and going on the premises or by damages resulting from the equipment (or improper use of it by an employee) injuring a patient or employee. If the RE and the practice are operated by the same legal entity, all the "eggs" are in the same "basket." This means that the claim will be against an entity that has something to lose—all of those valuable assets. By separating the RE from the practice, you have also insulated the practice from these risks.

3. If there is a claim against the Doctors personally, the LLC can provide (+2) protection from such claims due to the charging order protections that you can read about in Lesson #6 on personal asset protection.

Separation Involves LLCs And Lease-Backs

The actual tactic of separating ownership simply involves creating a new Limited Liability Company (LLC) and transferring ownership of the real estate or equipment to the new LLC. Because the RE is no longer owned by the operating practice, claimants suing the practice have no claim against the LLC that owns the RE. For this arrangement to be respected and to ultimately protect the assets, Doctors must:

1. Properly create the LLC, with the right language in its operating agreement and all formalities being followed by the owners.

2. Respect all entity formalities.

3. Transfer title of the RE to the LLC.

4. Create fair market value leases or license documentation between the practice and the LLC(s) and make actual rental payments.

5. Ensure proper tax treatment for all parts of the transaction.

6. Transfer all insurance policies for the RE to, and premiums paid by, the LLC.

7. Comply with all other formalities that evidence the ownership of the RE by the LLC.

Your Financial Incentive

As we noted at the outset of the chapter, there is also a way the LLC lease-back tactic can be part of your "practice as Engine" strategy as well. In other words, the LLC lease-back can actually allow you to create more wealth while also protecting the RE. In fact, it can help you build wealth without requiring you to work additional hours or see more patients.

For simplicity's sake, we will assume that you have a one-Doctor medical practice (although these techniques work equally as well for group practices). Let's assume today that you own the practice's office building in the same practice entity (PC). Tomorrow, you follow our advice and use the LLC lease-back technique for the practice office and follow all the proper formalities.

We would use an LLC that is initially owned by you and your spouse. Over time, you can gift ownership interests to children while maintaining 100% control of the LLC and the RE the LLC owns. Once the children are over the age of 18 (or age 24 if they are full-time students), their percentage of the LLC income will be taxed at their (likely) lower income tax rates. If you can take full advantage of this opportunity for tax bracket sharing (see Chapter 7-3), you can save tens of thousands of dollars in income taxes each year. Stretched out over a career, the savings (and growth on saved dollars) can reach well into the six figures.

LLC Lease Back For Office Property

Medical Practice (PC) — Fair market value rent → LLC Owns Real Estate
← Fair market value lease terms

Owned by Doctor; Annual gifts of LLC % to children Over 18/24, children % taxed at their rates

The Diagnosis

After learning that the way you manage your practice is likely inappropriate, you may have been chagrined. This chapter showed you one way to resolve this issue. By using multiple entities to protect business assets, you can take advantage of a strategy that millions of businesses worldwide have used for decades. Don't be discouraged that very few Doctors are familiar with this technique. Just because few of your colleagues use multiple entities doesn't mean that you have to forfeit an opportunity to turn your practice into a Fortress and an Engine. To continue your education on transforming your practice into a Fortress and an Engine, you should consider another strategy that few Doctors implement—protecting accounts receivable. This is the topic of the next chapter.

Protecting Your Practice's Accounts Receivable

Since a medical practice's Accounts Receivable (AR) is typically its largest and most vulnerable asset, one would think that most Doctors would focus on protecting it (Fortress) from the many lawsuit risks that Doctors, medical practices, and any operating business with employees and customers face. Unfortunately, this isn't the case. Also, since the Doctor earns the right to be paid weeks and often months before the AR is ultimately collected, one might think that most Doctors would try to apply the concept of Leverage to this unproductive asset (Engine) to get more out of the asset. Again, you would be wrong.

In this Chapter, we will explain the exposure of a practice's AR to claims against the Doctors and employees of the practice. Then we will compare and contrast two options for protecting the AR and leveraging this asset for further wealth creation.

How Doctors Lose Their Accounts Receivable

A medical practice's accounts receivable (AR) is the Doctor's most vulnerable asset when it comes to losing wealth in any claim against the practice. These claims can be medical malpractice claims, employment claims, healthcare related suits, or any number of financial risks to the practice. This financial risk exists because every case against a physician or the practice will include the medical practice as one of the defendants in the lawsuit. When there is a successful lawsuit against the practice, attorneys will look to corporate assets to satisfy the corporate debt. What is the biggest (and possibly only) liquid asset that a practice has? The Accounts Receivable (AR).

The accounts receivable has already been earned by your practice. You are only awaiting payment. Most medical practices "turn over" their AR every 60-90 days or so. This means the creditor only needs to wait 2 or 3 months, at most, to get access to your AR. It doesn't matter that the AR is used to pay salaries and expenses. Once there is a lien against the AR, it becomes the property of the creditor and you have to find other ways to pay salaries and expenses.

Protecting Accounts Receivable

It is important to understand how you can protect your AR. Basically, what you need to do is find a way to "encumber" the AR to protect them. In both of the techniques we will examine, there will be a loan to the practice where the AR will become the collateral or "security" for the loan. In this way, the AR will be encumbered. This means that the AR is owned by the lender until the debt is repaid. By implementing one of these two accounts receivable financing strategies, you may not only shield your AR, but you will turn a non-productive asset (the AR balance) into a productive asset that can be immediately invested. This can lead to financial Leverage that may result in greater retirement income for you and death protection for your family. This is another example of how the practice can help build assets (Engine) while protecting existing and future assets from claims (Fortress). Let's examine the basics of accounts receivable financing and the two different types of strategies you can use.

Accounts Receivable Financing

Accounts Receivable Financing or "AR Financing" is an arrangement where a lender makes a loan to a practice that pledges the AR as collateral for the loan. This way, the practice has a liability (the loan) that offsets the asset (the AR). Typically, the lender will file an official UCC-1 form to give notice to the world that their security agreement exists and that the lender is first in line as a creditor to the AR. This means that any future creditors, including claimants who eventually get any judgments against the practice, would not be able to successfully attack the AR. In this way, the practice can create an arrangement that would successfully dissuade any future creditor from going after the AR that rightfully belongs to someone else. This is an example of an asset protection "debt shield."

This is similar to what a bank does when it gives you a first mortgage on your home. Once the bank files their security interest, all subsequent mortgages come after their interest. If you have a home worth $1 million with a $1 million previously-filed first mortgage, no creditor (including a lawsuit plaintiff) would see any value in your home. This is because there is no equity for the creditor to attack.

The above description applies to both types of AR financing protection we will discuss in this Chapter. Beyond this basic similarity, there are substantial differences between the two strategies that significantly impact the Doctor's ability to practically apply the techniques in a cost effective manner. Let's consider the nuances of the two strategies so that you can make up your mind as to which might work best for you and your practice.

AR Financing Type 1: Unrelated Lender

In the unrelated lender AR financing structure, an outside lender (typically, a bank) makes a loan to the practice and takes the security agreement against the AR. There are a number of vendors for this type of AR financing in the U.S. In some states (most notably Texas and Florida), these lenders' programs have become fairly popular. Most of the programs we have seen work the same way, although there may appear to be significant differences among them.. Let's examine a number of factors involved in these types of programs:

1. Protection of the AR

As above, because the lender is an unrelated bank, the protection of the AR will be at the highest (+5) level of protection. However, this assumes that all the formalities are respected and followed. The most important formalities are that the collateral and security agreement make the AR the primary collateral for the loan and that the proper UCC filings are made. While all promoters of these techniques claim that they "do it right," we have reviewed many of these arrangements where we disagree with both the structure and the method of following the formalities.

2. Borrower

In most of the properly structured arrangements, the borrower is the medical practice. In some, the individual Doctors are the borrowers. It's a "facts and circumstances" determination.

3. Use of loan proceeds

There is a great deal of variability here. In most of the arrangements, the practice gets the loan and then creates a deferred compensation arrangement for the Doctors. If the practice owns the deferred compensation agreement, this may not protect the loan proceeds at all. In other arrangements, the deferred compensation agreement can trigger immediate ordinary income tax to the Doctor, even though the AR has not yet been received (discussed in point #4 below). How the funds get out of the practice, how they are taxed, and what the Doctor does with the funds are all very important considerations. Make sure to discuss this with experts who understand the nuances of tax law before agreeing to participate in such a plan.

In almost all cases, the proceeds of the loan will eventually be invested in some type of cash value life insurance policy. You will learn in Lesson #8 that insurance policies can significantly outperform mutual funds and other brokerage accounts when the investor is a high-income taxpayer. In addition, in the states where cash values in life insurance policies are given the highest (+5) level of asset protection, this is a great way to achieve full (+5) protection of the AR.

4. Tax issues

This is the one area where we're used to seeing claims made by the arrangement promoters that are not well founded. Some programs have made great strides toward handling this matter properly. However, this is not always the case. The two key tax issues here are the deductibility of the interest paid to the bank and, if there is a deferred compensation plan as part of the arrangement, the tax treatment of that plan. It is imperative that the Doctors get independent review of these issues and not rely solely on the promoter or bank, or any tax attorney or accountant who has a relationship or financial incentive to work with the program promoter or bank.

5. Protection of loan proceeds

As above, in many of the AR financing structures, the loan proceeds are invested in (+5) state-exempt assets like cash value life insurance policies and annuities. In states where such assets are not given (+5) protection, the protection of the proceeds is more challenging and may typically involve (+2) LLCs. Of course, this assumes that the loan proceeds are properly removed from the practice. Any assets that remain in the practice will not be protected.

6. Economics

This is the area where promoters were especially aggressive when initially selling these plans a decade or so ago. The promoters would sell these techniques based on projections of very low interest rates on the loans and very high rates of return in the policies and annuities. For the most part, the reality of the past decade has generated returns that are nowhere near these rosy projections. Nonetheless, there is the potential for some wealth creation in these techniques. Because interest rates and investment returns vary greatly from year to year, there will always be a significant opportunity for appreciation and a substantial risk of lost principal. This needs to be understood before you agree to any such arrangement.

7. Overall cost/benefit

We recommend that you look at the unrelated lender AR financing arrangement more specifically as a protection tool and less as an arbitrage play that will create significant wealth in retirement. We understand that the stock market has outperformed the prime rate over time, but we cannot be sure how these two indices will perform between today and the day you need the money. If the arrangement can be structured to protect the Doctor's financial downside and shield the AR effectively, we think that would be ideal. The additional valuable insurance protection these programs can afford (which most Doctors and their families need) can become the "icing on the cake."

AR Financing Type 2: Related Lender

In the related lender AR financing structure, a related lender (often, an irrevocable trust for the benefit of non-physician family members) makes the loan to the practice and takes the security agreement against the AR. Because the trust and family members (spouse and children, typically) are being paid market-comparable interest, the overall family economics are superior to the unrelated lender arrangement.

Let's examine a number of factors involved in these types of programs:

1. Protection of the Accounts Receivable

As above, because the lender here is a related entity, the protection of the AR will be examined more closely. Nonetheless, if done right, this technique could afford protection at levels of (+3/+4). This also assumes that all of the formalities are followed correctly. Most important are that the collateral and security agreement make the AR the primary collateral for the loan, that the proper UCC filings are made and that the loan is at a market-comparable rate (at Applicable Federal Rate, or AFR, at a minimum when dealing with family members). Making sure your arrangement follows the necessary guidelines is the job of the attorney who structures the arrangement.

2. Borrower

In these arrangements, either the practice or the Doctor could be the borrower.

3. Use of loan proceeds

There is a great deal of variability here. In most of the arrangements, the funds are ultimately invested either directly into some kind of cash value life insurance policy in the states where these policies' cash values are given the highest (+5) exemption protections or into an LLC that may then invest into life insurance or some security.

4. Tax issues

If the Doctor is the borrower, there will not be a deferred compensation arrangement. That means that the tax issues are much simpler. If the practice is the borrower, the same deferred compensation tax issues exist as they do with an unrelated lender. In both situations, interest deductibility is still an issue that needs to be addressed with your tax advisors.

5. Protection of loan proceeds

As above, the loan proceeds may be invested in (+5) state exempt assets like cash value life insurance policies and annuities. In states where such assets are not given (+5) protection, the protection of the proceeds is more challenging and may typically involve LLCs that offer a (+2) level of protection.

6. Economics

Because the trust and family members (spouse and children, typically) are being paid interest, the overall family economics are superior to the unrelated lender arrangement. This is because the practice will pay interest to family members instead of to a bank. This means that the funds stay "in the family." This technique will work in high or low interest markets, while the previous technique's success will be contingent on a long-term, low-interest rate environment. Also, this arrangement may be combined with a related debt shield of the home (see asset protection Lesson #6), and an estate plan, to become a centerpiece of the Doctor's asset protection plan.

7. Overall cost/benefit

The related lender AR financed structure, though a bit more complex at the outset, can be much more rewarding to the Doctor and his or her family. The main reason is that the interest payments are not "lost" to the bank. Rather, they are paid to a trust for the benefit of the family. In addition, this structure can also protect the Doctor's home as well. For this reason, the authors often work with attorneys who have experience with this technique and introduce them to our clients when appropriate.

The Diagnosis

For most practices, the single largest asset is the outstanding Accounts Receivable. This generally represents between 16% to 25% of a practice's annual revenue and 30% to 50% of a practice's annual profit. One successful lawsuit against the practice resulting from the actions of any of the partners or employees could wipe out up to six months of income for ALL of the partners. This significant risk necessitates the protection of the Accounts Receivable.

In this chapter, you learned that related and unrelated lender AR financing strategies are viable for protecting this valuable practice asset. If you meet with your advisory team, they should be able to explain the differences between each plan and help you determine which plan is right for your situation.

Using Qualified, Non-Qualified & Hybrid Plans

This chapter discusses two topics that are related and can contribute to the practice being both a Fortress and an Engine. However, the chapter is unique in that almost every Doctor takes advantage of the first option—qualified plans—while almost none utilize non-qualified or "hybrid" plans. We will discuss both popular qualified retirement plans and less common non-qualified plans here, so that you can be aware of options that are available to you and, hopefully, get more out of your hard work, build greater wealth and enjoy the fruits of your labor.

Use Qualified Retirement Plans

A "qualified" retirement plan describes retirement plans that comply with certain Department of Labor and Internal Revenue Service rules. You might know such plans by their specific type, including pension plans, profit sharing plans, money purchase plans, 401(k)s or 403(b)s. Properly structured plans offer a variety of real economic benefits, such as:

- The ability to fully deduct contributions to these plans.

- Funds within these plans grow tax-deferred.

- Funds within these plans are protected from creditors.

In fact, these benefits are likely the reasons why most medical practices sponsor such plans.

For this chapter, we will include IRAs as "qualified plans" even though, technically, they are not. We are doing this because IRAs have essentially the same tax rules as qualified plans and have the same attractions to Doctors who can use them.

As you will learn in Lesson #6 on asset protection, qualified plans and IRAs enjoy (+5) protection in bankruptcy—for asset protection purposes.

You can learn more about their tax benefits (and drawbacks) in Lesson #7. You will see that the obvious tax benefits may be outweighed by the less obvious tax drawbacks.

With qualified plans (not IRAs), they must be offered to all "qualified" employees (within certain restrictions). For a Doctor owner, there may be some economic costs to having a plan that you must offer to, and contribute for, everyone at the office or at related businesses. With these mixed benefits and drawbacks, it is surprising how many Doctors (nearly 100%) use qualified plans and ignore their cousins, non-qualified plans, which are far less restrictive. Review the following chart so you can better understand the pros and cons of qualified plans.

Benefits & Drawbacks of Qualified Plans

Benefits	Drawbacks
Tax deductible contributions	You must contribute to plan for all eligible employees
Highest level of asset protection (+5)	All withdrawals subject to ordinary income tax rates
Tax-deferred growth	Penalties for access prior to age 59½
	Must take minimum distributions at age 70½
	You are "betting" that future income tax rates are the same or lower
	May be taxed at 75% or more at death

Your Qualified Plan "Bet" on Future Tax Rates

In other parts of the book, we cover most of the benefits and drawbacks of qualified plans in more detail. Here, we want to make sure you understand the bet you are making on future tax rates when you rely on qualified plans heavily for your retirement. Since all amounts that come out of qualified plans (and SEP and roll-over IRAs, of course) are 100% income taxable, there is no way to know how good (or bad) a financial deal such a plan could be for you until you know the tax rates when you withdraw funds.

In other words, if you contribute funds to a qualified plan today (when the top federal income tax rate is 35%) and withdraw funds when income tax rates are at the same or a lower level, the deduction today and tax-free growth over time is likely a "pretty good deal" for you. However, if you withdraw funds from your plan and the top federal tax rates are 40%-50% or higher, then the qualified plan/IRA may be a "bad deal" for you. Certainly, future federal income tax rates of 50% or more could make qualified plans a very negative long term investment proposition for you.

[Clarification Point: Some folks may argue that, in retirement, doctors are likely to have less income and thus the plan distributions will be taxed at lower rates. While this may be likely for 95% of taxpayers, many doctors will build enough wealth in retirement and non-retirement assets to be in the top marginal tax rates in retirement. The second highest marginal income tax rate (2% less than the highest rate) goes into effect when a married couple earns TOTAL income of only $200,300 in 2008. If you are single, divorced or widowed, that second highest rate applies to income above $164,550. Do you think that your total income will be less than $164k or $200k when you add in retirement distributions, Social Security, rental income, and any investment gains from non-pension assets? In many cases, doctors are going to retire only when their retirement assets will generate incomes equal to their last year's salary. For most of our clients, this is the retirement game plan—retire only when they can maintain the lifestyle to which they have become accustomed.]

With this is mind, review the history of US income tax rates chart below. Putting aside politics, you must understand that it is certainly a possibility that tax rates can return to the levels they were for most of the 20th century. If they do, qualified plans utilized today by most doctors may turn out to be "losing bets" in the long run. Since we cannot know what future tax rates will be, we need to at least acknowledge the bet we are making and ask how we can reduce our risk and perhaps hedge against such a losing bet.

Federal Income Tax Rates

Year	Top Marginal Federal Income Tax Rate
1920	73.0%
1930	25.0%
1940	81.0%
1950	91.0%
1960	91.0%
1970	71.0%
1980	70.0%
1990	28.0%
2000	39.6%*
2010	35.0%
2013–on	39.6%**

*Source: Citizens for Tax Justice, May 2004.
**Scheduled.

A New Concept for Investing—Tax Treatment Diversification

Does the fact that our qualified plans today may turn out to be losing bets mean that we should abandon them? In most cases, the answer is "no." These plans generally have the strongest asset protection available and provide significant incentives for employees. We would strongly recommend, however, that EVERY doctor make investments that offer a hedge against potential tax rate increases.

The concept here is that you should have various "buckets" in which to grow wealth—and each bucket should be subject to a different tax treatment. Consider it a second, but equally important, diversification technique for your wealth—along with investment class diversification.

We spread our investments across different classes of investment so that, in the event something bad happens impacting one industry, the total portfolio is not affected. With tax diversification, a similar theory applies. If you have some investments that may be taxed as ordinary income, some that may be taxed at capital gains or dividend tax rates, and some assets that may not be taxable at all, you have flexibility. When ordinary income tax rates are very high, you may choose to spend assets that are taxed at low capital gains tax rates or not taxed at all. When rates are low, you may choose to pay those taxes now. For example, some real estate investors in the last few years have NOT made 1031 exchanges. They volunteered to pay the 15% federal capital gains taxes. Others deferred the tax and may have to pay future federal rates of 20% or 28% when they sell (if rates increase). The goal is to have flexibility so you are never at the mercy of one legislative change. Some savvy investors exchange and later fund their charitable remainder trust with the replacement real estate in order to avoid the capital gains taxes. This technique is explained in Lesson 9-8.

How to Hedge Your Qualified Plan "Bet" with Tax Treatment Diversification

Above, we have recognized that, if history is any indication of the future, federal income tax rates may rise, perhaps significantly, in the future. We also understand that our qualified plans are, in fact, a bet on such future tax rates staying close to the rates today or decreasing in the future. Because such a bet is risky at best, we would all like to find a way to hedge against it. We *can* hedge against federal tax increases, using tax treatment diversification. Such diversification can be accomplished in two ways: (1) by accumulating non-qualified plan after-tax investments and (2) by using non-qualified benefit plans that are taxed differently from traditional qualified plans. Let's examine each here:

1. Using After-Tax Investments

This technique is used by most doctors. It is simply investing one's after tax savings in a liquid asset class (securities, savings, CDs, etc.) that can be accessed in retirement. Because these assets can be sold without significant income tax—stock sales will typically trigger "capital gains" taxes, while savings, bonds and CDs trigger income taxes on relatively small interest payments—they are much better protected against a high future income tax than qualified plan distributions that are 100% income taxable. In this way, if income tax rates are very high for a period of retirement, you could use these types of assets to live on and not draw down significantly on the qualified plan assets at that time. Even more importantly, by having this asset class as part of your retirement game plan, you are not as exposed to the risk of income tax rates increasing in the future.

While this technique is certainly crucial, it still has one tax risk—that capital gains tax rates rise significantly. In fact, while we call this technique "after tax investments," this is actually a misnomer. That is because such assets will trigger capital gains taxes when they are sold and—for certain assets, like mutual funds—capital gains taxes are levied along the way as well.

Again, study the chart below. You will see that, at the time of publication, US federal capital gains tax rates are at the LOWEST point in the history of the tax. Putting politics aside, we do not think that it is unrealistic to expect that such rates will be higher at any point in the future. Again, does this mean that we should abandon this asset class? Absolutely not. However, it does make sense for most Doctors to examine a third tax asset class that can eliminate the risk of future income tax rate AND future capital gains tax rate increases.

Top Federal Capital Gains Tax Rate

Year	Top Federal Capital Gains Tax Rate
1940	30.0%
1942–1967	25.0%
1970	32.3%
1977	39.9%
1980	28.0%
1990	28.0%
2000	20.0%*
2010	15.0%
2013–on	20.0%**

Source: Citizens for Tax Justice, May 2004.
**Scheduled.*

2. Using Non-Qualified Benefit Plans

Non-qualified plans are relatively unknown to Doctors, despite the fact that most Fortune 1000 companies make non-qualified plans available to their executives. This type of plan should be very attractive to Doctors, as employees are not required to participate AND allowable contributions for the owners and executives (Doctors, in the case of a medical practice) can be much higher than with qualified plans. Because there are numerous types of non-qualified plans—from split dollar plans to 162 Executive Bonus plans among many others—we will keep our discussion here to one type of plan that has both qualified and non-qualified traits and, therefore, we call a "Hybrid" plan. This plan can provide you with excellent tax diversification as well.

This so-called "Hybrid" plan is a very flexible plan that has numerous benefits for a medical practice. As relevant here, the contributions are partially deductible and partially taxable at the outset—which is much better today than the "after tax investments" asset class and not as good as the qualified plan. The funds grow tax-deferred, which is the same as the qualified plan and better than the "after tax investments" class. Finally, in the future, when funds are accessed in retirement, they can be reached without tax—better than the "after-tax investments" and far superior to the qualified plan. In this way, the Hybrid plan avoids the risks of future income and capital gains tax rate increases in a substantial way—and can act as an ideal "hedge" against future income and capital gains tax increases.

In addition to playing the role as a future tax increase hedge, the "Hybrid" Plan has the following benefits:

- These plans can be utilized in addition to a qualified plan like pension, profit-sharing plan/401(k) or IRA.

- The funds in these plans can grow in the top (+5) asset protection environment in most states and always in a good (+2) environment at minimum, in other states.

- Maximum contribution levels are $100,000 per Doctor in practices with 10 employees or less. In larger practices, these levels can be even higher.

- In a group practice, not every doctor need contribute the same amounts—extremely beneficial for group practices with Doctors who want to "put away" differing amounts.

- The plan funding can be flexible.

- Employee participation requires a minimal funding outlay.

- There are no minimum age requirements for withdrawing income (no early withdrawal penalties).

- The transfer of assets at the Doctor's death is income tax-free to heirs.

To find out more about Hybrid plans, feel free to contact the authors.

The Diagnosis

Most Doctors in the U.S. utilize some type of qualified retirement plan, including an IRA, as part of a benefit plan. Certainly, these types of plans can serve both as a protective (Fortress) and wealth accumulation (Engine) tool. On the other hand, too few Doctors use, or even investigate, non-qualified or "hybrid" plans. This is unfortunate given the tax bet that qualified plans require—a bet that could be a losing one in the future. We hope that you make it a priority to hedge such a bet—and investigate other tax asset classes such as the plans described above.

The One Contract Your Practice Must Have

Though the odds of a premature death of a practice partner are not high, the same cannot be said about a life changing disability. Because both of these risks can have such devastating effects on the finances of the practice and the future income of the remaining healthy partners, we find it troubling that so few Doctors properly address this risk.

A medical practice is a business. As such, it is created for the purpose of generating financial benefit for its owners. Practice CEOs are supposed to take calculated risks and manage these risks to maximize long-term after-tax income. There is no excuse for them to completely ignore the potentially devastating risk of disability or death of physician-partners. Are you the de facto CEO of your practice? If so, how are you protecting against these risks?

Professional medical practices have ownership restrictions in most states that prevent non-Doctors from owning them. This means that, as compared to a regular business owner, a Doctor building a medical practice is not generally building wealth for his or her family. If you want to ensure that you do build wealth for the family through your practice and actually turn your practice into a "wealth building engine" for your family, you must draft, fully-execute, and fund a Buy-Sell agreement.

In this chapter, we will discuss the reasons why a premature death or disability of a partner is such a big risk and what the financial repercussions are of failing to address this issue. We will then discuss the "medicine" for such an ailment—the Buy-Sell Agreement. We also address the importance, and method, of funding the agreement and how to work with the right team of advisors. With all of this knowledge, you should be motivated and prepared to address this important issue in your practice.

Always Expect The Unexpected

As owners of a professional practice, Doctors can spend 10 hours per day, six or seven days per week getting their practices to the point where the practice provides a measure of security for their families. We know, because we have been there ourselves. Nonetheless, those who ignore one fundamental legal contract jeopardize all of their hard work. This very important legal contract is the Buy-Sell agreement. This is an agreement that all owners sign, agreeing how the practice will be valued at the time of one partner's death or disability, and how the purchase of the shares will be paid.

Without a Buy-Sell agreement, partners and remaining families have no guidelines as to how a practice will deal with an early death or the disability of a physician-owner. At a time when the family is grieving or caring for a disabled family member and possibly struggling to pay their bills, they will look to the remaining partners' practice to help them in their time of need. At the same time, the remaining partners may be struggling to get by without the services of a valuable partner. The last thing either of these two groups need is a struggle over money. In too many cases, the absence of a Buy-Sell agreement at the time of death or disability can cause bankruptcies for the families of all of the partners.

Let's consider some of the questions that Doctors should ask themselves:

- What would happen to my family if I died or was permanently disabled? Is it fair that I worked so hard to build the practice and all my family will get will be my outstanding accounts receivable?

- What happens if and when any of my partners die or become permanently disabled? How will their families fare?

- If I have another business and a partner dies or becomes permanently disabled, do I want the surviving family members as new partners? How will I buy them out at that time?

- What happens to my share of the practice if I decide I want 'out' of the practice or I decide to eventually retire? (We will discuss exit buy-outs at the end of this chapter.)

Let's look at a quick case study of Steve and David, involving only one of the many situations where a Buy-Sell agreement has great utility. As you'll see, their story of a two-person practice losing one partner is a pretty typical case.

Case Study: Steve and David

Steve and David are owners of a very successful surgery center. Steve has the clinical expertise that patients want, while David runs the operations and marketing. Their overall profitability results from their joint efforts. If Steve were to die prematurely, David would have to find a Doctor capable of doing what Steve does. With the new hire, it's unlikely that the person could duplicate Steve's results.

At the same time, Steve's widow would want to continue to take the same money out of the practice that the family received before Steve's death. In fact, if Steve's widow is raising a young family or has children in college, she may have to force a sale of the surgery center at a distressed price just to meet her needs. Maybe Steve's son fancies himself a savvy businessman and has his own ideas on how things should be run. Perhaps Steve's spouse wants to see Steve's son take over his father's place. It wouldn't matter that Steve Junior is incompetent. There are so many problems that can arise. Needless to say, it may be impossible for David to continue a profitable practice under such circumstances.

Special Issue for Medical Practices:
Why The Buy-Sell Is Needed for the Engine

Notice that the case study above was for a surgery center—not a professional medical practice. In the case of a professional medical practice, non-physicians generally cannot own the practice. So, at the time of a physician's death or disability, the remaining family has no right whatsoever to any of the practice's assets or future income.

This restriction means that a Doctor can work hard over a career to build a practice that can never be left to remaining heirs. In fact, this creates a huge "gap" in the wealth planning for most Doctor families when compared to clients who have similar sized businesses in other areas. The business owner builds the value of the business while building net worth for the family. The Doctor, on the other hand, is generally not doing that. The only way to accomplish this goal is to convince all partners to agree to a Buy-Sell Agreement and to fund that agreement. This is why the Buy-Sell Agreement is essential to making your practice a financial "Engine" as well as a "Fortress." Let's dig into the details of Buy-Sell Agreements so you can see how they should be used in your situation.

The Buy-Sell Agreement

A Buy-Sell agreement is an agreement that all practice owners sign agreeing how the practice will be valued at the time of one partner's death or disability and how the purchase of the shares will be paid. There are various ways to structure Buy-Sell agreements, depending on the goals and circumstances of the owners and the structure of the practice. In all arrangements there are some basics regarding the agreements that can apply to any type of practice. Specifically, the benefits different stakeholders and their families can gain from a Buy-Sell agreement are universal.

Practically speaking, Buy-Sells can be used for medical and non-medical corporations (PCs, PAs, and PLLCs all qualify whether they are "S" or "C" corporations for tax purposes), partnerships, limited partnerships, Limited Liability Companies (LLC), and other forms as well. To simplify the text, we will use the words "practice owner" generically to mean any type of physician practice, including shareholders in a corporation, partners in a partnership, and members in an LLC. In the following discussion, we will address the benefits to the living partners, to the practice and its remaining owners after a death or disability, and to the surviving family members who have lost a loved one.

Benefits To All Living Partners

From the standpoint of a healthy practice owner, the Buy-Sell agreement can provide the individual partner with an opportunity to negotiate and obtain the fairest or best price for his share of the practice. In the case of retirement or disability, the agreement can be an additional source of funds for each owner.

Benefits To The Practice And Remaining Owners

There are various benefits of the Buy-Sell agreement for both the practice and its remaining owners when one partner dies or becomes disabled:

A. Provide Continuation and Control

First, from the standpoint of the practice and its remaining partners, a properly planned Buy-Sell agreement will provide for the orderly continuation of the ownership and control of the practice. This continuation should survive the death, disability, divorce, or bankruptcy of any owner and should provide for a seamless transition in the event that any owner wants to retire and sell his or her ownership share.

B. Keep out Unwanted Owners

Second, the Buy-Sell agreement can prevent unwanted outsiders from becoming owners and can eliminate the need for negotiation with remaining spouses and children. The agreement may also perform the role of a succession plan by providing for continuity or orderly succession of practice management. As above, this is not as relevant for the professional practice as it is for surgery centers and other medically-related businesses where non-Doctors can be owners.

C. Provide Liquidity to Buy Out Surviving Family Members

Third, the Buy-Sell agreement is often used in conjunction with life and disability insurance policies to effectively provide liquidity for the practice to purchase the outstanding ownership interests of the disabled or deceased partner.

Benefits To Surviving Family Members

The Buy-Sell agreement benefits the family members of disabled or deceased partners in various ways:

A. Provide Liquidity to Surviving Family Members

For a deceased or disabled owner's family, the existence of a properly funded Buy-Sell agreement can assure the family a liquid asset rather than an illiquid minority interest in a privately-held practice that would be extremely difficult, if not impossible, to sell. As mentioned earlier, this can be extremely important as the remaining family may be burdened with estate tax payments or additional expenses to care for a disabled family member. The agreement itself may provide a valuation of the practice interest, which can be used for estate tax filing purposes. This may save the survivors the additional headache and expense of securing another valuation and fighting the IRS on that value.

B. Eliminate Practice Risks to Surviving Family Members

If one owner becomes disabled or dies, the Buy-Sell contract guarantees that the disabled owner's family does not have to become involved in the practice in order to protect the total family's interest. The Buy-Sell agreement frees the disabled or deceased owner and his or her family from the risk of future practice losses and creates funds that may be used to pay medical bills and living costs of his or her family.

Funding The Agreement

Because the Buy-Sell agreement contemplates a Buy-Sell transaction at the time of an owner's death or disability, insurance policies are generally recommended to fund the transaction. There are many reasons for this, including the following:

- Insurance policies pay a predetermined amount with proceeds that are available at exactly the time when they are needed. This means there will be no liquidity concerns for any of the involved parties who need money at this time.

- Proceeds will be available regardless of the financial state of the practice at that point (so long as premiums have been paid).

- The practice "Leverages" the cost of insurance premiums to create the proceeds. Therefore, it costs the practice less to buy insurance than it would cost to save money in a special buy-out side fund.

- The economic risks of early death or premature disability of any owner are shifted from the medical practice to the insurance company.

- Insurance proceeds are paid to the owner or owner's family income tax-free.

If the payment contemplated under the agreement is not a lump sum cash or periodic payment other than through a disability insurance policy, it is important to consider some type of security arrangement for the departing owner. These agreements might include personal guarantees from remaining owners, mortgages or security interests in real estate, a bank standby letter of credit, or even collaterally-assigned life insurance policies.

The Need For A Coordinated Team

Creating a Buy-Sell arrangement that fits a particular practice's circumstances requires expertise and experience. Expertise in areas of corporate and health care practice law, tax law, insurance products, and the valuation of practices are all absolute requirements. Just as important is experience in dealing with different owners and being able to negotiate and draft an agreement that meets the needs of all parties involved.

Too often, practice owners make one of two key mistakes in deciding who should oversee the creation of a Buy-Sell arrangement. These include:

1. Choosing a friend who is a lawyer, rather than an expert with experience in this area, to create the strategy and draft the document.

2. Failing to work with a coordinated team to implement the plan.

Once you realize that you need a coordinated team to administer the Buy-Sell arrangement, you have to find the right team. This team would involve the following:

- An *attorney* who has experience creating these types of arrangements.

- A *life and disability insurance professional* who has worked on these issues many times.

- A *practice appraisal firm*, whose expertise may be needed in the future for annual practice valuations.

The Diagnosis

As with any legal or insurance planning, the early bird is richly rewarded. Nowhere in practice planning is this truer than in the Buy-Sell agreement. The reason is not so much economic, but political. If this planning is done before any owner is close to a disability, divorce, retirement, or death, all owners are in the same position relative to each other. That makes the negotiation of a standard deal for all owners a much easier and smoother process. Planning early for a Buy-Sell agreement will truly benefit you, your family, and your practice. In order to avoid financial disasters, the agreement should be an essential part of your financial planning.

Captive Insurance Companies— The Ultimate Practice Tools

Many Doctors will build their wealth primarily through their professional practice. Typically, the practice is not only the vehicle that allows the client to use Leverage, but also the vehicle which creates the bulk of the client's annual income and long-term wealth accumulation. Given this fundamental importance, it is essential that Doctors do everything possible to protect the practice and maximize its Leverage potential. The best tool for achieving such protection and Leverage is the one we will discuss in this chapter—the captive insurance company (CIC). In this chapter, we will discuss what a CIC is, what benefits it offers, and how Doctors can use it to maximize the benefits they get from their practice planning.

The CIC

Early in the book, we stressed the importance of using tools that have multiple benefits. By using tools that offer multiple benefits, Doctors can compound their Leverage and achieve a number of planning goals more efficiently than if they tried to reach their goals one at a time. Of all the tools discussed in this book, the CIC can be the most efficient. For clients who own successful businesses or professional practices, the CIC often becomes the cornerstone of the ascent to a desired level of affluence. This is because the CIC affords the following benefits:

- Superior risk management for the practice.

- Reduction in the practice's insurance expenses to third-party insurers.

- The ability to capture profits on insurance policies.

- Highest levels (+4 and +5) of asset protection for CIC assets.

- Superior income tax treatment for CIC income (when the CIC is properly structured and maintained).

- Significant estate planning benefits (when the CIC is properly integrated with estate planning tools).

- Creation of a potential buy-out mechanism for older owners of the practice upon retirement.

The CIC we will discuss here is a fully-licensed insurance company domiciled either in one of the states that has special legislation for small captive companies or in an offshore jurisdiction which has similar captive legislation. Whenever a CIC is established offshore, it is critical that the CIC be compliant with all US tax rules and must be handled by captive managers, tax attorneys, or CPAs experienced in these matters.

CIC As A Risk Management Tool

The CIC must always be established with a real insurance purpose—that is, as a facility for transferring risk and protecting assets. The transaction must make economic sense. Beyond this general rule, there is a great deal of flexibility in how the CIC can benefit its owner(s).

First, clients can use the CIC to supplement their existing insurance policies. Such "excess" protection gives the client the security of knowing that the company and its owners will not be wiped out by a lawsuit award in excess of traditional coverage limits. As Doctors, you should be concerned with all types of lawsuits—from medical malpractice to practice risks to employment liability—and this protection can be significant. Further, the CIC may even allow the client to reduce existing insurance, as the CIC policy will step in to provide additional coverage if needed.

Using one's own CIC gives the client flexibility in using customized policies which one would not easily find when using large third-party insurers. For example, many clients would like a liability policy that would pay the client's legal fees (and allow full choice of attorney), but would not be available to pay creditors or claimants (what we call "Shallow Pockets" policies). This prevents the client from appearing as a "Deep Pocket" (a prime lawsuit target). Avoiding this appearance is a necessary asset protection strategy in today's highly-litigious society.

In addition, the CIC has the flexibility to add coverage for liabilities excluded by traditional general liability policies, such as wrongful termination, harassment, or even ADA violations. Given that the awards in these areas can be over $1 million per case, Doctors should understand the value of the CIC for this benefit alone. Let's see how two such clients used a CIC by looking at the Case Study of Justin and Harry:

Case Study: Justin and Harry Use CICs

Justin and Harry are Doctors who each own successful practices and surgery centers. Justin feels like he is paying too much for his group's medical malpractice and commercial liability insurance policies. After our firm introduced Justin to an attorney and actuary who specialize in CICs, he hired them to create a CIC to issue policies that cover the least significant, most common medical malpractice and commercial liability claims (under $100,000 per occurrence). These self-insured policies significantly reduced his existing insurance premiums because he then had much higher deductibles for his third-party insurance policies.

Justin believed he could reduce his insurance premiums to commercial insurance companies, implement successful risk management programs, reduce the claims of the center, and reduce his total overall payments and costs. Ultimately, he hoped that the CIC would help him increase the profits of the center. He was right. While a significant portion of the $1.5 million in total payments was paid out to cover claims, there was still over $1 million in his CIC reserves after five years.

Justin also created the CIC owned by a Trust for his family. This way he was able to build the wealth created by the CIC out of his taxable estate.

Harry had a different approach. He established a CIC to insure lesser risks that were not covered under commercial insurance. These policies included Medicare fraud defense, HIPAA litigation expense, and malpractice defense policies (which are available only to pay for the company's legal fees, but not to pay claimants). After five years, Harry's CIC did not pay any claims. At this point, the premiums are still growing as reserves of the CIC to be used to pay future claims.

Harry is also considering bringing younger partners into his practice. He plans on using the CIC as part of an exit strategy for his practice as well, with each new partner responsible for paying some of his buyout—from both the practice and the CIC.

The purpose of the case study is to demonstrate that clients can purchase policies from their CIC that are similar to policies offered by traditional third-party insurers or can purchase less common policies. In either case, CIC owners have an opportunity to enjoy powerful asset protection, tax, retirement, and estate planning advantages from using a CIC. In essence, the question for the client becomes:

**If you are going to use insurance to protect against risk,
why give away the potential profits, asset protection,
and tax and estate planning benefits when you do not have to?**

Let's more closely examine a few of the benefits of having a CIC.

CIC Compared To Self-Insuring—The "Rainy Day Fund"

Because our society has become so litigious, many Doctors have been "self-insuring" against potential losses like the ones named above. These clients have simply saved up funds to be used to pay any expenses that may arise from a risk. This is the proverbial "rainy day fund." While a rainy day fund may prove wise, the client would be better off using a CIC to insure against any risks. This is because premiums paid to the CIC enjoy the highest levels of asset protection (+4/+5), can be structured to grow outside the taxable estate, can be structured to layer into a practice exit strategy, and can enjoy tax advantages as well. None of these benefits are found with the "rainy day fund."

Avoiding Land Mines

The CIC structure must be properly created and maintained. If not, all risk management, asset protection, estate, practice and tax benefits may be lost. For these reasons, using professionals who have expertise in establishing CICs for clients is critical. It is especially important that the right attorneys and insurance managers are involved. While using such experts and a real CIC structure may be more expensive than some of the cheaper alternatives being touted on the Internet or at fly-by-night seminars, this is one area where "doing it right" is the only way to enjoy the CIC's benefits and be 100% compliant with Federal and local laws and regulations.

Who Can Afford A CIC?

Setting up a CIC requires particular expertise. As you might expect, the professionals most experienced in these matters charge significant fees for both the creation and maintenance of CICs. Set-up costs can be from $70,000 to $100,000 and annual maintenance costs another $30-50,000 per year. While these fees are significant (and often fully tax-deductible), the CIC's potential risk management, tax, practice, estate planning, and asset protection benefits often combine to make it a very attractive option for very successful Doctors. There is no better way for successful practice owners to Leverage their advisors than to work with them to create such a flexible and efficient planning tool as a captive insurance company.

The Diagnosis

Doctors face various financial threats that range from operational problems to exit strategy challenges and from lawsuit threats to increasing operational costs. Astute Doctors not only want to mitigate these risks, but to do so in an efficient manner. For these reasons, Doctors who own very successful practices use captive insurance companies (CICs). A CIC can be a valuable tool in addressing many of a Doctor's planning challenges at one time. In fact, perhaps no other tool described in this book can impact a client's overall wealth protection and long-term accumulation as much as a CIC. Once you read the rest of the book and understand all of the available planning options, you will have a greater understanding and appreciation of the value of a CIC.

Creating Your Practice's $1 Million Retirement Buyout

One of the most common complaints we hear from Doctors is that they are frustrated that their decades of hard work are not building anything of concrete financial value. In other words, Doctors are frustrated that their practice will not be "worth anything" when they retire. As a result, they cannot "sell it" and enjoy a lucrative exit from the practice of medicine the way other business owners can with their non-medical businesses.

It is certainly true that the days of an outside practice management firm coming in and purchasing a Doctor's practice for millions of dollars are long gone. On the other hand, there are a number of tactics a Doctor can employ to create a $1 million "buy-out fund." We are not talking about the funded Buy-Sell arrangement that applies to unforeseen circumstances such as a disability or premature death of a partner. The buy-out funds we will discuss here are mechanisms to exit a practice at the Doctor's chosen retirement time and take over $1 million out at that point. Of course, this would also be in addition to whatever the Doctor has in qualified retirement plans and other personal assets.

Buyout Funding Options

As you will see below, each of these tools require periodic funding over time. With the compound growth over an entire career, a Doctor can create significant retirement buy-out funds over 10, 20, or 30 years. A nice bonus is that the funds can grow on a tax-deferred or tax-free basis in most of these arrangements. With all of these tools, Doctors have two potential ways of funding them:

A. Solo Practice Model

Here, the Doctor in question simply takes advantage of one or more of the tools below and funds them from the practice. This approach is certainly better than not funding them at all, thanks to the asset protection and potential tax benefits that many of these tools afford. These options force the Doctor to build the buy-out fund with dollars that might otherwise be spent on personal consumption. Therefore, any and all of these tools can be used in the one-Doctor model.

B. Group Practice Model

In this model, in addition to the potential tax, asset protection, and forced savings benefits, Doctors enjoy another crucial benefit described earlier on in the book. They get to use other people's money (OPM) to achieve a long-term goal. OPM is involved here because each of these tools can be Leveraged in a way that older Doctors of the practice require the younger Doctors (partners or not) to contribute into these vehicles. While the contributions go partly to their own buy-out fund, part of it could also fund the buy-out of older Doctors. When these younger Doctors become more senior, they too will benefit from this arrangement and the funding by younger Doctors at that time. This "pyramid" model is common in professional firms outside medicine, such as consulting or law firms.

Buyout Funding Tools

As you will see below, all of the major buyout funding tools are arrangements that we have already described earlier in this Lesson. Let's examine each of them again briefly and review how they apply to the goal of creating a buyout retirement fund.

1. LLC Lease Back

A valuable piece of equipment or the practice's office can be transferred to an LLC and then leased back to the practice entity. As explained before, this provides asset protection for the practice (vis-à-vis claims from the property or equipment), the property/equipment (from claims against the practice), and for the Doctors (from both).

The LLC lease back works as a buyout funding tool through the rent paid by the practice to the LLC. Each month the practice will pay tax-deductible rent to the LLC. In the solo practice model, the Doctor could utilize a gifting program for the LLC interests and, over time, get the benefit of lower tax bracket "borrowing" of children or grandchildren. Proceeds remain inside the LLC, asset protected at a (+2) level. They can be managed by professionals in a tax-favored way and build up over time to create a buyout fund.

Even better, in the group practice model, the Doctors gain additional shares in the LLC for each year of service. This way, the older Doctors have more of an interest in the LLC accounts as they remain with the practice, and the younger Doctors help fund their value (as the rent can be an expense they all share equally). When the Doctor retires, he or she can redeem LLC interests for cash. The cycle continues as new Doctors join the practice and become young partners.

2. Unrelated AR financing

In the unrelated lender AR financing structure, an outside lender (typically a bank) takes the security agreement against the AR. This is typically in return for a loan to the practice. Often, the loan proceeds are invested in a creditor-protected life insurance policy as part of a deferred compensation arrangement for the Doctors.

In the solo practice structure, the opportunity for a buy-out fund comes from the deferred compensation arrangement. However, as cautioned before, because loan interest must be paid to the bank, the investments of the plan should be conservatively structured to meet the loan interest and principal obligations. Sometimes, it is difficult to generate a return that exceeds the interest costs of the loan. Taking too much risk here in an attempt to generate income to offset the loan payments is extremely unwise and can lead to further negative financial consequences. Remember, the reason you are entering into this transaction in the first place is to reduce—not increase—financial risks.

For the group practice model, there may be more of an opportunity for a buy-out fund, even if the policy is a very conservative one. This is because of the OPM factor. If younger Doctors share the burden of funding the policy of older Doctors, there is a greater opportunity for buy-out funds accumulating beyond the loan obligations.

3. Related AR Financing

In the related lender AR financing structure, a related lender (often an irrevocable trust for the benefit of non-physician family members) makes the loan to the practice and the trust takes the security agreement against the AR. Because the trust and family members (spouse and children, typically) are being paid interest, the overall family economics are superior to the unrelated lender arrangement.

This buyout fund arrangement generally only works with solo or two-person practices because the lender is related to the Doctor. It becomes too complex to have multiple trusts loaning funds to a practice with more than one or two Doctors. However, in the small practice scenario, this arrangement can provide solid asset protection and create beneficial buy-out funds within an LLC or exempt life policy as well.

4. Non-Qualified Plan/Hybrid Plans

Non-qualified/hybrid plans are benefit plans not required to be offered to all practice employees. While the contributions to the plan are typically not tax deductible, the funds in the plan can grow tax-deferred.

The non-qualified plan works as a buy-out funding tool through the contributions paid by the practice to the plan. Each month or year, the practice will make contributions to the plan for each participant. The funds can then grow in the plan tax-deferred. At retirement (no age restrictions as with qualified plans), the Doctor can withdraw their plan funds. The tax at that time depends on the plan. In the solo practice model, the Doctor simply has the practice make contributions to the plan and enjoys the tax-favored build up over time to create a buyout fund.

Even better, in the group practice model, the Doctors gain additional benefits by using the practice' contributions to fund the plan based on years of service. This way, the older Doctors have more of an interest in the fund as they remain with the practice. The cycle continues as new Doctors join the practice and become young partners.

5. Captive Insurance Company (CIC)

As explained in the last chapter, CICs are real insurance companies which insure the medical practice for a host of risks. In many cases, the Doctor's CIC can be just as profitable over their career as the medical practice. Thus, whether the Doctor owns the CIC himself (solo model) or all the Doctors in the practice own it, the CIC can create an enormous potential buy-out fund when any Doctor retires. In fact, the superior structure is one where the CIC is owned from the outset by one or more Trusts for the Doctors' families and the CIC establishes some type of benefit plan for the Doctors' buy-out fund. This layers in estate planning benefits as well as buy-out funding benefits.

The Diagnosis

Doctors cannot simply rely on a "white knight" firm to come in and buy their practices for $1 million on the day they want to retire. On the other hand, the idea that they "can't get anything for their practice" misses the point entirely. Doctors who plan for an exit can have a lucrative one—but they need to focus on the goal of creating a buy-out fund years before they retire and be diligent in their funding of one of more buy-out tools over time.

In this Lesson, you learned how not to structure your practice and how to utilize multiple entities to protect valuable real estate, equipment and accounts receivable. You also learned how retirement plans provide asset protection and why your practice MUST have a fully executed and funded Buy-Sell agreement. You also learned how successful practices benefit from captive insurance companies and million-dollar buyout programs. Now, we will focus our attention on personal asset protection strategies that every Doctor must consider.

Protect Personal Assets from Lawsuits

If one studies how the rich have treated their wealth throughout history, you will see signs of asset protection. Kings would build impressive castles to shield their wealth from invading armies or rival kings. Some would build walls around the towns that surrounded their castles. Others would even build moats around those walls. Today, this is exactly what Doctors need to do with their wealth. The threats may not be rival kings or armies, but the importance of protecting assets has not changed.

Over the last twenty-five years, a significant period of wealth accumulation in this country has fueled the growth in the field of asset protection. Asset protection as an endeavor is quite easy to define: "the structuring of one's assets in a way to shield them from lawsuits and other creditor threats." The goal of asset protection planning is simple, but achieving this goal can be quite difficult. Asset protection requires expertise from a number of disciplines and must be managed on an ongoing basis to be successful. As a family's situation or asset mix changes, so too will the plan need to change to adequately protect their wealth.

In this Lesson, we will begin by explaining the importance of asset protection, the sliding scale of asset protection, and common asset protection myths. Then, we will explain a number of tools and strategies that have helped Doctors protect their assets, such as:

- Business and personal insurance

- State and federal exempt assets

- Family limited partnerships and limited liability companies

- Various types of trusts

- International planning

- Strategies for protecting your home

- Strategies for protecting against divorce

To see which tools work best for protecting your assets, you will have to work with your Advisory Team and make sure there is at least one asset protection specialist in the group.

The Importance of Asset Protection

Until the last part of the 20th century, it might have seemed excessive to be concerned with protecting assets from potential lawsuits. Lawsuits were not particularly common and jury awards were reasonable. In the 1980s, the number of lawsuits in the United States skyrocketed and outrageous jury awards became commonplace. This has been especially the case in employment and medical malpractice claims—two areas where Doctors are specifically targets. As such, Doctors have realized that protecting their assets from lawsuits needs to be the focus of any financial plan.

The Lawsuit Explosion

Why are there so many more lawsuits today? It may be because many Americans see a lawsuit as a way to "get rich quick" rather than as a way to make someone whole and ultimately achieve justice for being wronged by another. In our society, many people believe that misfortune is an opportunity to place blame and seek financial reparations—even if that person wasn't at fault for the misfortune. Unfortunately, juries routinely adopt the idea that someone must pay for alleged wrong-doings and often disregard the facts of the case when reaching a verdict. Through emotion and bias, juries sometimes give away large sums of money to unfortunate victims, even when the defendants were not to blame for the misfortune.

To illustrate this point, let's consider the decisions reached in some cases you may have read about in your daily newspaper:

Claim: A woman sues a franchise eatery because the coffee she spilled in her lap was too hot.
Decision: Woman receives $2.6 million.

Claim: A trespasser is injured while burglarizing a home.
Decision: Burglar receives thousands of dollars.

Claim: A Pennsylvania woman sues a physician claiming to have lost her psychic powers during a routine set of tests.

Decision: Woman receives a jury award for $690,000.

After reading the large settlements these ordinary people receive, it seems rational that other people would begin to ask themselves, "Why not me?" The more press these cases receive, the greater the reinforcement of this belief. The greater the number of people who try to "work the system," the greater the number of people who will eventually succeed. Each new outrageous success gains more press, and the vicious cycle of lawsuits continues.

Knowledgeable Doctors realize that this lawsuit trend cannot be ignored. They insist on having their advisors devise financial plans that address the protection of their assets. They realize that they have something to lose if they are sued, and that the plaintiff often has nothing to lose. This is especially true in the United States legal system.

American Rule Of Legal Fees

Did you know that in virtually every other legal system in the world, a plaintiff who sues unsuccessfully has to pay the defendant's legal bills? That is correct. This rule, called the "British Rule," effectively keeps people from suing others unless they truly think they have a case with merit. If a plaintiff does not have a very good case, he risks not only paying his own attorney's fees, but also the defendant's.

This is obviously not the situation in the United States. In U.S. courts we follow the "American Rule," which dictates that each side pays their legal fees regardless of the outcome of the case. This rule was originally created so that people wouldn't be discouraged from suing big businesses. Though this rule may have had some positive impact, it has created two negative consequences:

1. As a plaintiff, you have a lot less to lose if you bring a meritless case. In fact, with the prevalence of contingency fee attorneys, plaintiffs are literally in a no-lose situation as they have no "skin in the game." This is because contingency fee attorneys do not charge their clients hourly fees. Their only compensation is a percentage of the judgment awards of the cases they win.

2. As a defendant, a winning outcome is still a losing proposition. We say this because a successful defense of a lawsuit still results in significant out-of-pocket defense costs and legal fees. In addition, a legal defense results in time out of work and an unquantifiable amount of stress.

Evidently, the American Rule of legal fees encourages civil lawsuits. Proponents of the system still claim that it allows the poor access to the legal system and is a method for Americans to redress injustices. They may be right. Nonetheless, an unwanted side effect of this rule is that it also allows thousands, if not millions, of frivolous and dubious lawsuits to be filed each year.

People Abuse The Legal System

Whether it is caused by the American Rule of legal fees or not, it is clear that many people simply abuse the legal system for personal gain. This trend is so severe in California that the legislature passed the Vexatious Litigant Act, a law establishing a list of people who routinely abuse the legal system by filing too many frivolous lawsuits. These same individuals cannot be denied their constitutional right to sue. However, this act restricts them from filing suits without attorneys unless they receive a judge's permission. This list is available to every lawyer in the state.

Who is on this list? The people on this list are those who, in the court's opinion, have repeatedly filed lawsuits lacking merit or have engaged in other frivolous and abusive tactics. Two offensive examples of people on this list are:

1. A Los Angeles-based claimant who filed over 200 lawsuits in seven years. Very few of the suits were successful.

2. Defensive plaintiffs. A court clerk recommended certain individuals for this list. These individuals made the clerk a lawsuit target and the clerk was then sued 11 times in two years—unsuccessfully. The clerk's reaction: "I do not exaggerate when I say I am extremely frightened by these people." (*The Sacramento Bee*, November 26, 1995)

The Diagnosis

At this point, we hope you realize what the wealthy have known for years. The American Rule of law has afforded people an opportunity to protect themselves through the courts. Unfortunately, many people have taken advantage of the system and a lawsuit frenzy has resulted in our country. In this litigious society, asset protection planning is an integral part of any comprehensive financial plan. For Doctors with greater liability than the average person, asset protection planning couldn't be more important. Luckily, it can be integrated into a financial plan to protect assets from lawsuits, allow the Doctors to spend more time making money, and provide peace of mind. In the following chapters, you'll learn the various tools and techniques you can implement to shield your wealth from lawsuits and other claims.

The Sliding Scale of Asset Protection

The most common misconception among Doctors regarding asset protection is the idea that an asset is either "protected" or "unprotected." This "black or white" analysis is no more accurate in the field of asset protection than it is in the field of medicine. In fact, asset protection advisors are very similar to physicians in how they approach any client or patient. In this chapter, we will discuss the way in which advisors measure a client's assets by using a sliding scale. Then we will suggest ways in which Doctors can protect assets, avoid high-risk assets and achieve a high level of protection.

The Sliding Scale And Scores

To measure the assets of a client, advisors use a sliding scale that indicates the client's "good" and "bad" financial habits. Like Doctors, asset protection professionals will first try to get a client to avoid "bad habits." For a medical patient, bad habits might mean smoking, drinking too much or maintaining a poor diet. For a client of ours, bad habits might include owning property in their own name, owning property jointly with a spouse or failing to maximize the percentage of exempt assets in an investment portfolio.

Like a Doctor who judges the severity of a patient's illness, asset protection specialists use a rating system to determine the protection or vulnerability of a client's particular asset. The sliding scale runs from—5 (totally vulnerable) to +5 (superior protection). As you have probably already guessed, our goal is to bring a client's score closer to (+5) for each of their assets.

When most clients initially come to see us, their asset planning scores are overwhelmingly on the negative side of the scale. The reason for this score varies. Typically, personal assets are owned jointly (-3) or in their individual name (-5). Both of these ownership forms provide little protection from lawsuits and may also have negative tax and estate planning implications.

Many medical practices themselves also have asset planning scores that are overwhelming negative. For practices, the worst way to operate a business or title assets is a general partnership (-5). For all other business entities, liability from operations is always a concern. For this reason, owning any business assets within an operating business is extremely unwise (-5).

Before asset protection specialists can achieve a high level of protection for their clients, they must first eliminate the high risk assets. There are many ways to protect assets, but the most efficient way to avoid high risk assets and achieve a high level of protection is to utilize exempt assets. This is mentioned briefly in the next section and then discussed in greater detail later in the Lesson.

The Best Protection: Federal & State Exempt Assets

Each state law identifies assets that are absolutely exempt from creditor claims in that state. Federal law also exempts certain assets. Because these assets are inherently protected by law, they enjoy the highest level of protection, a (+5) score on the sliding scale. These will be discussed in detail in Chapter 6-6.

Good examples of how state laws can protect assets are found in Texas and Florida, where the homestead exemptions are unlimited for personal residences (within certain rules) and the cash value in life insurance policies is completely protected. At the federal level, bankruptcy law affords (+5) protection for qualified retirement plans, like pensions and 401(k) plans.

Basic Domestic Legal Tools

In many states, the list of state exemptions is not very generous. Even in those states where the exemptions are broad, we need to make sure that the asset protection goals are balanced with wealth accumulation and investment goals. For these reasons, there will almost always be non-exempt assets in a client's asset mix. For these assets, we must use other protection tools.

In such a situation, the basic asset protection tools are family limited partnerships (FLPs) and limited liability companies (LLCs). FLPs and LLCs provide good asset protection against future lawsuits, allow you to maintain control and can provide income and estate tax benefits in certain situations. For these reasons, we call FLPs and LLCs the "building blocks" of a basic asset protection plan.

FLPs and LLCs afford asset protection scores somewhere between (+1) to (+3), depending on the circumstances.

Other Protection Strategies

Most Doctors can achieve the majority of their asset protection planning with a combination of exempt assets and legal tools (like FLPs, LLCs, and Trusts). However, Doctors who are worth more than $3,000,000, or who earn more than $500,000, almost always need additional planning strategies to help them protect their assets. More successful Doctors may utilize advanced techniques like:

Non-Qualified Plans

Certain Non-Qualified Plans used in a medical practice may provide asset protection benefits vis-à-vis creditors of the physician. In addition, these tools can offer tax-deferral and estate planning benefits. Most Doctors find these tools attractive because employees need not be covered in these plans to be successful. Revisit Chapter 5-4 for more on these tools.

Captive Insurance Companies

Structured offshore or domestically, Captive Insurance Companies can also reach the (+5) status when the shares are owned by a second entity like an irrevocable trust. Successful businesses can use such insurance companies to provide superior asset protection, risk management, efficiently fund a partner buy-out and potentially reduce income and estate taxes. This strategy was discussed in greater detail in Chapter 5-6.

Debt Shields And Collateralization

Debt Shield and Collateralization strategies are ideal for protecting equity in real estate, especially the personal residence and the medical practice's Accounts Receivable (AR). This technique helps achieve a (+1) to (+5) rating. The exact score depends on the funding vehicles used in this technique. When structured properly, after-tax wealth can be built while protecting the real estate equity or Accounts Receivable in a superior way.

The Diagnosis

Asset protection planning, like any sophisticated multi-disciplinary effort, has degrees of success. Nothing in life is 100% certain (except perhaps death and taxes—both of which are discussed in Lessons #9 and #7, respectively). For asset protection planning, this adage holds true. You can protect each personal or practice asset to different levels. Exempt assets offer the greatest level of protection with the least cost. Legal tools generally fill in the rest of the plan for the average Doctor. Successful Doctors may choose to add Debt Shields, Captive Insurance Companies or Non-Qualified Plans to complete the planning.

In your asset protection plan, make sure you understand the benefits and consequences of the various tools you employ. Your asset protection advisor can help you weigh the pros and cons of each potential strategy. Your advisory team can help explain how each asset protection strategy or tool may be integrated into your comprehensive financial plan. By addressing your asset protection concerns as part of comprehensive planning process, you will not only protect the wealth you have already built, but you may find more efficient ways to build greater after-tax wealth for your retirement and for future generations.

Asset Protection Myths

Every day, we speak to Doctors about how they can achieve the protection they desire in order to maintain their wealth. In these conversations, we hear many common myths. Perhaps you too hold some of these false beliefs. Five common myths are:

- "My assets are owned jointly with my spouse, so I'm okay."

- "My assets are owned by my spouse, so I'm okay."

- "I am insured, so I'm covered."

- "I can just give assets away if I get into trouble."

- "My Living Trust (or Family Trust) provides asset protection."

These myths are dangerous because they lull the individual or family into a false sense of financial security. This, in turn, may prevent the Doctor from taking necessary steps to truly protect the assets. Let's examine each of these common myths and dispel them.

Myth #1: "My Assets Are Owned Jointly With My Spouse, So I'm Okay."

Most Doctors hold their homes and other property in joint ownership. Unfortunately, this ownership structure provides little asset protection in both community and non-community property states.

In community property states community assets will be exposed to community debts regardless of title. Community debts include any debt that arises during marriage as the result of an act that helped the community. Certainly, any claims resulting from a medical practice, income-producing asset (rental real estate) or auto accident would be included.

Even in non-community property states, joint property is typically at least 50% vulnerable to the claims against either spouse. Therefore, in most states, at least 50% of such property will be vulnerable—and all of the other problems associated with joint property still exist in non-community property states.

Myth #2: "My Assets Are Owned By My Spouse, So I'm Okay."

One of the most common misconceptions about asset protection is that assets in your spouse's name cannot be touched. We cannot tell you how many Doctors have come to us with their assets in the name of one spouse and assumed that those assets were protected from claims against the other. This often happens when one spouse has significant exposure as a Doctor and one does not.

Unfortunately, simply transferring title of an asset to the non-vulnerable spouse does not protect the asset. The creditor is often able to seize assets owned by the spouse of the debtor by proving that the income or funds of the debtor were used to purchase the asset. To determine if the asset is reversible, three questions can be asked:

- Whose income was used to purchase the asset?

- Has the vulnerable spouse used the asset at any time?

- Does this spouse have any control over the asset?

If the answer is "yes" to any of these questions, then the creditor can be paid from these assets.

Myth #3: "I Am Insured, So I'm Covered."

While we strongly advocate insurance as a first line of defense, an insurance policy is 50 pages long for a reason. Within those numerous pages there are a variety of exclusions and limitations that most people never take the time to read, let alone understand. Even if you do have insurance and the policy does cover the risk in question, there are still risks of underinsurance, strict liability, and bankruptcy of the insurance company. In any of these cases, you could be left with the sole financial responsibility for the loss. Lastly, with losses that fall within the plan's coverage limits, you still may see your future premiums go up significantly.

Myth #4: "I Can Just Give Assets Away If I Get Into Trouble."

Another common misconception of asset protection is that you can simply give away or transfer your assets if you ever get sued. If this were the case, you could just hide your assets when necessary. You wouldn't need an asset protection specialist. You would only need a shovel and some good map-making skills so you could find your buried treasure later.

In recognizing the potential for people to attempt to give away their assets if they get into trouble, there are laws prohibiting fraudulent transfers (or fraudulent conveyances). In a nutshell, if you make an asset transfer after an incident takes place (whether you knew about the pending lawsuit or not), the judge has the right to rule the transfer a fraudulent conveyance and order the asset to be returned to the transferor, thereby subjecting the assets to the claims of the creditor.

If you have been sued or suspect that you may be sued, there are other ways you can protect yourself. Typically, reactive last minute strategies are not very effective and may be much more expensive than the highly successful strategies that can be implemented when there are no creditors lurking.

Myth #5: "My Living Trust (Or Family Trust) Provides Asset Protection."

There have been countless instances where clients have come to us with the impression that their revocable Living Trust provides asset protection. While you are alive, this is simply not true. Revocable Trust assets are fully attachable by any creditor as the trust is a grantor trust. Later in this Lesson you will read about Irrevocable Trusts and how they provide varying levels of asset protection for you and your heirs in addition to the estate planning they are primarily designed to achieve. A Living Trust may provide some asset protection, but that protection does not exist until one spouse dies.

The Diagnosis

Many Doctors develop a false sense of security as a result of dangerous asset protection myths. Owning assets jointly with a spouse or in your living trust will not protect them. Titling all of your assets in your spouse's name does not work. Relying on your ability to move assets when a problem arises is a terrible plan that can easily be overturned and may result in disastrous consequences. Relying on insurance to protect you will leave too many risks to your financial well-being.

Do not be concerned or alarmed if you believed any of these asset protection myths. Do not be disappointed if your perceived protection has just been proved inadequate. With the myths dispelled, you can now follow the proper steps to implement the right type of asset protection plan for you. The next chapters should be very helpful in this regard. We will start with a philosophical discussion, and some practical examples, of the best way to protect assets.

The Best Asset Protection is NOT Asset Protection

Too many physicians over the last 20 years have sought cookie-cutter asset protection plans to give them some "peace of mind." While we admire these Doctors' commitment to proactively managing their risk, we have to remind the Doctors we speak with that all "asset protection plans" are not created equal. In fact, many of these "plans" will not work if they ever are tested. Why is this? Essentially, it is because of a basic tenet of asset protection: for any asset protection plan to truly stand up to a challenge, it *must have economic substance*.

Looking at it from a different viewpoint, superior asset protection planning would involve tools that are primarily used by people for non-asset protection purposes. In this way, the best asset protection plan involves tools typically not thought of as "asset protection tools"; instead, they are "business planning tools." Stated another way, "the best asset protection is not asset protection."

Similar To Tax Planning

While few physicians realize this crucial fact of asset protection planning, leading attorneys in the field know it quite well. In fact, we are not alone, as tax attorneys and CPAs know this adage is just as true when it comes to tax planning.

Simply put, when determining whether or not a particular transaction with significant tax benefits was an illegitimate tax shelter or not, the IRS or tax court typically uses a simple test: "Would a taxpayer have done this deal if not for the tax benefit?" In other words, they are asking whether or not this transaction was simply done to save taxes or if it had another economic purpose. If there was such a purpose, the transaction stands. If the transaction was only tax-motivated, it fails.

This same test applies when evaluating whether or not a credit protection tactic will be upheld if ever challenged down the road. Here, the question is "did this transaction have an economic purpose, or was it simply done for asset protection purposes?" If you are using tools that millions of Americans use on a daily basis for non-asset protection purposes, you can convincingly answer yes.

Why This Is So Important

Over the last decade, many courts throughout the U.S. have become increasingly frustrated with "asset protection planning." Reading judges' decisions in this area, it is obvious what has created their frustration—the prevalence of firms marketing themselves as "asset protection" experts, promoting the idea that the judgments of U.S. courts can be frustrated by their planning. Is this surprising? No. Of course judges are not going to be happy about an area of planning that is designed to circumvent the execution of a judgment that their court rendered, and prevent a successful plaintiff from getting paid on a judgment.

The courts' frustration is most severe when the defendant has made transfers or engaged in transactions that seem "fishy," even if the transaction at issue was made well before the beginning of the lawsuit process. If the transaction comes too late, the judges can resort to remedies to undue "fraudulent transfers." However, even in cases where the transaction came well before any plaintiff's action, we have seen judges strain to circumvent the asset protection planning.

In fact, there are certain cases where courts have given more leeway to a claim of fraudulent transfer based on a "foreseeability" argument. On the logic of one particularly noteworthy case, a medical malpractice case could always be seen as "foreseeable." Taken to its logical conclusion, this position could support the argument that a Doctor who does procedures daily is aware of the possibility of mistakes. If this were true, a plaintiff suing a Doctor could attack asset protection transfers made years prior to the case.

By using "non asset protection" asset protection, you are not as vulnerable to this emerging trend in the law. The techniques explained in this chapter do not involve "transfers" at all. Given this, and "non asset protection" techniques with tangible and concrete economic substance, these tools and tactics are certainly among the strongest protection you can implement for the long term.

Asset Protection That Isn't

The best asset protection tools were not created as asset protection tools. They are tools that have other primary benefits and offer outstanding creditor protection as a secondary benefit. Which asset protection tools are not asset protection tools? Let's examine a few of them briefly here. They will all be developed further in other parts of the book.

Qualified Retirement Plans

The term "qualified" retirement plan means that the retirement plan complies with certain Department of Labor and Internal Revenue Service rules. You might know such plans by their specific type, including pension plans, profit sharing plans, money purchase plans, 401(k)s or 403(b)s. Properly structured plans offer a variety of real economic benefits: you can fully deduct contributions to these plans, and funds within them grow tax-deferred. In fact, this is likely why most medical practices sponsor such a plan. Keep in mind that distributions may be subject to tax and a 10% penalty if withdrawn prior to age 59.

What you may not know is that under federal bankruptcy law and nearly every state law, these plans are protected against lawsuits and creditor claims—enjoying (+5) protection status. Yet the overwhelming majority of millions of Americans who use qualified plans are not using them for asset protection purposes. This, then, is a great example of an attractive economic tool that just so happens to have tremendous asset protection benefits as well.

Non-Qualified Retirement Plans

Non-Qualified plans are relatively unknown to physicians, even though most Fortune 1000 companies make Non-Qualified plans available to their executives. These types of plans should be very attractive to physicians, as employees are not required to participate and allowable contributions can be much higher than with qualified plans, although not deductible. Once again, Non-Qualified plans are generally not used for asset protection purposes, but they may have such benefits. Read more about them in Chapter 5-4.

Captive Insurance Companies (CICs)

CICs are used by many of the Fortune 1000 for a host of strategic reasons. In this technique, the owners of a medical practice actually create their own properly licensed insurance company to insure all types of risks of the practice. These can be economic risks (that reimbursements drop), business risks (that electronic medical records are destroyed), litigation risks (coverage for defense of harassment claims or HCFA audits) and even medical malpractice (keeping some risk in the captive and reinsuring the rest). If it is created and maintained properly, the CIC is an insurance company—established in a real economic arrangement with its insured. Also, CICs enjoy tremendous creditor protection—although they are almost never created for this purpose. This was covered in depth in Chapter 5-6.

Cash Value Life Insurance (CVLI)

CVLI policies are purchased by millions of Americans each year for their tax benefits (generally tax-free growth, tax-free access and pays income tax-free to heirs), for family protection and for estate planning purposes. Nonetheless, in many states the cash value can enjoy the top (+5) protections. In this way, a physician can purchase a product that is widely recognized as a part of a financial plan and enjoy (+5) protections easily. Please seek the counsel of your qualified professional to discuss this further.

The Diagnosis

When asset protection is a by-product of other primary goals, the courts look more favorably on the planning. In this way, asset protection planning is very similar to tax planning (which is discussed in Lessons #7 and #9). Qualified Plans, Non-Qualified Plans, Captive Insurance Companies and Cash Value Life Insurance are just a few of the tools that have primary benefits other than asset protection, but offer Doctors outstanding asset protection.

If you have an "asset protection plan" that has no value other than creditor protection, you should be concerned. To help you analyze your situation and to see how well your asset protection plan would hold up to an attack, the authors offer a free phone consultation to everyone who purchases our book. If you visit us at www.ojmgroup.com and click "Free Consultation," you can schedule yours today.

The Mixed Blessing of Property and Casualty Insurance

As principals of a financial firm that provides all types of financial planning, business consulting, insurance analysis and product implementation, a number of the authors of this book, including the attorney co-authors, are very familiar with the benefits of insurance.

We all see Property and Casualty (P&C) insurance as an important part of any asset protection plan—both for the practice and personal assets. In this chapter, we will define P&C insurance coverage and discuss its uses and limitations in the context of asset protection planning.

What Is P&C Insurance?

There are two "categories" of insurance: Life and Health (L&H) and Property and Casualty (P&C). L&H insurance includes all life insurance and health insurance, as well as disability insurance and long-term care insurance. P&C insurance is designed to protect against property and casualty losses. Often, P&C insurance is referred to as "property and liability" insurance because it protects people from all types of liabilities. Examples of P&C coverage include: automobile, homeowners and renters, umbrella liability, professional liability, medical malpractice, general liability, flood, earthquake, premises liability, errors and omissions, products liability, and others.

P&C insurance is designed to "indemnify" the insured. The insurance industry's definition of "indemnify" is to "make whole" or to restore the status quo. In other words, if you suffer a loss and have P&C coverage, you will be "put back" into the same financial place you were before the loss (minus any applicable deductibles or co-payments). As such, P&C coverage will cover your legal bills and other loss adjustment expenses, as well as the actual loss. These other expenses may include the costs of adjusters, estimates, expert testimony, or other associated costs.

P&C insurance coverage is very important given today's litigious society and the "American Rule" of legal fees. As mentioned before, there is no out of pocket cost (or deterrent) to the plaintiff under this system, yet the defendant is responsible for the actual loss and associated fees. Therefore, if you didn't have P&C insurance but still won your case, you still might have tens—if not hundreds—of thousands of dollars in legal fees and related expenses. As such, it is usually worth buying insurance to avoid these costs and the inconvenience and aggravation, let alone the potential judgment or loss.

Best Uses Of P&C Insurance

As we mentioned above, there are various types of P&C insurances. The most common P&C insurances are homeowners (or renters) and automobile insurance. Average Americans generally have these forms of coverage because they have a mortgage on their home or because they have a loan or a lease on a car. Yet, in a way, one does not own the home or car yet—the bank or credit department does. As such, they require collateral. Buyers must insure the asset while they are paying for it. Once the debt on a home or car is paid off, there is no bank or finance company requiring insurance protection. Of course, we would never recommend completely dropping all insurance on the home. The odds are very slim that they will suffer a house fire or burglary, but the costs of insurance are very small relative to what clients could lose.

Another common type of P&C insurance is the umbrella liability policy. For a very reasonable premium, you can get an additional one to five million dollars of excess liability insurance on top of the liability protection you may have from your homeowners or auto policies. You should seriously consider an umbrella policy.

Other popular P&C coverage includes professional liability insurance and premises and products liability insurance. As a physician, medical malpractice insurance, premises liability insurance, and other overhead insurances are wise options, if not requirements.

Four Limitations Of P&C Insurance

While some P&C insurance always makes sense as part of the asset planning for every Doctor, there are limitations to this tool. That is why we typically recommend using the other asset protection tools we describe in this Lesson, in addition to any insurance. Let's examine these limitations individually.

1. Policy Exclusions

Often we find that clients are completely unaware of the "fine print" P&C exclusions and policy limitations. Of course, they often become aware of such exclusions after it is too late. For example, many clients fail to realize that their "umbrella" policy only applies if certain underlying insurance coverage amounts are in effect. If your liability limits on your homeowner's policy or auto policy are too low, then you'll have to pay out of pocket before the umbrella coverage is in effect.

Case Study: Andy's Daughter's Car Accident

Andy was sued for more than $150,000 when his teenage daughter was involved in a car accident while using his car. Andy was certain that his insurance policy covered his daughter. Only then did his insurance agent tell Andy that the policy no longer covered his daughter, since she had recently moved out of the house. There was an exclusion from coverage for child drivers if they did not reside in the same residence as the parents. Now, Andy alone faced a lawsuit which cost him over $150,000.

The lesson to be learned from Andy's story is simple: Know your policy and the limitations contained therein!

---

2. Inadequate policy limits

Even if your insurance policy does cover you on a particular lawsuit, the policy coverage may be well below what a jury will award. You must pay any excess above the coverage out of your own pocket. If you were hit by a large judgment, would your policy cover you completely?

3. Insurance forces you to lose control of the defense

Even if your insurance policy covers against a specific claim, you must consider the consequences of filing a claim. You have lost negotiating power because your insurance company will dictate when the case is settled and how much the case settlement will be. While this may not matter with a personal injury car accident lawsuit, a case against you professionally is another matter. Here you may not want to admit liability and settle, while your insurance company does.

On the other hand, if the claim involves your professional reputation, you may want to settle the case out of court and away from the public view. There is no guarantee that your insurer will see things the same way. In these situations, if you rely solely on insurance, you lose all ability to negotiate effectively.

4. Claims bring ever-higher premiums

An additional consequence of relying solely on insurance to protect you from lawsuits is that, once you make claims on the policy, your premiums rise. Given the dismal statistics, you will probably endure a number of lawsuits over your life—and your cost of insurance will rise with every claim, even if you are not at fault.

Recommendations To Manage Limitations

To manage the four limitations of P&C insurance as outlined above, we recommend the following preventive measures:

1. Know your policy

2. Don't skimp on coverage

3. Consider an umbrella policy

4. Utilize other asset protection tools

5. Own your own insurance company if you have significant risks in your practice or business (read Chapter 5-6 for more information).

The Diagnosis

Like every tool discussed in this book, Property & Casualty insurance has its place in a Doctor's comprehensive financial plan. Certain types of coverage, such as homeowner, auto, umbrella and medical malpractice for physicians, are compulsory. However, we caution Doctors not to rely on insurance for all of their protection. Much more must be done if you want to adequately shield assets and discourage claims from the outset. There are various exclusions within every policy and many risks (like employment liability) that are not covered in traditional insurance policies. You want to integrate insurance into your plan, but this is only one piece of the puzzle. In the next chapters you'll learn about powerful tools that you can use to protect all assets and potentially enjoy significant tax benefits at the same time.

Maximizing Exempt Assets

In the following chapters, we will explain a number of legal entities and techniques we use to protect the assets of our Doctor clients. This chapter on maximizing exempt assets precedes the following chapters because, in our view, clients should always reasonably maximize their use of exempt assets before moving on to legal tools, legal entities, and other techniques.

Despite their superiority to other asset protection strategies, exempt assets are not adequately used by most Doctors. This chapter will explain why many advisors don't recommend exempt assets as often as they should. Then we will discuss all of the exempt assets that can be valuable components of a comprehensive financial plan. Throughout the book, you will revisit many of these exempt assets as they provide additional benefits to asset protection. In a later Lesson, you will learn how sophisticated Doctors save time and money by leveraging exempt assets that offer additional benefits. For now, let's begin discussing why exempt assets are considered the "best" asset protection tool and then discuss the reasons why they remain underutilized in asset protection planning.

Exempt Assets: The "Best" Asset Protection Tools

We consider exempt assets to be the "best" asset protection tool for the following reasons:

1. No legal/accounting fees
Most of the tools in subsequent chapters involve the creation of legal entities that require set up and ongoing legal fees, state fees, accounting fees, and even additional taxes. Using the exempt assets described in this chapter involve **none of these significant costs** and affords better protection as well.

2. No loss of ownership or control
The legal tools of the following chapters typically require giving up some level of ownership or control to family members or even third-party trustees. **By using exempt assets, you can own and access the asset at any time while enjoying the highest (+5) level of protection.**

3. Superior Protection
The legal tools explained later offer protection that ranges from (+1) to (+5). **Exempt assets always enjoy the top (+5) protection up to their exempt amount.**

Why Exempt Assets Are Underutilized

Given the clear benefits of exempt assets, one would think that exempt assets would be preferred over other tools in an asset protection plan. Surprisingly, this is often not the case. The reason for this may be that most asset protection planning is implemented by an attorney who is not familiar with the financial tools a multi-disciplinary team could offer.

There are various planning pitfalls that can arise when you do not have the benefit of a coordinated, multi-disciplinary team to help implement your plan. Attorneys generally do not understand many of the exempt asset classes, such as cash value life insurance and annuities. You cannot expect an advisor to recommend something he doesn't understand.

This doesn't mean that one attorney could not recommend an adequate asset protection plan. What it does mean is that the plan created by one attorney may not be efficient, because the plan may be limited only to legal solutions. If you were more skeptical, you might point out that attorneys are generally not licensed to sell such financial products. Is it unrealistic to expect an attorney to have a bias against the use of exempt assets for asset protection when the implementation of those assets does not require any legal work?

Is it unreasonable to expect attorneys to focus their asset protection recommendations around the use of legal documents that may generate thousands of dollars in legal fees? This is not a conspiracy against, nor is it an indictment of, attorneys—we, as an author group, include a number of attorneys. However, we are attorneys who appreciate multi-disciplinary planning and recognize the value of financial, as well as legal, solutions. **The reason we wrote this book with attorneys and the consultants of the OJM Group is that we believe 100% in a multi-disciplinary approach to asset protection planning.**

The lesson here is simple. Your asset protection plan, like the rest of your financial plan, MUST be handled by a coordinated, multi-disciplinary team that carefully considers all planning options to help you efficiently achieve your goals. The absence of exempt assets in a plan is always a warning sign that the planning is not coordinated.

Federally Exempt Assets

Federally exempt assets are those assets that are protected under federal bankruptcy law. Federal law protects certain assets from creditors and lawsuits if the defendant is willing to file bankruptcy to eliminate the creditor. In a Chapter 7 Bankruptcy, the debtor will be able to keep any assets that federal law deems exempt. The two significant asset classes that federal law protects are qualified retirement plans (QRPs) and IRAs. The term "qualified" retirement plan means that the retirement plan complies with certain Department of Labor and Internal Revenue Service rules. You might know such plans by their specific type, including profit sharing plans, money purchase plans, 401(k)s or 403(b)s. IRAs are very similar to such plans with several technical differences, and are now given exempt status under the federal law as well.

While this protection is (+5), you must recognize that this federal protection only applies if you are in a bankruptcy setting. If you were simply sued and a creditor was trying to take the funds in your pension or IRA, bankruptcy protection would not apply. You would have to take the step of filing for bankruptcy to shield the asset. This might be too great a cost for the protection.

If you do not file for bankruptcy, this federal protection would not apply. The amount of value in the QRP or IRA that would be protected outside of bankruptcy would be governed by applicable federal and state law.

Let's look at the applicable federal law. In 1992, the U.S. Supreme Court, in <u>Patterson v. Shumate</u>, 504 U.S. 753 (1992), held that a participant's interest in an ERISA (Employee Retirement Income Security Act)-qualified pension plan was excluded from the participant's bankruptcy estate and could not be used to satisfy the participant's creditor claims.

Outside of bankruptcy, if a Doctor's retirement plan is an ERISA-qualified pension plan, so the logic goes, creditors should not be able to reach that asset either.

To understand the level of protection of QRPs and IRAs in your state, contact us at www.ojm-group.com. We work collaboratively with attorneys in every state on our planning with clients.

State Exempt Assets

State exemption leveraging is a fundamental part of a financial plan and one which every Doctor client should take seriously. The most significant state exemptions are:

1. Qualified Retirement Plans (QRPs) and Individual Retirement Accounts (IRAs)

2. Primary Residence (or Homestead)

3. Life Insurance

4. Annuities

Important Note: We will make general comments regarding state exemptions below. If you want to know how your state exemptions work, please call us at 800-554-7233.

Qualified Retirement Plans and IRAs:

To recap, if a retirement plan is a pension plan covered by ERISA and meets the qualifications under the Internal Revenue Code, a Doctor's benefits under the plan will be protected from creditors' claims. Even if the plan is not covered by ERISA, but meets the definition of private retirement plan as described in the statute, a Doctor's benefits will be exempt from creditors' claims *unless* the plan is a self-employed retirement plan or IRA (including a rollover IRA), in which case the benefits will be exempt only to the only necessary for the support of the Doctor and the Doctor's dependents at retirement.

Primary Residence: Homestead

Many Americans consider the home to be the family's most valuable asset. You may have thought you knew the laws that protect your home. Perhaps you have previously heard the term "homestead", and assumed that you could never lose your home to bad debts or other liabilities because of this homestead protection. The reality is that few states provide a total (+5) shield for the home.

Most states only protect between $10,000 and $60,000 of the homestead's equity. Some states, such as New Jersey, provide no protection, while other states, such as Florida and Texas provide unlimited protection (with some restrictions). Given today's real estate values and the equity that many doctors have in their home, and it is clear that most states' homestead exemptions provide inadequate protection.

To determine how well a homestead law protects your home, you should compare the protected value to the equity. In order to do so, subtract the value of any mortgages from the fair market value of your home. For example, if you live in a home with a $300,000 fair market value and have a $150,000 mortgage, then your equity is $150,000. If your state protects only $20,000 through its homestead law, then you still have $130,000 ($150,000 of equity—$20,000 homestead) of vulnerable equity.

Homestead protection is often automatic, but may require additional action in some cases. Each state has specific requirements for claiming homestead status. In some states, you must file a declaration of homestead in a public office. Other states set a time requirement for residency before homestead protection is granted. Never assume your home is protected. You may be wrong and your inaction may cost you the protection you deserve. Your asset protection advisor can show you how to comply with the formalities in your state.

Life Insurance: Protected Everywhere

All 50 states have laws that protect varying amounts of life insurance.

For example:

- Many states shield the entire policy proceeds from the creditors of the policyholder. Some also protect against the beneficiary's creditors.

- States that do not protect the entire policy proceeds set amounts above which the creditor can take proceeds.

- Many states protect the policy proceeds only if the policy beneficiaries are the policyholder's spouse, children, or other dependents.

- Some states protect a policy's cash surrender value in addition to the policy proceeds. This can be the most valuable exemption opportunity.

- If the policy is purchased as part of a fraudulent transfer, a court can undo the policy. This is the same for any other fraudulent transfer.

One of the reasons for the under-utilization of life insurance as an exempt asset is that most clients—and advisors—do not understand the financial value of cash value life insurance. If they did, they would use it as a wealth accumulation and protection tool more often. Be sure to read the Lesson on Investments.

Annuities: Shielded in Many States

Another exempt asset in many states is the annuity. Annuities are insurance contracts that offer the upside of investment appreciation, tax-deferred growth, and principal protection. This diverse list of benefits makes annuities important components of asset protection and wealth accumulation plans.

The Diagnosis

The easiest and cheapest way to achieve the highest level of asset protection is to use exempt assets. For this reason, it makes sense that every Doctor who is interested in asset protection should attempt to maximize his or her use of exempt assets. However, to use exempt assets properly within a comprehensive financial plan, you may need insurance product, home loan, qualified plan, tax and asset protection expertise. This is another example of why you need a multi-disciplinary team to help you achieve your financial goals.

Practically, the laws in most states do not afford you enough exemptions to place every dollar of your wealth into exempt assets. For this reason, you will have to utilize legal strategies as part of your asset protection planning. The next chapter will discuss the two most common asset protection tools—the Family Limited Partnership and the Limited Liability Company.

Family Limited Partnerships and Limited Liability Companies

While (+5) exempt assets may be the most effective asset protection tools, most clients will need to go beyond the use of exempt assets in their quest to protect assets. They will make use of legal tools as well. Of all the legal tools we use to shield assets, the two we use most are family limited partnerships (FLPs) and limited liability companies (LLCs). Of course, having family members play a role in these tools is common—that's why we use the "F" in front of the "LP." However, using family members in this way is NOT required. Whether you use family members or non-family members, these entities can provide you solid asset protection. In this chapter we will discuss the similarities of the two tools, how they protect assets, and three tactics Doctors should use to incorporate FLPs and LLCs into their plans to build and preserve wealth.

FLPs and LLCs: Similarities and Differences

We have combined FLPs and LLCs in this chapter because they are very similar. You can think of them as closely related, like brothers and sisters, as they share many of their best characteristics. In fact, unless we make the point otherwise, we will use these tools interchangeably—if a case study refers to a FLP, you can generally assume that an LLC could have been used and *vice versa*. Similarities between the FLP and LLC include:

1. They are both legal entities certified under state law
Both FLPs and LLCs are legal entities governed by the state law in the state in which the entity is formed. Many of these laws are identical, as they are modeled after the Uniform Limited Partnership and Limited Liability Company Acts, which have been adopted at least partially by every state. As state-certified legal entities, state fees must be paid each year to keep an FLP or LLC valid.

2. They both have two levels of ownership
FLPs and LLCs allow for two levels of ownership. We'll call one ownership level "active ownership"- that is, the active owners have 100% control of the entity and its assets. In the FLP, the active owners are called "general partners", while in the

LLC the active owners are called "managing members"" (Note Well: Managers of LLCs do not have to be "owners".)

As you may have already guessed, the second ownership level is "passive ownership"—the passive owners have little control over the entity and only limited rights. The passive owners are called "limited partners" in the FLP, and are called "members" in the LLC.

This bi-level structure of ownership allows a host of planning possibilities because clients can then use FLPs and LLCs to share ownership with family members without having to give away any practical control of the assets inside the structures. Why is it optimal to be able to give away ownership but still maintain control? Asset protection reasons will be discussed in great detail in this chapter and estate planning benefits will be explained in Chapter 9-5.

3. They both have beneficial tax treatment

In terms of income taxes, both tools can elect for "pass through" taxation, meaning neither the FLP nor the LLC is liable for income taxes. Rather, the tax liability for any and all income or capital gains on FLP/LLC assets "passes through" to the owners (partners or members). Also, as discussed in the income tax and estate planning Lessons, both entities allow the participants to take advantage of "income sharing" and "discounting" techniques in the same ways.

4. They both have the beneficial 'charging order' asset protection benefit

While state laws do vary slightly, those based on the Uniform Acts provide "charging order" protection to FLP and LLC owners. The "charging order" will be discussed later in this chapter.

Two Differences Between The FLP And LLC

1. Only the LLC can be used for a single owner

Most states now allow single-member (owner) LLCs, while a limited partnership in every state must have at least two owners. Thus, for single clients, the LLC is often the only option. Also, if we are considering having an FLP or LLC protect a home, then the single member LLC is one alternative. Since the home is a significant asset, both financially and emotionally, there is an entire chapter devoted to protecting it, in Lesson 6-10

2. The FLP's general partner has liability for the FLP

While a general partner has personal liability for the acts and debts of the FLP, a managing member has no such liability for his/her LLC. For this reason alone, asset protection experts always recommend using an LLC rather than an FLP when the entity will own "dangerous" assets, i.e., those likely to lead to lawsuits.

"Safe" assets, conversely, are those which are unlikely to lead to lawsuits. Common safe assets include cash, stocks, bonds, mutual funds, CDs, life insurance policies, checking or savings accounts, antiques, artwork, jewelry, licenses, copyrights, trademarks and patents, among others.

"Dangerous" assets are those which have a relatively high likelihood of creating liability. Common dangerous assets include real estate (especially rental real estate), cars, RVs, trucks, boats, airplanes and interests in closely-held businesses. Since FLP general partners have liability exposure and LLC managing members do not, it usually makes sense to use an LLC rather than an FLP to own dangerous assets.

How FLPs And LLCs Protect Assets

FLPs and LLCs are asset protectors because the law gives a very specific and limited remedy to creditors coming after assets in either entity. When a personal creditor pursues you and your assets are owned by an FLP or LLC, the creditor cannot seize the assets in the FLP/LLC. Under the Uniform Act provisions, a creditor of a partner (or LLC member) cannot reach into the FLP/LLC and take specific partnership assets.

If the creditor cannot seize FLP/LLC assets, what can the creditor get? The law normally allows for only one remedy: the "charging order." The charging order is something a creditor can have served to a debtor. In other words, the creditor must legally be paid any distributions that would have been paid to the debtor. The charging order is meant to allow the business to continue operating without interruption and provide a remedy for creditors to be paid. Oftentimes, the best the creditor will usually be able to do is obtain a charging order when assets are owned by an FLP/LLC. You will see that the charging order is generally a very weak remedy.

Of course, this discussion assumes that, in transferring assets to an FLP or LLC, you do not run afoul of fraudulent transfer laws. We introduced the concept of these laws in the introduction of this Lesson. It also assumes that one remains in compliance with state laws and does not use the FLP/LLC as an alter ego of one's personal business affairs.

The Limitations Of The Charging Order

As mentioned earlier, the charging order is a court order which instructs the FLP/LLC to pay the debtor's share of distributions to his/her creditor until the creditor's judgment is paid in full. More important, <u>everything we will describe below assumes that your FLP or LLC operating agreement is properly drafted and all formalities are followed</u>. If these are handled, the charging order neither:

- Gives the creditor FLP/LLC voting rights

- Forces the FLP general partner or LLC managing member to pay out any distributions to partners/members.

While the charging order may seem like a powerful remedy, you do need to understand and consider its limitations. It is a temporary interest that may have to be renewed. In addition:

1. It Is Only Available After a Successful Lawsuit

First, the charging order is only available after the creditor has successfully sued you and won a judgment. Only then can your creditor ask the court for the charging order. It must be noted that once the threat of a charging order exists, and even while a lawsuit is proceeding, FLP/LLC assets are completely untouchable and available for you to use (so long as you avoid fraudulent transfers).

2. It Does Not Afford Voting Rights—So You Stay in Complete Control

Despite the charging order, you remain the general partner of your FLP (or managing member of the LLC). You make all decisions about whether the FLP/LLC buys assets, distributes earnings to its partners or members, shifts ownership interests and so forth. Judgment creditors cannot vote you out because they cannot vote your shares. Thus, even after creditors have a judgment against you, you still make all decisions concerning the FLP/LLC, including whether to pay distributions to the owners.

3. The Creditor May Have to Pay the Tax Bill

The real "kicker" is how the charging order may backfire on creditors for income tax purposes. Because taxes on FLP/LLC income are passed through to the parties who are entitled to the income, the FLP/LLC does not pay tax. Each partner/member is responsible for his/her share of the FLP/LLC income. This income is taxable regardless of whether the income is actually paid out.

If a creditor with a charging order against an FLP partner or LLC member goes to the step of "foreclosing" on the charging order, the creditor's interest will then become permanent. This also has the effect of making the creditor liable for all of the income attributable to the charged interest. At this point, the creditor "steps into your shoes" for income tax purposes with respect to the FLP/LLC interest—resulting in receipt of your tax bill for income taxes on your share of the FLP/LLC income. This tax liability will exist even though the creditor will likely never receive any income. Once this occurs, creditors will be very motivated to settle—as they have swallowed the tax "poison pill" without even realizing it.

Case Study: William and Donna are Protected By FLPs

Let's examine the spouses William and Donna. Assume that William is an oncologist. After two years of employment, William's assistant, Maribel, sues William for sexual harassment and wins an award of $750,000. William's general business insurance package does not cover this type of lawsuit. Once Maribel discovers, through a debtor's examination, that William and Donna's assets are owned by their LLCs, what can she do?

She cannot seize the vacation home, stocks or cars owned by the LLCs. The state law provisions prohibit that. She also has no fraudulent transfer claim to cling to in an attempt to undo the LLCs because the LLCs were created in advance of her claim. She can get a charging order on William's 39% share of the LLCs, but William and Donna would still control the LLCs. Maribel would probably not receive any distributed profits, only a tax bill on dividends paid out by the stocks that William and Donna never distributed. This charging order will not sound too inviting to Maribel, will it?

Maribel could look only to William's assets not owned by the LLCs. Because William had an incomplete asset protection plan and retained personal ownership of copyrights and business interests in a film company worth about $75,000, William settled the judgment for just that—$75,000 cash. William and Donna's LLCs helped them avoid financial disaster and settle the claim for pennies on the dollar. Moreover, they never lost control of their assets.

You may wonder why we have such protective laws for limited partnerships and limited liability companies. The charging order law, which can be traced back to the *English Partnership Act of 1890*, is aimed at achieving a particular public policy objective—business activities of a partnership should not be disrupted because of non-partnership related debts of the individual partners. The rationale for this objective is that if non-debtor partners and the partnership were not at fault, why should the entire partnership suffer? American law has adopted this policy for over 100 years, culminating in the charging order law of the Uniform Limited Partnership and Uniform Limited Liability Company Acts. (Note Well: The same is not true for general partnerships!)

Three Tactics For Maximizing FLP/LLC Protection

You now understand the basic strategy for using FLPs/LLCs: you put your assets into the FLP/LLC and they will be protected from personal creditors. This is basic "outside" asset protection. Assets "inside" the FLP/LLC are also protected against outside threats to you. Beyond this, consider these three basic rules:

1. Don't put all your eggs in one basket

One never knows when a court of law is going to make a surprise departure or deviation from accepted legal norms or precedents. One never knows when an asset within a single FLP/LLC could cause a lawsuit. Life is full of uncertainties. Because our clients understand that they cannot control court decisions or the litigious nature of society, they protect their assets by using multiple FLP/LLC arrangements (among other tools discussed in this Lesson) in different states to title their assets. Titling your assets in different legal entities makes it more difficult for any creditor to come after your entire wealth because they may have to conduct more investigations, file more motions with the court, and perhaps even travel to different states. The more entities used, the more difficult it will be for your creditors to attack your wealth. As a result, creditors will be more likely to negotiate more favorable settlements.

2. Segregate the dangerous eggs from the safe ones

Separating safe assets from dangerous assets increases the "inside" asset protection for the safe assets. In other words, since no dangerous assets are within the same entity as the safe assets, a lawsuit arising from a dangerous asset will not threaten the safe assets if the safe assets are in their own LLC. As we explained in the beginning of the chapter, dangerous assets should be owned by an LLC rather than by an FLP because LLCs give better "inside" protection. The general partner of an FLP can be personally liable for acts within an FLP but the managing member of an LLC cannot be personally liable for the acts within the LLC.

3. If possible, use LLCs or FLPs in the most protective states

Not all LLCs and FLPs are created equal. It is true that LLCs and FLPs vary greatly in their asset protection, estate and tax benefits based on the experience and expertise of the attorney drafting the operating agreement. However, the point here is that some states have much more protective language in their LLC or FLP statutes. For example, in Wyoming, there is no charging order language in the LLC statutes. Thus, a creditor cannot even get a charging order against a Wyoming LLC.

Some statutes are much more creditor-friendly, while others are more debtor-friendly. In addition, many states have adopted uniform language. However, the examples in those states have illustrated the fact that each state's courts may make a different interpretation of the statute. Further, over time, courts in the same state may have a change of opinion. Thus, our Doctor clients use legal entities domiciled in jurisdictions that offer the best law and they make sure that a member of their team is an asset protection expert, keeping an eye on developments in the field so that they can switch state domiciles if necessary.

The Diagnosis

Since exempt assets generally can't protect 100% of your assets, we have to find other techniques to the fill the remaining void. FLPs and LLCs are two of the most frequently employed asset protection tools we use to manage the wealth of Doctors and their families. We would be surprised if you did not use at least one as part of your new comprehensive financial plan. These tools not only protect assets, but they also can offer income and estate tax benefits. Taxes and the preservation of one's estate will be discussed in depth in Chapter 9-5.

FLPs and LLCs certainly have their limitations and are not cure alls. This is why we need to consider other tools as part of our comprehensive planning. Trusts are another set of tools that offer asset protection, tax and estate planning benefits. These asset protection tools are discussed in the next chapter.

Using Trusts to Shield Wealth

In addition to exempt assets, FLPs and LLCs, there is another tool that can be used to protect Doctors' assets and maintain their wealth—a Trust. A Trust is a legal entity that is often misunderstood by many Doctors. In this chapter, we will explain what a Trust is and the asset protection role Trusts play in the planning of physicians.

What Is A Trust?

A Trust is essentially a legal arrangement where one person holds property for the benefit of another. The person who holds the property is the Trustee. He or she "holds" the property for the benefit of the beneficiary or beneficiaries. A Trust is created by a Trust document that specifies that the Trustee holds property owned by the Trust for the benefit of the beneficiary of the Trust. The Trust document also establishes the terms of how the Trust should be administered and how the Trust assets should be distributed during the lifetime of the Trust as well as after the Trust is terminated.

The following definitions and classifications should help you understand a Trust and how it functions.

1. Grantor: The Grantor is the person who sets-up the Trust. He or she is usually the person who transfers property into the Trust. A Grantor may also be called the *Trustor* or *Settlor*.

2. Trustee: The Trustee is the legal owner of the Trust property. The Trustee is responsible for administering and carrying out the terms of the Trust. He or she owes a fiduciary duty to the beneficiaries—an utmost duty of care that he or she will follow the terms of the Trust document and manage the Trust property properly. A Trustee may be a person, such as a family member or trusted friend. The Trustee can also be an institution, such as a professional Trust company or the Trust department of a bank. When there is more than one Trustee, they are called *co-Trustees*.

The Trustee is the legal owner of any assets owned by the Trust and has "legal title" to the assets owned by the Trust. For example, assume that Dad wants to set-up a Trust for his children, Son and Daughter. Dad wants his brother, Uncle, to serve as Trustee. If Dad transfers his house into the Trust, the title to that house will be with "Uncle, as Trustee of the Dad Trust."

3. Beneficiary: The beneficiary (or beneficiaries) is the person (or people) for whom the Trust was set-up. (In the example discussed above, the beneficiaries would be Son and Daughter.) While the Trustee has legal title to assets owned by the Trust, the beneficiary has *equitable title* or the right to the Trust property. The beneficiary can sue the Trustee if the Trustee mismanages the Trust property or disobeys specific instructions in the Trust. The beneficiary may be the same person as the grantor, and can possibly be the same person as the Trustee. For asset protection purposes, the Trustee, beneficiary and grantor cannot all be the same person.

4. Funding: Funding the Trust means transferring assets to the Trust. A Trust that is "unfunded" has no property transferred to it. It is completely ineffective. You must title assets to the Trust if you want Trust protection as with any other legal entity/ asset protection tool discussed previously. To title real estate to the Trust, you must execute and record a deed to the property to the Trust. Bank and brokerage accounts can be transferred by simply changing the name on the accounts. Registered stocks and bonds are changed by notifying the transfer agent or issuing company and re-questing that the certificates be reissued to the Trust. Other assets, such as household items, furniture, jewelry, artwork, etc., are transferred by a simple legal document called an *assignment* or *Bill of Sale*. Your asset protection specialist can transfer assets simply and quickly.

Revocable Living Trusts: Illusory Asset Protection

Revocable Living Trusts (also called "Family Trusts" or "A-B Trusts") allow the grantor of the Living Trust the flexibility to make changes to an estate plan and to avoid unnecessary probate expenses. Probate is an unnecessary expense and hassle for Doctors and is discussed in detail in the sixth Lesson. Revocable Living Trusts also effectively sidestep the hidden dangers of joint tenancy, which is discussed in the sixth Lesson. However, many people mistakenly assume that these Trusts provide asset protection benefits.

During your lifetime, Living Trusts provide absolutely no asset protection. This is because Living Trusts are revocable. While revocability and flexibility are valuable characteristics for almost all financial planning tools, these characteristics render the Revocable Trust useless for asset protection purposes. Remember this simple rule: *Revocable Trusts are vulnerable to creditors*. Let's explore the main reason why Revocable Trusts offer no protection.

Creditors Can "Step Into Your Shoes," Revoke the Living Trust, and Seize Trust Assets

Revocable Trusts are useless for asset protection because Revocable Trusts allow the grantor to undo the Trust. If you wanted to unwind a Revocable Trust and use the funds for yourself, you could do so. Because of this, a creditor can essentially force the grantor of the Trust to do this. If the grantor's creditors want to seize assets owned by a revocable Trust, they need only petition the court to "step into the shoes" of the grantor and direct the funds of the Trust back to the debtor. The Trust assets will no longer be owned by the Trust, but by the debtor personally. The creditors then have all the rights and privileges to seize these assets now owned by the debtor.

Irrevocable Trusts: The Asset Protectors

While Revocable Trusts offer no asset protection, Irrevocable Trusts are outstanding for asset protection. Once you establish an Irrevocable Trust, you forever abandon the ability to undo the Trust and reclaim property transferred to the Trust. With an Irrevocable Trust, you lose both control of the Trust assets and ownership.

Of course, this discussion assumes that in transferring assets to any Irrevocable Trust, you do not run afoul of fraudulent transfer laws. We introduced the concept of these laws in the introduction of this Lesson. Now, let's discuss why and how Irrevocable Trusts can protect assets. (Note: Transferring assets to an irrevocable trust may have serious gift tax issues; please consult your tax counsel.)

Why Irrevocable Trusts Protect Your Assets

Irrevocable Trusts protect assets for the same reason that Revocable Trusts do not. As mentioned earlier, Revocable Living Trusts do not provide asset protection because creditors can "step into your shoes" and undo such a Trust. The logic here is that if you have the power to undo your Trust, so do your creditors.

An Irrevocable Trust results in the opposite. Because an established Irrevocable Trust cannot be altered or undone, your creditors cannot "step into your shoes" and undo the Trust any more than you can. Assets in an Irrevocable Trust are immune from creditor attack, lawsuits, and other threats against the grantor (the person who created the Trust).

Two Clauses Your Irrevocable Trust Should Have

There are two clauses that are extremely important for an Irrevocable Trust to include so that you can properly protect your assets. These clauses are not necessarily important to protect the Trust creator, but work to shield the beneficiaries from their creditors.

Spendthrift Clause

The spendthrift clause allows the Trustee to withhold income and principal—which would ordinarily be paid to the beneficiary—if the Trustee feels that the money could or would be wasted or seized by the beneficiary's creditors. This clause accomplishes two goals. First, it prevents a wasteful beneficiary from spending Trust funds or wasting Trust assets. This is especially important to many Doctors who set up Trusts with their children as beneficiaries. If you worry that money in a Trust for your children would be wasted if not controlled, then use a spendthrift clause. The Trustee can then stop payments if your child spends too quickly or unwisely.

Second, the spendthrift clause protects Trust assets from creditors of the beneficiaries. Beneficiaries may be young now, but as adults they will face the same risks we all face: lawsuits, debt problems, divorce, a failing business, etc. The spendthrift clause protects Trust assets from your children's creditors by granting the Trustee the authority to withhold payments to a beneficiary who has an outstanding creditor. If the beneficiary and Trustee are at "arm's length", the creditor has no power to force the Trustee to pay the beneficiary. The creditor only has a right to payments actually paid by the Trustee. He cannot force the Trustee to make disbursements.

Anti-Alienation Clause

The anti-alienation clause also protects Trust assets from the beneficiary's creditors. Specifically, the anti-alienation clause prohibits the Trustee from transferring Trust assets to anyone other than the beneficiary. This, of course, includes creditors of the Trust beneficiary. Thus, while the spendthrift clause allows the Trustee to withhold payments if a creditor lurks, the anti-alienation clause goes one step further—it prohibits the Trustee from paying Trust income or principal to anyone but the named beneficiary.

Combine Irrevocable Trusts with Debt Shields

As you may recall from Lesson #5 (and you will see again in Chapter 6-10), Doctors can protect assets by using "debt shields" or "collateralization" of a valuable asset. Basically, you can protect an asset by making that asset the collateral for a loan. This can be done by using an unrelated lender, such as a bank or credit facility, or by using a "friendly" lender. Often, an ideal "friendly" lender is an irrevocable trust for the benefit of your children. In the case of the "friendly" lender, you would be paying interest to your family, rather than to an outside organization. This way, your debt costs stay in the family—thus making additional debt more palatable for most physicians.

Using an irrevocable trust and a debt shield can be an ideal way to protect a Doctor's home in states where homestead protection is limited. This same technique can also protect other real estate and even a practice's accounts receivable.

The Diagnosis

Once Doctors have maximized their investment within exempt assets, they move on to FLPs,

LLCs and Trusts. When trusts are structured properly and funded with assets, they can provide significant estate planning and asset protection benefits. With a strong advisory team Trusts can be combined with LLCs to offer potential income tax benefits and leveraged estate planning benefits as well. When Trusts are combined with friendly loans and LLCs, Doctors can achieve asset protection for otherwise difficult-to-protect assets (like the primary residence or practice accounts receivable). Work with your team of advisors to see how Trusts can be integrated into your comprehensive financial plan to maximize your efficiency when addressing your specific planning goals.

International Planning

Over the last decade, an increasing number of Doctors—though still a small minority—have looked internationally for solutions to their comprehensive financial planning. It isn't necessarily a bad thing that international planning is limited to a small group, as there are numerous pitfalls that can snare naive Doctors. In this chapter, you'll learn what to do (and what to avoid) in international planning, and about specific tools used by top attorneys in their international planning. In addition, we will discuss the major pitfalls some clients endure as a result of inadequate international planning and advisors who lack international financial experience. We will conclude the chapter by discussing how international trusts and LLCs are effective financial tools for protecting assets.

Onshore Partnerships With Offshore Trust Ownership

We often may recommend a trust that is known as a foreign integrated estate planning trust (IEPT)—one created by a Doctor who establishes a trust in a country other than the Doctor's domicile. On this subject, the authors recognize attorney Barry Engel, who was very helpful to the following discussion. The Doctor's domicile is referred to as the home jurisdiction. For most physician clients, this is the United States.

One of the reasons that a foreign IEPT is one of the strongest asset protection vehicles available is that, if it is properly structured and properly administered, the final legal battle can be forced into one or more foreign jurisdictions with favorable asset protection legislation.

Under the typical foreign IEPT, there are two trustees, one of whom is an individual domiciled in the home jurisdiction (a.k.a. the domestic trustee). The second trustee is usually a corporate trustee (a.k.a. the foreign trustee), domiciled in a jurisdiction of the foreign IEPT's applicable law. The foreign IEPT agreement provides the domestic trustee with the power to take binding action so long as the foreign trustee is notified by the domestic trustee of any action taken.

As long as the Doctor's legal seas are calm, the foreign trustee's duties and activities are relatively passive. However, in the event of a legal threat against the Doctor, the foreign trustee has the express power and authority to fire the domestic trustee.

To obtain charging order protection and discounts for federal gift tax purposes and allow the Doctor to have control over certain designated assets, many planners combine a foreign IEPT with a domestic family limited partnership (FLP). The foreign IEPT is usually the 99 percent limited partner and the Doctor is the one percent general partner. Typically, a Doctor will establish a foreign IEPT at the same time that he or she creates a domestic FLP.

Once the FLP is formed, the Doctor gifts the 99 percent limited partnership interest to the foreign IEPT. However, since the Doctor retains full control over the assets and the investment decisions of the FLP as the general partner, the Doctor retains full control over the assets and the investment decisions of the FLP.

There is a common misconception that a foreign IEPT must invest most or all of its assets abroad. This is not true. While there are a number of good reasons for at least a portion of the assets of a foreign IEPT being invested abroad, more typically the bulk of the assets remain invested within the U.S. while there are no threats against the Doctor or the foreign IEPT assets, which is usually all of the time for most physician clients.

Dangerous International Pitfalls To Avoid

As you might imagine, in our business, we see too many Doctors who use international planning for the wrong reasons. Often, people are so anxious to avoid taxes, shield assets improperly, or get rich quick that their otherwise reasonable judgment is clouded. Consequently, people engage in planning which they would never do here in the U.S. Combine these desires with the virtually unregulated international jurisdictions (i.e., no reporting to the IRS, no SEC or NASD disclosure requirements, no state attorney generals remedying fraud, etc.), and one has an area ripe for potential abuse.

Offshore Planning Strategies

As explained in this Lesson, (+5) asset protection can be achieved in the U.S. through the use of exempt assets. Beyond this, legal tools are used. In this way, international entities have many of the same asset protection features—most common are the LLC and the Trust. Thus, the "right" way to protect assets internationally is to use the same structures and strategies one would use domestically. The practical problem you can encounter in doing so is that those entities are located in foreign nations. In these jurisdictions, American attorneys are unable to practice and are unfamiliar with the law.

Unfortunately, while creating legitimate international asset protection plans is not difficult for experienced advisors, many Americans forego such planning and simply try to "hide" wealth in these international centers. Rather than use an entity like an LLC, they simply set up bank or brokerage accounts in countries where there is little, if any, reporting. No one is the wiser, right?

The problem with this "no entity" approach is that in any litigation—civil lawsuit, divorce, or even governmental case—there will eventually be some type of formal inquiry of assets. This might occur by way of a "debtor's exam" after a successful lawsuit, a bankruptcy filing, a list of assets for a divorce settlement, etc. For the "no entity" approach to work, the client would have to omit the international assets or lie about their existence. This amounts to perjury, bankruptcy fraud, or obstruction of justice, depending upon the forum of the case. Thus, the ultimate success of many "hidden" offshore planning strategies relies on the clients' ultimate decision to commit perjury or some other crime. Smart clients realize this potential pitfall and have a group of advisors who ensure that this will not happen.

Going Offshore to Avoid Tax Is Illegal

As explained above, Americans are liable for taxes on all income earned offshore. However, it is true that many international banks, mutual funds and other financial institutions will not report earnings/interest to the IRS. This is the chasm where many greedy clients—or unscrupulous advisors—operate. This is also where tax evasion—a federal crime—is committed.

While the client is required under U.S. law to make the necessary tax reporting on income earned internationally (and advisors should instruct their clients to do so), many clients may keep quiet and hope that they are never caught. Failure to report offshore income can subject a client to substantial penalties and interest expenses. This "hide the ball" strategy is used not only by knowing clients, but also by shady advisors who concoct ever more sophisticated schemes, like moving money from one Trust to another company to a third foundation and so on, in hopes of avoiding detection.

Although the pitch may seem complex and impressive, astute Doctors know to always ask the following question: If the income will eventually accrue to my benefit, how come I don't have to report it to the IRS? They know that they must steer clear of these schemes unless they want the cloud of a possible tax evasion indictment hanging over them for years to come.

Going Offshore To "Get Rich Quick" Can Lead You To Scams And Frauds

The desire to get rich quick leads many clients into problems most pervasive in the investment arena. Here, scam artists and fraudsters abound, poised to take advantage of the next client who wants to "get rich offshore." The savvy Doctor understands that any investment that offers truly outstanding returns is on the radar screen of the world's most sophisticated financial institutions and their super affluent clientele. Then, the investment is reserved for the financial institution's billionaire clients. They know that the only thing that can be achieved from chasing fantastic returns in international markets is a significant, if not complete, loss of principal. Let's explore how some of these mistakes happen.

International LLCs And Trusts

Used properly, these tools can be used to achieve a high (+4/+5) level of protection. Compared to exempt assets, which do not have professional, government or accounting fees, these tools are expensive. However, they may be the best non-exempt options for Doctor clients who must have the top level of protection.

A number of jurisdictions have adopted LLC legislation over the last decade, most notably Nevis. Also, many jurisdictions have international Trust (IT) laws as well. Common uses of these tools include:

To Own International Insurance Policies

One of the leading international financial planning strategies today is purchasing a permanent (cash value) life insurance policy offshore. In terms of tax planning, if the policy is U.S. tax-compliant, then all of the growth within the policy will accumulate tax-free. Further, the proceeds will pay out to the beneficiary income tax-free and the client can take loans against the accumulated cash values during his life, tax-free. This is similar to the benefits of a domestic cash value life insurance policy, which you can read more about later in this book.

For Multi-Generational Planning For An International Family

Let's say the goal of a client is to create a nest egg for future generations like children, grandchildren and beyond. And let's say it is important that the nest egg be asset-protected in an ironclad way. In this circumstance, an international Trust would be an ideal tool. This would be especially appropriate if the trust was created in a country where the law does not limit the duration of Trusts under the "rule against perpetuities," found in many of the states. By using an IT, the client from an international family could literally secure the family's ability to enjoy the fruits of the gift for hundreds of years, as long as other tax issues were addressed by an experienced tax expert.

The Diagnosis

We live in a global economy. There are financial options for all of us to consider all over the world. With developments in technology and communication, it is possible (if not easy) to access international vehicles. The benefits of international planning in our global economy can be significant. These benefits can come in the form of increased levels of asset protection (+4 or +5) or intriguing investment opportunities that may offer excellent diversification for your portfolio (see Lesson #8). However, there are a number of scams and frauds to be avoided offshore. Even if you avoid scams and frauds, you are not "out of the woods" just yet. International tax and reporting laws are highly complex. There are many areas where an individual or advisor could make a mistake.

Though all areas of planning require the assistance of advisors, no area of planning requires greater expertise than international planning. Make sure your team of advisors has an asset protection expert who can help you navigate the tricky waters of international planning and that your tax advisors are familiar with international tax laws. With the right expertise and strategy, international planning can help protect liquid assets, real estate and possibly your home. For solutions to protect the home, you should read the next chapter.

Protecting Your Home

Along with retirement accounts, the family home is often the most valuable asset of most Doctors. Even beyond its pure financial value, the home has great *psychological* value as well. In fact, we find that most of our clients who engage in asset protection planning often begin with the question: "How can I protect my home?" That is why we thought it important to dedicate an entire chapter to discussing this asset and how to protect it from outside threats.

This chapter will discuss the pros and cons of state Homestead Law, LLCs/FLPs and the Debt Shield. You may be surprised to find out that something you always feared could actually be your ally in your quest to protect your most valuable asset.

State Homestead Law

As you learned in earlier, every state has some type of homestead protection law. In most states, such as New Jersey, New York, and California, the level of protection is very low when compared to what real estate is worth (New Jersey $0, New York $100,000, California $50-$100,000). On average, state homestead laws protect about $30,000-$50,000 of equity—typically much less than the home value of most Doctors.

Tenancy by the Entirety

Tenancy by the Entirety ("TBE") is a form of joint ownership available in a number of states, although its effectiveness is diminishing. The protection falls between (+1) and (+3), depending on the state and its court interpretations. Inherent within TBE, there are number of risks. These include:

1. Joint Risk
TBE provides no shield whatsoever against joint risks, including lawsuits that arise from your jointly-owned real estate or acts of your minor children.

2. Divorce Risk

If you rely on TBE for protection and you get divorced before or during the lawsuit, you lose all protections from TBE.

3. Liability Risk

If you rely on TBE for protection and one spouse dies before or during the lawsuit, you lose all protections from TBE.

4. Death Risk

TBE is a poor ownership form for estate planning purposes because, at the death of the first spouse, the entire value of the home will automatically be entered into the surviving spouse's taxable estate.

For these reasons, we do not generally recommend TBE alone as a protective tool. We generally combine Tenancy by the Entirety with the Debt Shield technique that is discussed later in the chapter.

LLCs And FLPs

LLCs and FLPs are two tools that could potentially protect a primary residence. In fact, many advisors regularly recommend these techniques to their clients who want to protect their homes. The drawbacks of these methods are perfect examples of why multidisciplinary planning is a necessity for Doctors. Let's look at some of the problems with doing asset protection planning in a vacuum with respect to the home.

Drawbacks Of LLCs And FLPs For The Home

In Chapter 6-7, we discussed LLCs and FLPs in detail. We will assume that this is fresh in your mind so you can see why owning real estate in an LLC would be attractive. However, when it comes to the primary residence, these entities are not very common choices of clients.

Unlike other assets, the family home has unique tax attributes—most notably, the deductibility of the mortgage interest and the $250,000 per person ($500,000 per couple) capital gains tax exemption. By owning the home within an LLC or a FLP, both of these tax benefits may be lost. However, this seriously impacts the asset protection of the structure as well—so these need to be balanced.

Qualified Personal Residence Trusts

When using a qualified personal residence trust (or QPRT), the owner transfers ownership of the home to the QPRT irrevocably. While this is certainly effective for both asset protection and estate planning purposes, it comes with a significant cost—you no longer own your home. In fact, when the term of years is up (typical range of years for a QPRT is 5 to 20 years), you have to pay rent to the Trust just to live in the home. Also, homes with mortgages on them present further tax difficulties as well. For these reasons, while the QPRT is a strong asset protection tool, we typically do not advise using it for most younger clients whose main concern is asset protection, not estate planning. Nonetheless, if it can be implemented correctly, a QPRT receives a rating of (+4) or (+5) level of protection.

The Debt Shield Concept

The debt shield can be the most effective way to shield the equity of the home. Essentially, using a debt shield means getting a loan against the equity in your home. For many clients, this is counter-intuitive—they want to pay down the mortgage as much as possible. While this may have an emotional appeal, for asset protection purposes, it is the exact opposite of what you want to do in states where home equity is exposed and homestead protections are minimal.

For most Doctor clients, using a "debt shield" does not mean taking a new loan on their home at all—rather, understanding that they may not want to rush to pay down their existing mortgages quickly. Here, the decision on whether (or to what extent) to pay down a mortgage they already have is examined from the asset protection perspective (could the funds be invested in another better-protected asset?) and wealth accumulation perspective (could the funds be invested in another better-performing asset?). When getting a new loan is involved, the analysis is identical.

Types of Debt Shields

As you will read in the Lesson on practice strategies, and earlier in this Lesson on trusts, "debt shields" can be implemented by using an unrelated lender, such as a bank, or by using a "friendly" lender. Often, an ideal "friendly" lender can be an irrevocable trust or a family LLC. While the asset protection may be slightly stronger for an unrelated lender debt shield, the economics can be much greater, and risks much reduced, when using a related lender.

Asset Protection

From an asset protection perspective, the transaction is simple—use the debt shield to move the equity from the vulnerable asset (the home) to a better-protected asset (e.g., exempt asset, LLC, FLP, etc.).

Economics

From an economic perspective, the transaction is also simple. Is the cost of the equity move (the after-tax interest cost) higher or lower than the ultimate repository asset of the loan proceeds? Also, how "safe" is what you are investing in with the loan proceeds? Of course, paying interest to a related entity, such as a Trust for the benefit of family members, is certainly a lot different than paying it to an unrelated bank.

Your economic analysis for an unrelated lender might be to ask, "What if the funds I gain by shielding my home could be invested in such a way that I had the opportunity to earn more within the investment than the loan interest would cost?" In this way, you would make money by shielding the home—through the concept of leverage we developed in the second Lesson.

The Diagnosis

For most Doctors, there is no more financially valuable and psychologically important asset than the family residence. Some states offer great homestead protection, but most offer inadequate protection of this valued asset. If homestead does not protect your home adequately, you should focus on this as part of your plan or accept the fact that your most valued asset is completely exposed. For older clients who are most concerned with estate planning, a QPRT may be an option.

For Doctors who are not ready to give their homes away to their children, some type of debt shield will likely be the most appropriate strategy. For Doctors who already have attractive loan rates on their homes and don't want to refinance their homes, the "friendly" debt shield which essentially pays children the interest may be the most attractive option. For more on this technique, speak to your advisors or contact the authors.

Divorce Protection

Of all the risks to Doctors, the most common threat to financial security may be divorce. According to *Divorce Magazine*'s (www.divorcemag.com) statistics from 1997, 50% of all first marriages in the United States end in divorce. Remarriages end in divorce 60% of the time. Undoubtedly an emotionally devastating experience, divorce can be a financially disastrous experience as well.

Divorce protection is not about hiding assets from a soon-to-be ex-spouse. Nor is it about cheating or lying to keep your wealth. Rather, it concerns resolving issues of property ownership and distribution before things go sour. By agreeing in advance what will be yours and what will be your spouse's, you save money, time and emotional distress in the long run. In fact, this type of asset protection planning inevitably benefits all parties, except the divorce lawyers of course.

Divorce planning is also about shielding family assets from the potential divorces of children and grandchildren. Given the statistics enumerated above, it is almost a certainty that either a child or grandchild of yours will get divorced. Thus, for purposes of intergenerational financial planning, this is a crucial topic, unless you want to give half of your legacy to the ex-spouses of your heirs. This is a lesson wealthy families have known, and addressed, for decades. Wealthy families do not have a secret to avoiding divorce. Wealthy families do have a secret to avoiding the financial losses that can be associated with inevitable divorces. This chapter will discuss why divorce can be so financially devastating, the pros and cons of prenuptial agreements, irrevocable Trusts and ways to protect your children from divorce.

Why Divorce Can Be A Financial Nightmare

Most Doctors do not have to read newspapers to see how financially devastating a divorce can be. While high-profile divorces involving tens of millions of dollars illustrate the point dramatically, most of us need only look to family or friends to see how a divorce turns into financial upheaval. The prevailing attitude toward divorce can be illustrated by a scene from the movie, *The First Wives Club*. In the film, Ivana Trump explains her theory of divorce to three ex-wives, played by Goldie Hawn, Diane Keaton, and Bette Midler. "Don't get even," she says. "Get everything!"

Combine this fight-for-everything attitude with the terrible odds of facing a divorce, and you have a very serious threat to financial security. In fact, a divorce threatens not only former spouses, but also their families and possibly their business partners as well. To truly understand how a divorce affects the finances of the participants, you must first understand how property is divided when the marriage is dissolved.

Community Property States

Many of the country's Western states have Community Property law. Community Property law stipulates that if there is no valid pre- or post-marital agreement, the court will equally divide any property acquired during the marriage other than inheritances or gifts to one spouse. Even the appreciation of one spouse's separate property can be divided if the other spouse expended effort on that property during the marriage, and the property actually appreciated concurrent or subsequent to the effort so expended. Based on these facts, it is obvious that *how* the asset is titled is not the controlling factor. Instead, *when* the asset was acquired and *how* it was treated are far more important factors in determining how the asset will be treated.

Equitable Distribution States

Non-community property states are called "equitable distribution" states because courts in these states have total discretion to divide the property "equitably" or fairly. The court will normally consider a number of factors in deciding what is "equitable," including the length of the marriage, the age and conducts of the parties, and the present earnings and future earning potential of each former spouse. The danger of equitable divorces is that courts often distribute both non-marital assets (those acquired before the marriage) as well as marital assets (those acquired during marriage), in order to create a "fair" arrangement. In this way, courts often split-up property in ways that the ex-spouses never wanted or expected.

Can A "Pre-Nup" Protect You?

A premarital agreement (a.k.a. prenuptial agreement, premarital contract, ante-nuptial agreement, etc.) is the foundation of any protection against a divorce. The premarital agreement is a written contract between the spouses. It specifies the division of property and income upon divorce, including disposition of specific personal property, such as family heirlooms. It also states the responsibilities of each party with regard to their children after divorce. Finally, these agreements lay out the respective responsibilities during marriage, such as the financial support each spouse can expect or which religion will be used to raise future children. The agreement cannot limit child support because the right to child support lies with the child and not the parent.

Irrevocable Spendthrift Trusts: Ideal Tools To Keep Assets "In the Family"

As mentioned earlier, Irrevocable Trusts are very effective asset protection tools because the grantor no longer own the assets owned by the Trust. In other words, the grantor has transferred the property with no strings attached. Because the grantor neither owns nor controls the property, future creditors, including an ex-spouse, cannot claim the property. Moreover, the grantor can make children, grandchildren, and even future great-grandchildren, beneficiaries of an Irrevocable Trust. However, even though they can benefit from Trust assets, the Trust can be drafted so that their creditors, including divorcing ex-spouses, cannot get to Trust assets.

Nonetheless, using an Irrevocable Trust should not be taken lightly. Giving away assets forever with no strings attached can prove to have serious consequences when protecting against divorce, lawsuit, or other threats. When would such a strategy make sense? It would make sense in circumstances where you would have inevitably given away the assets to certain beneficiaries anyway. For example, the Trust might be used for assets which (1) you will leave to your children or grandchildren when you die; and (2) you do not need for your financial security. For a more detailed example, consider Irving's case study.

Case Study: Irving's Trust Protects His Summer Home

Irving, a plastic surgeon, bought a summer home in Malibu. He and his first wife had three small children. Unfortunately, they divorced about six years into their marriage. In the settlement, he received the summer home.

Fifteen years later, Irving was ready to marry again, now in Santa Fe. Both he and his prospective spouse had been married previously and understood divorce. Irving considered a premarital agreement to keep the summer home as his separate property. He had planned to give it to his three children, but wondered whether working on the home would jeopardize this plan if he later divorced.

After speaking with Irving, we noted three important points:

1. Irving's handiwork on the home might make it marital property;
2. Irving's children and their families used the home throughout the year; and
3. Irving had a lawsuit from a failed real estate venture.

Given these points, it was clear that the best strategy for Irving was to have an Irrevocable Trust own the summer home, which would give beneficial interests of the home to all three children equally (which already occurred).

By using an Irrevocable Trust to own the summer home, Irving protected the home against possible future divorce and also shielded it from other creditors and lawsuits. By including spendthrift provisions, Irving protected the home from his children's creditors, as well. This will insure that the summer house stays in the family for generations.

Protect Your Children From Divorce

When your children or grandchildren come to you, giddy with exciting news about their recent engagements, the last thing they want to hear you ask is "Are you going to sign a pre-nuptial agreement?" In fact, if you weren't paying for the wedding, you might lose your invitation for making such a statement.

As you learned earlier, the secret to protecting assets from divorce is keeping them as "separate property" and not commingling them with community or marital property. You can't trust your children to do this, so you are going to do it for them—without requiring the consent of your child or the future (or existing) spouse.

By leaving assets to your children's Irrevocable Trusts, with the appropriate spendthrift provisions, rather than to them personally, you can achieve this goal. Of course, if the children take money out of the Trust and use it to buy a home or other property, that property will be subject to the rules of their state. To illustrate this point, let's look at the example of Rob and Janelle.

Case Study: Janelle's Divorce and Her Inheritance

Rob and Janelle were college sweethearts who got married right after graduation. Within a few years, their romance quickly turned sour and Rob could no longer handle the physical and emotional abuse. However, during their three-year marriage, Janelle received a sizeable inheritance and used it to pay off the couple's home. When they filed for divorce, Rob's attorney successfully argued that his time and labor on the house, and the fact that he lived in it except when Janelle occasionally kicked him out and he had to stay at his mother's, made half of the equity in the home (or $100,000) Rob's fair share. Though Rob and all of his friends will argue the $100,000 was a small consolation for what he endured, Janelle's grandparents certainly didn't intend for Rob to receive their inheritance.

What could Janelle have done differently to ensure that she protected her assets? Her grandparents could have left her the inheritance through an Irrevocable Trust that only allowed her to take out so much money per year. In that case, she would have used the interest from the inheritance to pay the mortgage down each month. If she did so, the corpus of the inheritance would have remained separate property and would not have been part of the divorce settlement. In the short three years of their marriage, they would have had next to no equity in their home and Rob would have left the divorce with what he brought into the marriage and his wounded pride—but none of Janelle's grandparent's life savings. It is left to the reader to determine what is equitable—we aren't marriage counselors. We are only trying to help you reach your desired objectives.

In a nutshell, a little proactive financial planning can go a long way to making sure that a divorce doesn't completely disrupt a family's financial situation.

The Diagnosis

In this Lesson, we discussed the importance of asset protection in our litigious society and how the sliding scale of asset protection can help you assess how protected (or unprotected) your assets may be. We dispelled myths that may have given you a false sense of security, then discussed the ways you can protect your assets. We explained philosophical requirements for any asset protection plan and shared information about exempt assets and legal tools. We explained how FLPs, LLCs, Trusts and international planning could be part of your planning. We even discussed how to protect your home and how to protect your family from divorce.

Now that you are well-informed in the area of asset protection, you are ready to learn how to build wealth. In the next Lesson, you will learn how to legally reduce taxes. Then, you will learn how to invest wisely, how to avoid estate taxes, and how to move forward with your planning. If, while on your educational journey, you have questions about anything you read, feel free to email us at odell@ojmgroup.com or mandell@ojmgroup.com. We can forward questions on to our co-authors.

Legally Reduce Taxes

You don't have to be a Doctor to want to legally reduce your taxes. Judge Learned Hand once said: "Anyone may arrange his affairs so that his taxes shall be as low as possible... There is not even a patriotic duty to increase one's taxes." The difference between moderately and highly successful physicians is that the latter group always considers the tax impact of anything they do.

Doctors should understand that every additional dollar earned will be decimated by federal, state and local taxes that may approach 50 cents. Physician families should also know that up to 50% of the family's after-tax net worth will be subject to federal estate and state inheritance taxes every time wealth transfers from one generation to the next. The Internal Revenue Code (IRC) is structured in a way that makes it almost impossible to accumulate wealth and pass it to future generations without significant friction. This is why your ability to work less and enjoy more of your hard earned dollars is directly related to your ability to manage taxes throughout your career, into retirement and at your death.

You can't possibly expect to manage taxes unless you understand taxes first. Every Doctor should read the next chapter, "Uncle Sam's Pieces of Your Pie," to learn exactly what taxes threaten wealth accumulation. This will help you better understand the motivation for, and benefits of, the strategies in the subsequent chapters. These are tools that may help you reduce, defer or even eliminate some of these taxes while providing you, your family or your practice additional financial benefits. By learning and implementing the techniques in this Lesson, you will be able to reduce unnecessary taxes and build wealth more quickly. If you and your family can reduce taxes and enjoy more of every hard-earned dollar, you will be able to work less and get more out of your career in medicine.

Uncle Sam's Pieces of Your Pie

You can't expect to successfully overcome any challenge until you fully understand the challenge itself. In this chapter, we will explain how great an impact taxes have on your finances. We will also share techniques successful business owners have used to reduce unnecessary taxes for decades. If you need any additional motivation to save taxes, we know dozens of families that have been able to save tens of thousands to hundreds of thousands of dollars per year during their lifetimes, and millions of dollars in taxes at the time of death, by integrating these strategies into their comprehensive financial plans. Let's get started by examining where and how all of this tax revenue is generated by looking at four types of taxes:

- Incomes Taxes

- Taxes on Investments or Capital Gain Tax Rates

- Estate Taxes

- Income In Respect of a Decedent (IRD)

Income Taxes

Every citizen pays income taxes on salaries and other income. Do you know exactly how income taxes are computed? Most people believe that they move from income tax bracket to income tax bracket—increasing the percentage they pay on each dollar earned as they move forward. The truth is that every individual (in the same filing category) pays the same tax rate on the first $15,100 of income. As a taxpayer's income crosses a threshold into the next tax bracket, only the dollars earned within that bracket are taxed at the higher rate. The next table illustrates how income tax is determined for married couples that filed jointly in 2008.

2010 Federal Income Tax Table—Married Couples Filing Jointly

If taxable income is over:	But not over:	The tax is:
$0	$16,750	10%
$16,750	$68,000	15%
$68,000	$137,300	25%
$137,300	$209,250	28%
$209,250	$373,650	33%
$373,650	no limit	35%

To better understand how income tax is tabulated for families, let's look at the example of Mike and Gina.

Mike and Gina are married and file jointly. Mike makes $240,000 per year, while Gina runs an in-home business that generates $10,000 per year. For simplicity, the table below assumes they have no deductions and they live in a state with 0% state income tax. Based on their salaries, they have $250,000 of total adjusted gross income that generates federal income tax liabilities of $60,321.

Marginal Tax bracket	33%
Effective Tax Rate	24%

Let's also assume that Mike and Gina spend $12,000/month on various expenses and they save the rest.

Gross income	$250,000
Income Tax	$60,321
After-Tax Income	$188,771
Expenses	$144,000
Savings	$44,771 for retirement

If Mike and Gina put away $40,000 of his salary into a tax-deductible vehicle (like a retirement plan), it would look like this:

Gross income	$250,000
Deduction	$40,000
Taxable income	$210,000
Taxes	**$47,121**
Net income	$162,879
Expenses	**$144,000**
Savings	$18,879

Gina and Mike have $40,000 in pretax retirement savings to add to the $18,879 of after-tax savings for a total of $58,879 in total savings instead of the $44,771 they had before!

Beware: Present Income Tax Rates Are Very Low and May Rise

As we write this book, federal income tax rates are at one of the lowest points in the history of the U.S. income tax. See the following table.

Federal Income Tax Rates

Year	Top Marginal Federal Income Tax Rate
1920	73.0%*
1930	25.0%*
1940	81.0%*
1950	91.0%*
1960	91.0%*
1970	71.0%*
1980	70.0%*
1990	28.0%*
2000	39.6%*
2010	35.0%
2013–on	39.6%**

Source: Citizens for Tax Justice, May 2004.
**Scheduled.*

Doctors need to understand the information presented in the table above and what it means. In short, tax rates are currently at a historical low and will likely rise (possibly significantly) in the future. You may recall when the highest marginal federal income tax rates were as high as 70%+. Could the largest U.S. deficit in history lead to higher rates sooner rather than later? Are you willing to bet your hard earned money that rates will not increase again?

Taxes on Investments

Once you earn money and pay income taxes, you aren't done with tax payments. This is only the tip of the tax iceberg. You may spend the money you earn (after taxes) on purchases and have to pay sales tax; or buy real estate and pay annual property taxes. Another possibility is that you save the money and invest it in some type of investment. Common investment choices include savings accounts, certificates of deposit (CDs), money market funds, stocks, bonds, mutual funds, cash value insurance policies and real estate. A detailed discussion of investments is offered in Lesson #8.

Most investments can generally be classified as either income or growth vehicles. In some cases, an investment may offer both. Income investments are those that offer some type of regular return (income) to the investor. Your bank accounts, CDs and money markets give you an interest payment each year. If you own traditional bonds, you receive a coupon every six months or year. If you own rental real estate, you may collect rental income. All of these interest payments, bond coupon payments and rent checks are added to your income for the purpose of calculating taxable income discussed above. If you are in a 33% marginal federal income tax bracket, then you will have to pay federal tax of 33% on those payments. If you are in a 35% marginal tax bracket, then you will pay 35% of the investment gain in taxes on that investment income. Of course, if you are not in an income tax-free state (most are not), you could pay up to 10% in additional state income taxes as well.

Not all investors require immediate income from investments. When you don't need current income from investments, you can afford to invest in riskier investments in search of greater long-term appreciation. Many of these investments are discussed in great detail in Lesson #8. We will offer a short discussion here to help you understand why it is so important to manage taxes on investments.

When you invest in a particular company, by buying stock your money is used to help grow that firm. The company who receives your investment will reinvest the proceeds to potentially increase the net worth (value) of the company. As the value of the company increases, the value of your shares in the company will also increase. You do not receive a regular check from the company. Rather, you have the right to sell your shares of the company. If you realize this type of profit on your investment, you are responsible for taxes on your "capital gains."

For tax purposes, capital gains can be categorized as long term or short term. Short term is defined as realized (sold) appreciation of an asset that you owned for less than one year. If you have a short-term gain, it is treated exactly the same way (for tax purposes) as the interest, coupons and rental income above. If your income puts you in a marginal federal tax bracket of 33%, your short-term capital gains would be taxed at 33% (plus any applicable state income taxes). Of course, you only need combined earned income and investment income of $200,300 to qualify you for the 33% federal tax rate. Most physicians will pay federal taxes of 33% or 35% or even 39% in 2011 (or sooner if tax rate hikes become law).

If you hold an asset for more than one year, the government gives you a benefit. You can pay long-term capital gains tax rates on your realized appreciation. Presently, these federal rates are 10% of the growth (for individuals who are in the lowest tax bracket—not physicians) and 15% for all other taxpayers (plus applicable state taxes). This benefit gives an incentive to investors to keep their funds invested. This stability is much better than the constant buying and selling which could significantly disrupt business. This tax incentive also acts as a deterrent to potentially unethical short-term trading.

Back to the example of our happily married couple who filed jointly—Mike and Gina. Let's say that Mike and Gina invest $70,000 of savings into a 5% money market. This generates a $3,500 interest payment annually. They must add this $3,500 to their income. Because they are in a 33% marginal tax bracket, the additional federal income tax liability will be $1,155. The $3,500 growth will only really be worth $2,345 (a real 3.33% return, instead of the 5% they thought they were getting) to them after-taxes.

Beware: Present Capital Gains Tax Rates Are Very Low and May Rise

As we write this book, capital gains tax rates, like ordinary income tax rates above, are at the lowest point in the history of the U.S. capital gains tax. See the following table:

Top Federal Capital Gains Tax Rate

Year	Top Federal Capital Gains Tax Rate
1940	30.0%
1942-1967	25.0%
1970	32.3%
1977	39.9%
1980	28.0%
1990	28.0%
2000	20.0%*
2010	15.0%
2013–on	20.0%**

Source: Citizens for Tax Justice, May 2004.
**Scheduled.*

Like the table presented earlier in the chapter, Doctors need to understand the information in the table above as well. Tax rates are low now and could easily become much higher in the relatively near future. Since your planning is long term, you must take the high probability of an increased capital gains tax rate into account in your planning.

Is Uncle Sam's triple dip enough? No, it isn't. After you pay your income taxes, sales taxes for your purchases and property taxes on real estate, and taxes on all of your investment gains, there is still more tax to be paid.

Estate Taxes

When you pass away, Uncle Sam levies an estate tax on those of you who might be worth more than $1,000,000 at the time of your death (assuming you live until at least 2011). That $1,000,000 includes the combined value of your home, retirement plans, real estate, brokerage accounts and insurance policies. While the rates might be between 40% and 55%, for estimation purposes, we will assume the estate tax rate to be about 50% for ease of calculation throughout the book. That means that half of what you think you will leave your children could go to taxes. For a complete description of the estate tax, how it works, why the supposed "repeal" is a fairy tale and how to avoid the unnecessary costs associated with it, please read Lesson #9, which focuses on estate planning.

IRD: The Only 70% Tax Trap

Lastly, there is a combination of taxes that severely threatens those of you who hope to be worth over $1,000,000 and who might die with a retirement plan or an IRA you would like to leave to your children. There is something called "income in respect of a decedent" (IRD).

No tax discussion is complete without mentioning IRD. IRD means the taxation of income earned by a deceased person who didn't pay tax on the income before passing away, or hadn't received the money before passing away. This is income which would have been taxable to the decedent had the decedent lived long enough to receive it. These income items include unpaid salaries, bonuses and commissions as well as retirement plans and IRA balances and variable annuity appreciation. Statistically, the retirement plan and IRA balances are by far the most significant assets that may be subject to IRD.

The following pie chart shows an example of how a retirement plan may be distributed at the time of death:

Distribution of Qualified Plan / IRA

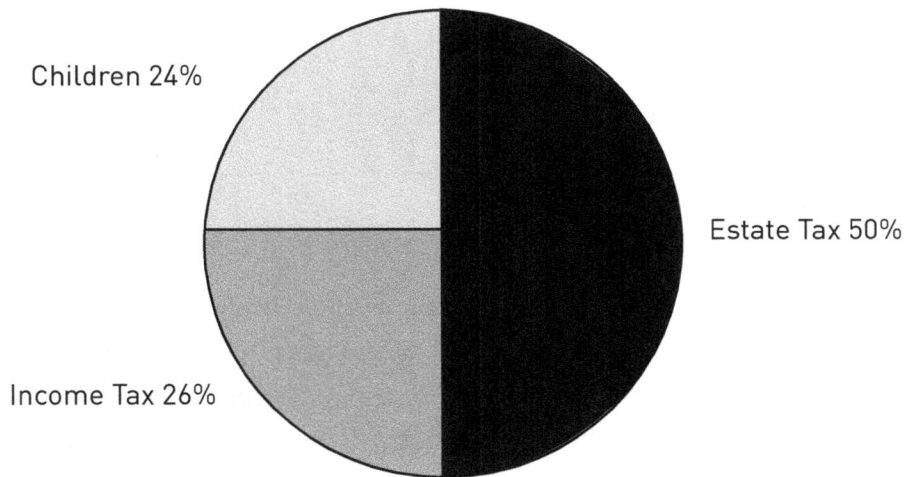

Children 24%

Income Tax 26%

Estate Tax 50%

Based on this figure, you should be aware that it is possible for less than $250,000 of a $1,000,000 retirement plan or IRA to reach your children after all taxes are paid.

The Diagnosis

It may seem crazy that there are so many ways that you can lose your wealth to taxes. Our tax laws are the most complex system of rules created by mankind. We will never master them. The best we can hope to do is attempt to manage the system. It is hoped that you understand how much money is at stake and will take this section very seriously. Managing taxes may prove to be the most important Lesson for Doctors to master. In the next chapter, we will learn practical ways to legally reduce taxes.

Use Retirement Plans

There are socially beneficial reasons for the creation of tax incentives surrounding qualified retirement plans. If you see a long history of tax benefits being afforded to a particular behavior or asset, this is generally because Congress believes that the behavior or asset provides some economic benefit to society as a whole. We will revisit additional tax benefits for investments later in this Lesson and in Lesson #8. In the case of retirement vehicles, the theory is that by encouraging people to fund their own retirement, the government (and the rest of us taxpayers) will not have to support them in retirement.

Two retirement tactics for Doctors to consider are:

1. Maximizing available qualified retirement plan contributions for all members of the family.

2. Maximizing investments in vehicles that are similar to qualified retirement plans for all members of the family.

As you learned in Lesson #1, Doctors must Leverage assets, capital and advisors if they want to work less and build more. By creating separate business entities to own real estate, equipment and liquid assets, Doctors are able to create employment opportunities for members of their family. By creating income opportunities for family members, you can accomplish two things:

1. Generate effective wealth transfers to junior generations.

2. Create opportunities for such family members to make tax-deductible contributions to their own retirement plans.

Maximizing The Use of Qualified Plans

Since tax deductible retirement plan contributions are limited for each person, having additional family members earning income within a family business or practice allows multiple tax-deductible contributions. This technique reduces the total tax liability for the family. In an earlier

Lesson, you learned that qualified retirement plans were afforded the highest level of protection from creditors (+5). The use of multiple contributions also affords physician families a greater level of asset protection for their total wealth, as more money will be invested into this exempt asset class. In addition to the reduced taxes and increased family savings, this strategy helps protect those savings from lawsuits (see Lessons #5 and #6). All of these benefits are integral for long term, sustainable affluence.

There are many types of tax-deductible retirement vehicles. They fall into one of two categories: defined contribution plans or defined benefit plans.

> **Defined contribution plans** restrict the amount you can contribute to the plans on an annual basis. These include all forms of IRAs (individual retirement accounts), profit sharing plans, money purchase plans, 401(k) plans, and others.

> **Defined benefit plans** restrict how much can be in the plan at any time. The broader category of defined benefit plans includes fully insured defined benefit plans which are also known as 412(i) plans. Typically, defined benefit plans are used to help older individuals catch up on lost contributions.

The choice and implementation of the right plan for the situation will be determined by your planning team. The benefits of that planning will vary widely depending on each family's circumstances and the ages and salaries of the employees.

Maximize The Use Of Vehicles Similar To Qualified Plans

Another tactic Doctors should employ is to use tools and techniques that mirror many of the benefits of retirement plans. Since retirement plan contributions are limited, Doctors need to utilize alternative saving and investment methods to meet their significantly higher long-term retirement needs. A common strategy to enhance long-term retirement income and reduce taxes on investment gains is to invest in cash value life insurance. This will be discussed in detail in Lesson #8 where we discuss how certain investments offer important benefits to Doctors. If you want to maximize long term, tax-efficient retirement income, you should definitely take time to review Lesson #8.

The Diagnosis

Retirement plans are a great way to achieve a high level of asset protection, while reducing current tax liabilities. In addition, the use of vehicles like cash value life insurance policies can help Doctors avoid taxes on investment gains and enhance retirement income while protecting assets from lawsuits all at the same time. Other vehicles, like Family Limited Partnerships and Limited Liability Companies, can also offer tax benefits. These are discussed in the next chapter.

"Borrow" Lower Tax Rates

In the last chapter, you learned that by creating income opportunities for family members you increase the family's total capacity for tax-deductible retirement plan contributions. This reduces a family's total income tax burden. By shifting the ownership of income-producing assets to family members in lower marginal income tax brackets, you can also reduce total family income taxes even further.

How FLPs And LLCs Reduce Taxes

In the asset protection Lesson (#6), you learned that family limited partnerships (FLPs) and limited liability companies (LLCs) are effective asset protection tools when exempt (+5) assets will not suffice. In addition, if used properly in the right situations, FLPs and LLCs can also save tens of thousands of dollars in income taxes each year.

By gifting interests of the FLP or LLC to family members who are in lower marginal income tax brackets, the parents are effectively "income sharing." A percentage of the income generated within the FLP will be taxed at the lower rates of the partners who are in lower marginal tax brackets. Typically, these are children or grandchildren. As long as the child is over 18 years old (or 24 if a full-time student), the child's share of the income will be taxed at a rate that is presumably lower than that of the working parents. (For more detailed information on this topic, revisit Lesson #5). Let's see how this works by reading the case study of Danny and Rina.

Case Study: Danny and Rina's LLC Reduces Income Taxes

Danny and Rina had annual taxable income of $100,000 from their rental real estate, which was worth $1 million. In a 40% combined state and federal tax bracket, their total income tax on this income came to $40,000. To reduce their taxes, they set up an LLC.

The LLC was funded with the real estate. Danny and Rina appointed themselves as managing members, so they would have 100% control. They gifted a 3% membership interest to each of their four children (Zach, Elgin, Earvin & Jerry) for a total of 12% removed from their estate. Because each child's interest would be valued at about $20,000 (3% x $1,000,000, less the minority valuation discount), no gift tax applied to the transfers to the children. Danny and Rina made these 12% transfers to their children annually for 5 years.

Under the LLC agreement, the children were taxed on their share of the LLC's income; which, after five years, became 60%. Thus, in year five, 60% of the LLC's taxable income would be taxed at the children's lower tax rates. So, when the LLC assets earn $100,000 in income, 60% of that income was taxed at the children's rate—15%. Thus, their tax bill for operation of the LLC was $16,000 (40% on $40,000, the parents' share) plus $9,000 (15% on $60,000, the children's share). Danny's family tax savings would therefore be as follows:

Total tax with the LLC, Year 5:	$25,000
Total tax without the LLC, Year 5:	$40,000
Year 5 family income tax savings with the LLC:	**$15,000**

It must be remembered that there were also savings in years one through four! What's more, under the LLC agreement, the managing members did not have to distribute any LLC income to the members. This was totally within the discretion of Danny and Rina as managing members. Thus, Danny and Rina could pay all LLC taxes with the income and reinvest the remaining proceeds.

Use Tax-Efficient Investments

Tax-efficient investments are used by wealthy families across the country to build wealth and protect assets. In the beginning of this Lesson, you learned that taxes on investment gains could significantly stunt long-term appreciation. You also learned that taxes on investment gains in states with state income taxes could be as high as 40%-44% of the short-term growth and 20%-24% of the long-term growth. To explain how a small differential in after-tax returns can have a significant impact over a long period of time, we would also like to add a simple law of finance to help you.

> **"The Law of 72"** states that 72 divided by the annual after-tax rate of return of an investment will give you the number of years it takes an investment to double in value.

Under the Rule of 72, an investment that returns 9% per year doubles in value every 8 years. In 24 years, a $100,000 investment that grew by 9% per year would be worth $800,000. What would happen if this investor paid less attention to taxes? Would it make that much of a difference? Let's see. $100,000 invested at 6% (because 33% of the 9% pretax gain was lost to taxes) would take 12 years to double in value. At the end of 24 years, this investment would only be worth $400,000. **If your investments lose 33% of the return to taxes, you could end up with half as much money in your investment account at the end of 24 years.** Half? That is a significant reduction indeed! Is the possibility of doubling your savings reason enough to pay attention to taxes on your investments now?

Savvy Doctors have always focused on after-tax investment returns. This is why they have so much money. Sometimes, tax management means investing in vehicles that are tax-exempt. Other times, it means hiring advisors who take a more active role in managing taxes within an investment portfolio. It can also mean investing to generate losses to offset gains. These are important Lessons Doctors must master to get the most out of their investments.

The Diagnosis

In Chapter 6-7, you learned that limited partnerships and limited liability companies are favorite asset protection tools of asset protection advisors to Doctors. In this chapter, you learned how to use these same tools to "share" income with family members in lower tax brackets. In Lesson #9, you will learn how these tools can be valuable estate planning tools as well. This is an example of how one tool can offer numerous benefits. You will learn more about this important philosophy in Lesson #8. For now, let's focus on more ways to save unnecessary taxes by getting the government to pay for some of your health insurance costs. This is the topic of discussion in the next chapter.

Let the IRS Subsidize Your Long-Term Care Insurance

In this chapter, you'll learn how to reduce taxes while providing an important financial planning tool for your family—long-term care insurance (LTCI).

Conventional financial planning wisdom tells us that the reasons for buying long-term care insurance are twofold:

1. To make sure you have enough money to pay for potentially devastating medical costs later in life and still have enough money to support your retirement (covered in Lesson #4).

2. To protect your estate from high medical costs, so you can leave an inheritance to your children and grandchildren (covered in Lessons #4 and #9).

What's more, you can also deduct your long-term care insurance premiums and reduce your taxable income. As an individual taxpayer, you can deduct up to the eligible amount of the LTCI premium. The following table shows the eligible tax-deductible premium in 2008.

Eligible Tax Deductible LTC Premium in 2008

Attained Age	Limitations on Premiums
Age 40 or less	$3100
Age 41—50	$580
Age 51—60	$1,150
Age 61—70	$3,080
Age 71 and older	$3,850

Source: Internal Revenue Code §§213(d)(1)(D), 213(d)(10))

If you have your own practice entity, you can possibly take much larger deductions for LTCI than indicated in the table above. A C-corporation can deduct all LTCI premiums for owners and employees. If you do not have a C-corporation (i.e., you have an S-corporation, LLC or partnership), you can only deduct additional LTCI expenses by covering employees and their spouses. Theoretically, you could employ your spouse and achieve the maximal tax deduction you desire by offering LTCI to your spouse (as an employee) and you (as the spouse of an employee). This way, you can get a 100% deduction for LTCI premiums without having to change your practice to a C-corporation. The basic guidelines regarding LTCI paid through a business by the employer are:

- Employer provided LTCI treated as accident and health plan. Source: IRC §7702B(a)(3).

- Deductible by employer (subject to reasonable compensation). IRC §162(a)

- Total premium excluded from employee's income (not limited to eligible premium). IRC §106(a)

The reason why deductions for long-term care insurance are allowed is because LTCI is considered to be a form of health insurance that pays for a variety of health costs, which may or may not be covered by Social Security, Medicare, Medicaid, Medi-Cal or your state plan. The details of long-term care insurance and our recommendations on what to look for in an LTCI contract are covered Chapter 4-4 on LTCI, which should be read to get a full understanding of how LTCI will help you and your family.

You may wonder "Doesn't Medicare pay these expenses?" The answer is "Yes... and No." That is, the State of California for instance will pay for a senior's medical bills, but only after that individual has depleted all but $2,000 of the patient's net worth. This means that if a retirement plan or any investments are titled to an individual, or have been titled in the individual's name in the last 5 years, the state will require those assets to be sold to pay for medical costs. In addition, the state will then take all but $30 per month of the individual's income as reimbursement for the coverage.

It isn't hard to see how this so-called "Medicaid spend-down" could deplete someone's assets very quickly. We don't know about you, but we could not live on $30 per day—let alone $30 per month—and we certainly wouldn't subject our parents to that poor of an allowance. As a result, we have purchased long-term care insurance for our parents.

Caution: The numbers above refer only to the state (Medi-Cal) or Medicare paying for some of your LTCI. You should also keep in mind that Medicare only pays after you spend 3-days in a hospital, for nursing home care only (not in-home care), for needs that are "medically necessary" (custodial needs are the most common and are NOT covered) and for only 20 days. Thereafter, Medicare only pays a daily benefit of $105 that ceases if the patient is not improving. For more detailed information on Medicare, please visit www.medicare.gov.

The Diagnosis

Because of the work of Doctors like you, we are living longer. The longer we live, the more likely we are to develop a condition that may require sustained, costly medical attention. Unfortunately, government programs will not adequately protect us. As a result, we have to protect ourselves with long-term care insurance. If we structure our business affairs properly, we can get a tax deduction for helping ourselves. The tax code also allows us to use deductions for helping others. This is covered in the next chapter on charitable planning.

Use Charitable Planning

The will to give is strong in many people. As a society, we cherish the right to give to the charitable institutions of our choice. The will to give is what we refer to as "charitable intent." We all want to give something back. Often, the biggest hurdles to giving are that we do not know how to give or we assume that our family will suffer as a result of our giving. Our goal in this chapter, and in Chapter 9-8 on charitable planning, is to show you a few ways to make charitable gifts that benefit the charity and your family at the same time. This is possible because of the tremendous tax benefits the IRS grants for charitable gifts. Before we examine the ways to use charitable giving to reduce income taxes, let's take a look at the basic tax rules regarding charitable giving.

Direct Gifts

Direct gifts are gifts that are made to a charitable organization for their immediate use. The federal tax code provides for current income tax deductions for gifts to charities that have qualified under 501(c)(3) as a charitable organization. The tax rules governing charitable giving are rather complex. Our explanation will be rather simplistic, but should give you a basic understanding.

The IRS distinguishes between "public charities" (universities, hospitals, churches, etc.) and "private charities" (private family foundations are the most common). What's the difference? If the gift is given to a public charity, you can deduct the amount of the gift against your adjusted gross income (AGI) up to a maximum of 50% of your AGI. If the gift exceeds this amount, you can apply the excess as deductions against future year's income for 5 additional years.

If the gift is to a private charity, then you can only deduct a maximum of 30% of your AGI but this also can be applied forward 5 years. Let's see how public and private charities differ in the case study of Charitable Chris.

Charitable Chris: Give to Foundation or Alma Mater

Chris is a retired cardiologist who created a small private family foundation a few years ago to give something back to the community. He involved his children in the foundation and realized some significant tax benefits. Now Chris has $60,000 worth of highly appreciated stock he doesn't need to support his retirement needs. As a result, he would like to make a gift to charity. His annual AGI is only $30,000 per year from the consulting work he does. Chris is considering gifting the stock either to his family foundation or to his alma mater where he sits on the board.

If he gifts the stock to the foundation, he will only be able to deduct $9,000 per year from his tax return (30% of AGI). If he gifts to the university, he will be able to deduct $15,000 (50% of AGI). Because he can only carry the deduction forward 5 years, he'll only be able to apply $54,000 (6 years x $9,000) worth of deductions using the family foundation but he'll be able to use all $60,000 (4 years x $15,000) of deductions if he gifts to the university.

Indirect Gifts

Indirect Gifts are often called "split interest" or "planned gifts" because some of the benefit from the gift is for the benefit of the charitable organization and some of the benefit of the assets being gifted will be retained by the grantor (or donor) and his or her family. The real beauty of charitable giving from the family perspective is that the IRS also allows tremendous tax benefits for "indirect gifts"—those left to charity through a trust or annuity. In fact, the IRS also allows deductions for indirect gifts through irrevocable charitable remainder or lead trusts, and through charitable gift annuities, which provide lifetime income to the donor as guaranteed by the charity and monitored by the state. By using an indirect gift, charitable planning can truly be a win-win-win situation: you win, your family wins and your favorite charities win.

Common Charitable Giving Scenarios

The following are the most common charitable giving scenarios, where it makes financial sense for a family to consider charitable planning because of the tax benefit:

Sale of a highly appreciated asset: Many Doctors or their parents, especially those over 60, hold highly appreciated assets—usually real estate or stocks that have grown enormously in value over time. Even more problematic is where there are few assets making up the bulk of someone's net worth. This is often the case where there is a closely held family business or a family farm. Regardless of the asset, you may want to sell the asset but don't want to pay the capital gains tax, thus reducing the after-tax value of the asset by up to 24%. Through the use of charitable planning strategies, you may be able to unlock some of the appreciation and significantly reduce the capital gains tax while benefiting a favorite charity as well.

Need to generate family income from investment assets: The past ten years have seen unprecedented growth of personal wealth in the form of portfolio apprecia- tion. However, when clients seek to re-shuffle their asset allocation to produce more income and diversify their portfolios, they will be hit with a substantial tax on their gains. By giving to a charity you have the chance to be creative in your approach to convert paper gains to cash flow, save taxes, and turn non-deductible items into tax deductible ones while addressing charitable objectives at the same time.

Estate Planning: The most powerful benefits of charitable planning can be enjoyed when used as part of a multi-disciplinary financial plan. As you'll learn in Lesson #9 (Estate Planning), when you die, your family could pay as much as 40-60% in federal and state estate taxes, plus income tax on IRD assets such as pensions and IRAs. Charitable giving mitigates many of these taxes. In Chapter 9-8, we'll address charitable planning as it pertains to estate planning in more detail.

The Most Common Charitable Tool: The Charitable Remainder Trust

Let's assume you have one highly appreciated asset you would like to sell but are reluctant to do so because of the significant capital gains taxes you would owe. At the same time, you are look- ing for ways to reduce your current year's taxable income and would like to receive an ongoing income stream. Moreover, you would like to diversify your overall investment portfolio. Usu- ally, this would mean selling that highly appreciated asset, paying the high taxes and reinvesting with a substantially reduced amount. In this situation, the Charitable Remainder Trust (CRT) may be an ideal option for you.

- Used properly, a CRT can potentially:

- Reduce current income taxes with a sizable income tax deduction.

- Eliminate immediate capital gains taxes on the sale of appreciated assets, such as stocks, bonds, real estate and just about any other asset.

- Increase your disposable income throughout the remainder of your life.

- Create a significant charitable gift.

- Reduce estate taxes that your estate might have to pay upon your death, thus leaving more for your heirs after your lifetime.

- Avoid probate and maximize the assets your family will receive after your death.

- Protect your highly appreciated property from future creditors

Think of a CRT as a tax-exempt trust that provides benefits to two different parties. The two different parties are the individuals receiving income and the chosen charity or charities. The "income beneficiaries" (usually you or your family members) typically receive income from the trust for either their lifetimes or a specified number of years (20 years or less). At the end of the trust term, the chosen charity will receive the remaining principal to utilize for its charitable purposes.

How A CRT Works

A CRT is an irrevocable trust that makes annual or more frequent payments to you—typically until you die. What remains in the trust then passes to a qualified charity of your choice.

A number of tax saving advantages may flow from the CRT. First, you will obtain a current income tax deduction for the value of the charity's interest in the trust. The deduction is permitted when the trust is created even though the charity may have to wait until your death to receive anything. Second, the CRT is a vehicle that can enhance your investment return. Because the CRT pays no income taxes, the CRT can generally sell an appreciated asset without recognizing any gain or paying any tax on the sale. This enables the trustee to reinvest the full amount of the proceeds from a sale and thus generate larger payments to you for the rest of your life.

Using Life Insurance For "Wealth Replacement"

Many people would be more motivated to make gifts to charities, but they are afraid that they won't leave an adequate inheritance to their heirs. Doctors need to understand that they can make donations during their lifetimes, save income taxes, and find a way to leverage the tax deduction to achieve a similar, or sometimes larger, inheritance for their heirs than if they hadn't utilized charitable planning. This concept of using life insurance for "wealth replacement" will be discussed next.

A CRT is eligible for the estate tax deduction if it passes assets to one or more qualified charities at the time of one's death. If you wish to replace the value of the contributed property for heirs who might otherwise have received it, you could use some of your cash savings from the charitable income tax deduction to purchase a life insurance policy on your life held in an irrevocable life insurance trust for the benefit of your heirs. This is called a "wealth replacement trust."

Often, through the leveraging effect of life insurance, it is possible to pass on assets of greater value than those contributed to the trust. In this way, your heirs are not deprived of property they had expected to inherit. In fact, your heirs may find it advantageous to receive cash, in the form of proceeds from a death benefit, as opposed to an asset that they did not wish or know how to manage. Let's see how this works:

1. You gift a highly appreciated asset to the CRT. You receive a current income tax deduction that you can use to reduce your income tax liability for up to 5 years.

2. The CRT sells the asset. Neither you nor the CRT pay any taxes on the sale. 100% of the value of the asset is preserved and invested in a tax-free environment.

3. You receive a larger annual distribution from the CRT than you would have received if you had paid taxes on the sale of the asset and invested the proceeds in a taxable environment.

4. Although the annual distribution is taxable, it is taxed in accordance with how it was earned in the trust. This form of taxation is beneficial given the lower dividend and capital gains tax rates. The income beneficiary will save a significant amount in taxes each year.

5. After the death of all income beneficiaries, the remaining assets from the CRT go to your selected charity.

6. A "wealth replacement trust" can be funded with insurance to replace those assets given to charity and give the family even more than they would have received had no charitable planning been done.

The CRT's "Cousin"—The Charitable Lead Trust (CLT)

When it comes to charitable trusts, CRTs seem to get all the attention. But the cousin of the CRT, the charitable lead trust (CLT), also can provide significant charitable and tax benefits, particularly in an environment of lower interest rates.

With a CLT, sometimes called a "charitable income trust," you transfer cash or income-producing assets to the trust. The trust then pays out income earned by the assets to a designated charity or charities. The payout may be an annual fixed dollar amount set at the time of the transfer—called "an annuity trust"—or an amount based on a percentage of the assets in the trust at the time of each annual payout—called a "unitrust."

At the end of a specified number of years, the remaining assets in the trust are distributed to the non-charitable beneficiary, usually someone other than you or your spouse. It could be your children, grandchildren, other family members or a trust for the benefit and protection of any of these heirs. This timing is, in effect, the opposite of the CRT, in which the donor receives current income from the trust assets and the assets go to the charity at the end of the designated time.

Gift tax may be due at the time the assets are transferred to the trust, because non-charitable beneficiaries (your family) will ultimately receive the assets. However, this can often be planned so that no gift tax will be due. This is because (1) the gift is discounted as the beneficiaries won't receive the gift for some time; and (2) you receive a gift-tax deduction because a charity is receiving the income from the assets (the deduction is based on the amount transferred into the trust and the amount of time the assets are to remain in the trust). Furthermore, the gift won't be taxed at all if its discounted value is less than your remaining applicable gift tax exclusion.

Keep in mind that CRTs and CLTs can be established not only during life, but also after death, i.e., testamentarily. Your team of advisors can help you determine whether it is better to establish CRTs/CLTs during your life or after your death.

The Diagnosis

If you have a charitable intent and want to reduce current income taxes, capital gains taxes, or even estate taxes, then you should seriously consider charitable planning techniques. Often, you and your family will stand to benefit as much as the charity itself. The right team of advisors can help you understand the costs and benefits of charitable planning and manage all of the complex issues. If you want to find out ways to more efficiently invest for the other people you take care of—your children—you should read the next chapter on tax-efficient educational funding.

Tax-Efficient Educational Planning

In Lesson #1, you learned Doctors all use leverage when they leveraged their education to increase their earning potential. This increased level of education is directly responsible for your significant income. From our experience, most highly educated professionals would like to give their children every opportunity to gain as much education as possible. Why not do this in as efficient a manner as possible?

The average cost of a 4-year education at a private college for a student graduating in 2000 was $85,356. With a 6% inflation estimate, the estimated cost of a 4-year private education for the graduating class of 2020 will be over $273,000. Of course, if your child goes to an Ivy League school, like many children of physicians do, the total cost of the undergraduate degree could be well over $500,000. If you consider that most physician families pay almost 44% in income taxes AND between 15% and 44% in taxes on capital gains and dividends, it may seem almost impossible to save for a child or grandchild's education while also putting away funds for retirement. In this chapter, we will discuss five types of tax efficient college investment options that you should consider to preserve your wealth.

Tax Efficient College Investment Options

If you have children or grandchildren who might go to college, graduate school, medical school or law school, there are tax efficient ways to save for this future expense. The short list of potential tax-efficient investment options includes:

1. 529 College Savings Plans

2. 529 Prepaid Tuition Plans

3. Uniform Gifts to Minors Act/Uniform Transfers to Minors Act (UGMA/UTMA) Trusts

4. Cash Value Life Insurance

5. Coverdell Plans (formerly Education IRAs)

Because the Coverdell plan contribution limits are $2,000 per year and that amount is completely inadequate for high-income earners like physicians, we will exclude it from out analysis. To compare and contrast the first four plans, we want to consider each of them across a number of metrics. Then, we will offer a qualitative discussion about the contribution limits, tax benefits, access and flexibility of each plan to help you understand why Doctors should use some plans more than others.

To do so, let's consider the following table.

Comparison of Tax-Efficient Educational Funding Options

	529 Savings Plan	529 Prepaid Plan	UGMA / UTMA	Cash Value Insurance
Income Limitations	None	None	None	None
Maximum yearly contribution per beneficiary (all numbers double when gifts come from two parents or grand-parents)	annual federal gift tax exclusion (up to 5 years in advance)	annual federal gift tax exclusion (up to 5 years in advance)	annual federal gift tax exclusion	Umlimited as policy is owned by parents
Account earnings	TAX-FREE, if used for qualified expenses	TAX-FREE, if used for qualified expenses	Taxable	TAX-FREE
Ability to change beneficiaries	Yes	Yes	No	Yes
Contol of withdrawals	Owner of account	Owner of account	Transfers to child when child reaches legal age	Owner of account
Investment options	Ready-made portfolios of mutual funds	Tuition units guaranteed to match tuition inflation	Wide range of securities	Various. Depends on policy chosen.
State tax deductible contributions	Varies by state	Varies by state	No	No
Qualified use of proceeds	Any accredited post-secondary school in the U.S.	Varies by state	Unlimited	Unlimited
Penalties for nonqualified withdrawals	10% penalty withheld on earnings	10% penalty withheld on earnings	No	No
Taxation of qualified withdrawals	Tax-free	Tax-free	A portion may be exempt; income may be taxed at child's rate	Tax-free
Ownership of assets for financial aid purposes (may vary by institution)	Account owner	Student	Student	Exempt for student aid

Reducing The Comparison To 3 Plans

The first thing we want to make clear is that we are skeptical of prepaid tuition plans. Though these plans allow parents to "lock in" tuition rates at the state universities and colleges when they make contributions, we see the inflexibility of the plans as a major issue. If it is so hard to get children to clean their rooms or take out the trash, we find it hard to base the success of a plan with hundreds of thousands of dollars in it on our ability to convince our children to attend one of a few colleges we chose for them when they were two years old. We can't make that assumption. Practically speaking, we will compare 529 plans (not prepaid tuition plans) to UGMA/UTMA plans. Then, we will compare 529 plans to cash value life insurance.

Basics of 529 Plans

529 plans allow an individual to make annual tax-free "gifts" of $13,000 to any person. It also allows a couple to make such gifts of up to $26,000 per year to each child. With the 529 College Savings Plan, an individual can make 5 years worth in advance. Total benefits include:

- Contributions over $26,000 for a married couple (and $13,000 for an individual) are allowed—gift tax-free.

- You, the donor, control the withdrawals.

- You may change the beneficiaries.

- You receive any tax benefits.

- You direct the type of investments (from a short list of choices).

- The money grows tax-free.

Contributions Over $26,000 May Be Allowed—Gift Tax-Free

You may already know that an individual can make annual tax-free "gifts" of $13,000 to any person and that a couple can make such gifts of up to $26,000. With the 529 College Savings Plan, an individual can make 5 years worth of gifts in one year without paying a gift tax. The 529 Plan allows you to allocate those gifts over the next five years. Thus, a couple can gift $130,000 tax-free in one year to a 529 Plan for each child or grandchild.

Total proceeds in a 529 Plan are capped. The amount differs from plan to plan but many caps range from $220,000 to $260,000. This means that a set of parents could gift $130,000 to a 529 Plan AND a set of grandparents could gift an additional $130,000 to the same child's 529 Plan and no gift taxes would be paid. Larger amounts could be gifted, but gift taxes would apply.

When you compare the 529 Plan to the Educational IRA (now called a Coverdell Plan) whose annual contribution limit is $2,000, there is no question as to which is the better choice.

YOU Control The Withdrawals And Beneficiaries

Unlike an UGMA account or Education IRA, you control the withdrawals and may change the beneficiaries of a 529 Plan. If one child doesn't go to college or receives a scholarship, you may change the Plan to benefit someone else. You can also make these changes as often as you like, as long as the beneficiaries are related. In fact, you can even name yourself the beneficiary if you plan to go back to school.

If you change your mind and want to withdraw the funds and use them yourself, you may do so. The only penalty is that you must pay a 10% penalty in addition to ordinary income taxes on any growth of the funds in the plan.

YOU Receive The Tax Benefits

The funds in a 529 plan grow on a tax-free basis. Because annual capital gains and dividends are not taxed in the 529 Plan, the account balance has the potential to grow faster than if invested in comparable taxable investments. If you consider that dividends and short-term capital gains are taxed at rates that may be as high as 44% in some states, the 529 plan could grow twice as quickly as a UGMA or UTMA that offers no real tax deferral benefit.

You may also be able to reduce estate taxes by using a 529 plan. The plan's high contribution limit provides a convenient way to effectively lower the taxable value of your estate. As you'll learn in Lesson #9, federal estate taxes can be as high as 55% for Doctor families who may not pass wealth to the next generation until after 2011. In light of this fact, the ability to reduce your taxable estate while providing educational funding for family members should be very attractive.

You Direct The Type Of Investments

Some 529 Plans allow you to invest in a variety of stock, bond, and money market funds. You may have a choice of a growth portfolio or a balanced portfolio. There's even a company that offers an "Age-Based Portfolio" that focuses on growth in the early years of the child and automatically re-balances every few years to focus more on capital preservation as college approaches. There is no extra fee for this added service.

Shortfall Of The 529 Plan

If you make your scheduled contributions, don't mind the risk of the stock market and don't die, the 529 Plan is a much better alternative than just saving money in your brokerage account with the intention of cashing it in to pay the bills later. However, we can't guarantee that you will live to see all of your children go to college or graduate school and we can't invest in a 529 plan without subjecting our funds to market risk. For these reasons, you may want to consider some type of life insurance as part of your college savings plan. There are two plans to consider. If you are going to invest in a 529 plan, you should also invest in a decreasing term life insurance policy. If you need $1,000,000 because your two young children will someday attend Ivy League schools, then you should buy a $1,000,000 decreasing term policy that reduces by your annual contribution amounts. To illustrate this point, let's refer to the following:

Year	Child's Ages	Amount in 529 Plans	Amount of Term Insurance
1	2 & 4	$40,000	$1,000,000
2	3 & 5	$84,000	$950,000
3	4 & 6	$132,400	$900,000
5	6 & 8	$244,200	$800,000
10	11 & 13	$637,500	$500,000
15	16 & 19	$1,279,000	$0

If you are very concerned about the stock market's volatility and don't want it to have a significant impact on your children's educational funds, you should consider a whole life policy with a AAA-rated insurance company. This is a relatively stable investment and will grow at a steady rate. Even in 2001, one of the worst years in recent stock market history, one AAA-rated insurance company paid over 7.5% on its whole life policies. In addition to the tax-free cash accumulation inside such a policy, there is also a minimum death benefit to protect against an early death. When your children eventually attend college, you can then use tax-free loans to withdraw money from the policy and keep the death benefit intact.

Unconventional Wisdom—Life Insurance As An Investment

The last few pages focused on the benefits of 529 plans versus UGMA and UTMA plans. Now, let's compare the 529 to cash value life insurance. The only benefit the 529 has over the insurance policy is that, in some states, the 529 plan offers a state income tax deduction for low income contributors. Generally speaking, this could give the 529 plan a grade of an A+. Practically, this benefit may be very limited. The few states that offer a state income tax deduction also have either a phase out of the deduction for high-income earners or they limit the state tax deduction to a couple thousand dollars per year. Even if you move to a state that offers a deduction, the deduction will likely not apply to you because you earn too much.

The tax pendulum could swing back the other way when using a 529 plan if your children earn academic or athletic scholarships, choose to attend a less expensive school or don't attend college at all. Let's look at an example of how this could create a tax problem for the parents.

If the parents invest $100,000 into the 529 plan that grows to $200,000 and they don't want to spend the funds for a child's education, they could be subject to income taxes and penalties that total $50,000 or more. The flexibility of a 529 plan is excellent if you are talking about transferring funds from one child's plan to another child's plan. However, the flexibility of using the funds for other things is quite poor.

Let's look closely at how life insurance fairs in a comparison to the 529 plan. First, let's look at contribution amounts. Unlike all of the other college funding options, there is no practical maximum on how much a parent can invest in a life insurance contract. We have seen affluent clients invest over one million dollars per year into insurance policies. There are financial underwriting guidelines, but there should be very little problem contributing much more than the $13,000 or $26,000 per year limit of the 529 plan.

Second, let's look at the tax benefits of the life insurance policy. Like the 529 plan, the funds grow without taxation. Also, if you compare withdrawals from the 529 that are used for educational expenses to policy withdrawals and loans, those are also equal. The big difference is in the situation where you want to use the 529 values for something other than qualified college costs. Where the 529 plan is fully taxable plus a 10% tax penalty, there is no tax on any withdrawals from an insurance policy if you don't violate modified endowment contract (MEC) guidelines or lapse the policy (which the insurance professional on your team should be able to help you easily avoid). This tax benefit leads into a discussion of flexibility below.

Third, the life insurance policy offers you much more access and flexibility. Not only can you use the funds for anything you like, but you can also protect your children at the same time. If you make $100,000 of contributions to a 529 plan and die, your children will get no more than $100,000. If you contribute $100,000 of premiums to a life insurance policy and die, your heirs may get $2,000,000 or more. When you finish reading this book, you will see at least a handful of uses for life insurance. When you compare this to the sole tax penalty-free use of 529 plans, it is obvious to see how life insurance can be a much more valuable component of your financial plan.

To look at a review of the different options, please consider the following:

	529 Savings Plan	529 Prepaid Plan	UGMA/ UTMA	Cash Value Insurance
Contribution Limits	B+	B+	B-	A+
Tax Benefits	B- to A+	B- to A+	B-	A-
Access (reversibility)	B-	C-	F	A
Flexibility of Plan	B-	C-	F	A+

The Diagnosis

If you have children, grandchildren or nieces and nephews whom you would like to assist in funding their education, or if you or your spouse might go back to school, you may consider a

529 College Savings Plan. If you are looking to build an efficient, flexible financial plan that can easily be altered to manage different issues as they arise, you should consider funding cash value life insurance as a funding vehicle for college savings planning. There is much more detailed discussion of insurance policies for this and other purposes in Lesson #8.

Avoid the Only 70% Tax Trap—Pensions and IRAs

There is one type of asset that can generate a tax that can be as high as 70%—your retirement plan. This results from a combination of income and estate taxes being applied to retirement plan balances at death. By leaving less than 30% of your retirement plan assets to your heirs, it will be very hard to achieve a high level of affluence for the future generations of your family.

One of the "common sense" lessons you will hear repeated in the financial media is that you should contribute as much as you can to your retirement plans (pensions, profit-sharing plans, IRAs, 401(k) plans, etc.). The conventional wisdom is that because you get an income tax deduction and tax-deferred growth, these plans are a huge tax win for the client.

In Chapter 9-6, we will offer an in-depth discussion of this tax problem. This discussion includes the following: that tax rates may be higher when you finally retire, you may not need the funds in retirement; how double taxation can impact retirement plan assets; and how to avoid this terrible tax trap.

The Diagnosis

If you are participating in a retirement plan and may someday have a sizeable pension balance, you should be concerned that your heirs may unnecessarily have to pay the 70% tax on IRD. No tax discussion is complete without mentioning IRD. No financial plan should disregard this potential tax trap. When you are finished reading this tax Lesson, you should make a point of reading Lesson #9 to learn more about protecting your hard earned money from this avoidable and unnecessary tax.

Determine When Your Tax Advisor Is Helping or Hurting You

As previously highlighted in the Case Study for Chapter 3-3, some years ago, David Mandell's former law firm was retained by a long time client to perform a self-audit. The client, an extremely successful businessman, had reason to believe that his firm may have made a mistake in tax reporting. If he had underpaid taxes, he wanted to review the situation and bring it to the attention of the IRS and volunteer to pay any missing taxes to avoid some potential penalties. He hired the firm to do an audit of his personal and corporate income tax returns for a period of five years. What the firm found was shocking.

Even though this client had used four different accounting firms for his various returns (including a well-known 500 person firm), the taxes he had paid were far from what he owed. Luckily for him, it was an overpayment—in the neighborhood of over $2 million!

That is correct. Because of the self-imposed audit, the client learned that he could legally file amended tax returns and claim a multimillion-dollar refund. Lucky for him, he was concerned about poor tax advice and spent the money to hire David's former firm to perform the audit (even though he thought he would owe more, not less tax).

Lessons To Be Learned

While the above case is extreme, it is not unusual. It demonstrates the two ways millions of taxpayers get in trouble with tax planning by relying on tax professionals who (1) incompetently cause unjustified underpayments of tax; or (2) are so conservative or close-minded that they actually "cost" the client through gross overpayments of tax.

When you add the federal, state and even municipal taxes, Doctors pay marginal income taxes at the rate of 40% to 45%. At these rates, the following question becomes very important: **Does your tax advisor—CPA, attorney, or other professional—suffer from one of the drawbacks below?**

Incompetence: Not Admitting When an Area is Beyond His or Her Expertise: This is the most obvious issue for any advisor. While it may be obvious to avoid the incompetent advisor, the signs of incompetence are not so apparent. If you do realize it, it is often too late.

Lack of Multi-disciplinary Skills: Skilled in One Area, but Not the Other: More common is the situation where the client's advisor is skilled in one area of practice but not knowledgeable about another tax area. This is understandable. Tax planning is like medicine. Each area has become so complex that one can only hope to become an expert in one discipline. In the medical arena, most patients and physicians realize this and readily accept the idea that patients are regularly referred to other specialists. A gastroenterologist would no sooner make diagnoses of skin conditions than a dermatologist would handle a digestive disorder. Yet this is what happens all the time in the tax area.

When an advisor is faced with an issue beyond his expertise, he tends to do one of the following:

1. Admit his lack of knowledge and refer the client to another expert.

2. Try to quickly get up to speed on the issue (on the client's dime).

3. Simply reject any recommendations that he does not understand.

Too often, we see tax advisors resort to the third option, rejecting a potentially beneficial strategy for their client because it is out of the advisor's area of expertise. We see accountants and attorneys who refuse to work as part of a multi-disciplinary team. Often, this is because they fear losing the client to another advisor if they admit that what the other advisor recommends actually makes sense. While these advisors will never actually tell the client not to listen to another professional, their behavior speaks for them when they reject another professional's suggestions with arcane arguments and references that they know the client will not be able to evaluate on his own.

The Diagnosis

Certainly, there is no easy answer to the dilemma of how to choose a competent tax advisor who has a great deal of experience working with Doctor clients, can handle complex planning, and fits comfortably between overly-aggressive and overly-conservative. We are not suggesting that you abandon your present CPA or tax attorney. We are merely suggesting that you take an active role in your tax and estate planning, bring new solutions to your advisor or bring in other professionals to assist your advisor in a coordinated team approach. Since you are the client who will ultimately pay for the planning (or lack of it) that is put into place by your advisors, it behooves you to make sure that your planning fits your needs and tax goals.

Avoid Poor Investment Outcomes

Just as avoiding poor medical outcomes is an obvious goal for physicians, so too should avoiding poor investment outcomes be an obvious financial goal. Similar to medicine, the application of this obvious financial goal is much more complicated than you would think. One reason for the difficulty is that wisdom and luck are often hard to differentiate. Historically, many unwise investments have performed well, at least for a short period of time. Remember, Enron was the investment community's darling at one time. To measure the wisdom of an investment strategy, one does not measure performance over a short period of time. A more accurate measure of an investment should take place over a complete market cycle—which is defined as a bull high to a bear low and back again, or vice versa.

Let's look at this another way: If you applied the modified Machiavellian concept of "the ends justify the means" to an investment scoring philosophy, you would say that the person who purchased a lottery ticket and won $25,000,000 was a smart investor and the millions who spent the same $1 on losing lottery tickets were failures. You should instead look and compare the probabilities of success with the risks, complexity of the investment and interaction with the other elements of the plan to determine the wisdom of the investment philosophy. Doing this, you might come to the more reasoned conclusion that none of the investments in lottery tickets were wise—one was simply lucky. Picking individual high-risk equities in hopes of finding one that "hits it big" is another example of a lottery mentality with similar appeal to the unwise. Like the lottery, this strategy has a very low probability of success.

The applications of the numerous principles discussed throughout this book are the keys to successful investing. Lesson #6 on asset protection showed you how to protect your investments from lawsuits. Lesson #7 on tax planning showed you how to reduce unnecessary taxes. Lesson #9 on estate planning will show you how to pass your wealth onto your heirs with as little tax and complication as possible.

This specific Lesson is going to explain how to avoid bad outcomes so you can preserve as much of your principal and investment gains as possible. This Lesson will help you avoid the most common physician investment mistakes by teaching you some important investment fundamentals, explaining how these may or may not apply to Doctors, and explaining some common and not-so-common, investment alternatives. More specifically, this Lesson will explain the limitations of a Nobel Prize winning investment theory that most investment firms follow, the real costs of taxes and inflation, the pitfalls of mutual funds for the wealthy and discuss alternative investment strategies that address these concerns. This Lesson will also discuss specific investments that address all of these concerns, making them important investments for building and protecting wealth.

A Nobel Prize Is Not Enough

Many investment advisors may boast that their strategy is based on a Nobel Prize-winning theory. Though this statement may seem impressive, it has two faults:

1. Nearly everyone's strategy is based on that same theory.

2. The theory itself has a number of limitations that were acknowledged by the Nobel Laureates themselves.

The purpose of this chapter is threefold. First, we will give you a very basic understanding of this Nobel Prize-winning investment theory. Second, we will point out the limitations of the theory. Third, we will suggest how to make the theory work within a Doctor's comprehensive financial plan.

The Modern Portfolio Theory and Capital Asset Pricing Model

In 1990, the Nobel Prize in Economics was awarded to Harry Markowitz, Merton Miller and William Sharpe for their Modern Portfolio Theory ('MPT') and Capital Asset Pricing Model ('CAPM'). With apologies to Messrs. Markowitz, Miller and Sharpe, we would like to offer simplistic summaries of MPT and CAPM. There are three concepts you must understand before you can put them together to form the MPT and CAPM. Those are:

1. Types of Risk

2. Risk vs. Reward

3. Diversification of Investments

Types of Risk

CAPM divides the risk of any investment into two types of risk - specific risk and market (or systematic) risk. Specific risk is unique to an individual investment; while systematic risk affects all investments in the "market" and is also known as "market risk." Let's look at examples of each:

Specific Risk: Do you remember the Tylenol scare of 1982? Someone tainted a number of bottles of Tylenol with cyanide. This obviously affected the stock price of Johnson & Johnson, the maker of Tylenol. The risk of this type of occurrence is an example of specific risk because it didn't have an effect on all makers of analgesics in the market, just Johnson & Johnson.

Market or Systematic Risk: You've no doubt heard or read about the stock market crash of 1929. That incident affected all investments in the market. The risk of a crash is certainly the most extreme example of market risk. A more current example is what has happened between January 2, 2008 and March 3, 2009. The Dow Jones Industrial Average was down 49% (from 13,261.82 to 6,764.81). In this time, very few stocks saw a rise in value.

When you make an investment, that investment is subject to both market and specific risk. In a portfolio of investments, you are subject to market risk, which affects the whole portfolio, and a combination of specific risks that affect each individual investment distinctly.

Risk vs. Reward

Over an extended period of time, rewards are generally higher for those who take more risk. Individuals who start their own businesses and are ultimately successful will probably make considerably more money than those individuals who took the less risky route and went to work for someone else. The entrepreneur risked his time and money. If successful, he will be rewarded handsomely for the risk he took.

Doctors and lawyers bypass the opportunity to make money right out of college. Instead, they spend more money going to medical school or law school and delay their income-producing careers by another 3 to 7 years. For this risk of time and money, they are generally rewarded with higher income opportunities than other college graduates. Within the medical field, for example, some Doctors pursue even more education and defer income to become surgeons. Within the surgical field, there are plastic, neurological, orthopedic and dermatologic surgeons who undertake additional training. Within those specialties, there is additional training as orthopedic surgeons may become spine specialists or dermatology surgeons may go on to learn the Mohs surgery procedure. Usually, an increased investment in time and money (risk) leads to greater income potential (reward).

Diversification Of Investments

Diversification is a business school term for "not putting all of your eggs in one basket." When applied to investments, it has two meanings. First, it means diversifying among asset classes. This is more popularly known as asset allocation. Asset allocation involves investing in a combination of stocks, bonds, real estate, cash and other investment classes. Diversification also applies to the individual investments made within each asset class—not investing in just a few stocks, just a few bonds or in one or two parcels of real estate. As an example, most investment managers recommend a portfolio of at least thirty securities to achieve a minimally acceptable level of diversification.

Earlier, we explained the idea that an investment portfolio is subject to (1) market risk and (2) the specific risks of each of the assets in the portfolio. One interesting finding of the CAPM & MPT is that in a "well-diversified portfolio," all specific risks cancel each other out. In other words, specific risk can be diversified away. Investors can reduce the overall risk in their portfolios by spreading their risk across and within different asset classes. At face value, this makes perfect intuitive sense. More significant, the mathematical proof for this statement and the subsequent model for creating the "most efficient" set of portfolios were worthy of a Nobel Prize.

How Do The CAPM And MPT Work For You?

CAPM and MPT provide a mathematical model for minimizing systematic risk in any investment portfolio. Once an investor determines the level of risk he or she is comfortable assuming (we call this risk tolerance), he or she can follow the mathematical model to construct a portfolio that will optimize the risk-reward balance. In other words, by following this theory, the investor can maximize his expected returns for any level of risk. All such "maximized" portfolios exist on what financial people call "the efficient frontier."

Certainly, we are not going to contend that the findings of three Nobel Laureates are incorrect. Rather, we are going to point out the acknowledged limitations in their theory and offer additional insights that might help you.

As acknowledged by the laureates, CAPM and MPT are designed to work in a simplified world where:

- **There are no taxes or transaction costs**
- **All investors have identical investment horizons**
- **All investors have identical perceptions regarding the expected returns, volatilities and correlations of available risky investments**

As there is no such thing as a simple world, these three components actually present the limitations of CAPM and MPT as financial tools that provide wise investment advice. We will now discuss these problems and suggest ways that Doctors can overcome them in an effort to avoid bad investment outcomes.

Problem #1: All Investors Pay Different Taxes & Transaction Costs

The first limitation of the theory involves taxes and transaction costs. Obviously, we consider tax to be a significant concern of Doctors. If we didn't, we wouldn't have devoted an entire part of this book (Lesson #7) exclusively to this topic. If all of your investments are in a non-taxable account, like an IRA, you don't have to worry about taxes until you begin taking distributions. You could look to maximize the pretax returns on your portfolio for a given amount of risk because taxes have no impact until you take withdrawals.

A common situation is to have a portion of the total investment portfolio in a retirement account and a portion in a taxable account. If this is true for you, you will need to determine which investments will be made in the tax-favored accounts and which investments will be made in taxable accounts. If you are in your prime earning years and are in the 30% to 35% federal income tax brackets, the following rules should suit you well:

1. Hold all interest-bearing and dividend-producing assets within a tax-favored account. Otherwise, as much as 44% of the earnings will go to paying income taxes each year. You are better off deferring the tax and earning money on the government's dime.

2. Hold all long-term growth assets in your taxable accounts. If you don't intend to sell these assets for at least one year, you will only pay 15%-24% capital gains taxes when you sell. You can control the deferral of taxes by controlling recognition of gains. If you hold these assets in a pension account, you would be taxed at up to 35% federal (plus state) when you make withdrawals. Why pay the government twice when you don't have to do so?

These are just basic strategies to supplement the CAPM and MPT when taxes are an issue. There is much more to be learned about taxes in the chapters within Lesson #7.

Problem #2: All Investors Do NOT Have Identical Investment Horizons

Another obvious problem with the CAPM and MPT is that all investors do NOT have identical investment horizons. Some investors need their money in 30 days and some don't need it for 30 years. The investor who needs his money in less than a month would be well served by a CD or money market. When an investor doesn't need the money for 30 years, he should have nearly 100% of his investments in equities (stocks) and other long-term investments.

If you have assets that you do not need for five years, you can afford to take some risks with those assets and should seriously consider investing in the stock market. If you need the money in less than a year, cash equivalents are your best option. For the assets that need to be accessed in 1 to 5 years, some combination may work well.

Problem #3: All Investors Have Very Different Perceptions Of Risk And Expected Returns

In English, the environment where the CAPM and MPT work best is one where everyone has the same knowledge of all assets and the same access to purchasing assets. Yet, investors have very different perceptions of expected returns, volatilities and correlations of available risky investments. For stocks and bonds, where there is more research available than you could possibly read, perceptions of the risk of any given stock are broad. People can't even agree on the value or the risk of certain stocks.

As far as availability, there is a also a very wide gap. If you are only investing $100,000, you may be restricted to mutual funds that can have very high transaction costs and taxes. If you have more than $500,000 to invest, you have access to unique products that have considerably lower transaction costs than the investments that are available to smaller investors. If you have $5 million or more, you can access products that others can only dream of buying. These may include small businesses and initial public offerings, to name a few.

For those of you with real estate investments, you know the gap in knowledge between buyer and seller is a key competitive factor for the investor. Many professional real estate investors have admitted that over 50% of their profits are a direct result of a buyer or seller not understanding the real estate market. The CAPM and MPT call for a percentage of your portfolio to be invested in real estate assets. However, for the real estate expert who understands this market better than most, we would deviate from the strategy and recommend he (or she) stick with what he (or she) knows best to maximize profit from the advantage in this arena.

For the investor with little knowledge of real estate, we would avoid investing in real estate (other than your home)—unless you hire professional real estate advisors as part of your team. There are two reasons for this. First, the time necessary to manage the property or the costs to pay someone else to do so will reduce the earnings the property generates. Second, there is no reason to jump into a market where you have a distinct disadvantage. This adds risk to your portfolio instead of reducing it as you had hoped by utilizing the CAPM and MPT.

In addition, the recent real estate and credit crashes have demonstrated two reasons why leverage is so important—especially in real estate. If you had very little equity in a property, you could have walked away from your debt and the property with a very small loss. If you had a lot of equity in a property, it has been very difficult to get it out lately. Many institutions just are not lending. Unless you have a lot of leverage, your real estate investments can be very illiquid. These are all points that a good real estate investment advisor should be sharing with you.

Doctors need to understand what they know and what they don't know. By understanding the investment landscape (if not the investments themselves), Doctors can avoid unnecessary risk in an investment portfolio. In the next chapter, you will learn how to avoid decimation of wealth by taxes and inflation.

The Diagnosis

CAPM and MPT have contributed greatly to the field of portfolio selection. In fact, these theories are the basis for a significant percentage of institutional investors and mutual fund managers. They have also played a large role in the field of financial risk management. However, as you saw from this chapter, there are problems with the practical application of these theories. You should work with an experienced financial planner and investment advisor who can help you apply these theories to your particular situation while integrating them into your comprehensive financial plan by working with the other members of your advisory team. As you will learn from the remainder of the book, you may wish to invest in a vehicle that offers you other benefits in addition to capital appreciation—like asset protection, tax deferral, or protection against a premature death. These are the types of investments the remainder of this Lesson will address.

Taxes, Inflation & Your Investments

In Lesson #2, you learned that most printed material and consulting firms focus their efforts toward Average Americans. Doctors need to understand that this has never been truer than in the world of finance. Though most of the money in the world is owned by a very small percentage of the people, almost all of the advertising is directed at the Average American. As such, it can be very misleading and detrimental to the uninformed Doctor. Consider the following.

"XYZ fund returned 18.6% last year." "My money manager has beat the S&P consistently for 5 years." "In this magazine, we'll profile the 'best returning' mutual funds." As financial professionals, we read and hear these types of statements on a daily basis. Why? Because everyone looks at the investment returns as the "currency" of investing. This is the popular way of comparing money managers, mutual funds, CDs, bonds and other investments. What most people fail to consider is the impact that taxes and inflation have on those investments as well as the risk involved in each investment. When you consider that ALL investments and financial professionals report their Pre-Inflation/Pre-Tax returns, it is easy to see why some people realize no additional purchasing power from their investments—they simply don't understand what they are really getting out of their investments!

Uncle Sam Back For Another Helping: Taxes

The last chapter discussed how taxes were not considered in Markowitz and Sharpe's Nobel Prize winning Capital Asset Pricing Model of investments. A new development in the mutual fund arena is that mutual funds may have to report AFTER-TAX gains, not Pre-Tax gains. How much will that change the numbers? A lot! Consider what Lipper, a mutual fund tracking firm, concluded:

"Over the past 20 years, the average investor in a taxable stock mutual fund gave up the equivalent of 17 percent to 44 percent of their returns to taxes."*
*CNN/Money.com 4/17/07

Without boring you with the math, this number means that some mutual funds sell most of their holdings within one year of purchasing them. This is also called "portfolio turnover" and can be used to compare different investments. This means you get much more short-term capital gains tax treatment (28%-44%) on your appreciation than you do long-term capital gains tax treatment (15%-24%). For example, if your mutual fund appreciated by 11% last year, it probably cost you close to 4% in taxes. Which number is more important to you, the 11% the investment firm reported or the 7% you actually received?

Mutual funds are not the only tax problem. Do you have CDs, money markets, or bonds? All of the income from these vehicles will be taxed as ordinary income. This will likely be taxed at rates between 27% and 35%, not to mention up to 10% of state income tax. For this reason, 5% to 6% in dividend or interest income may only be worth 2.5% to 4.0% after taxes. While this is depressing, it isn't the end of your problems.

Inflation: When A Dollar Is Only Worth 50 Cents

You would always rather have a dollar today than a dollar tomorrow, right? There is an area of finance and economics that deals with this simple concept. They call it the "time value of money." Time value of money allows us to compare the value of a dollar over different periods of time. When determining the present value of future dollars, many people want to know what a dollar in the future will buy them in today's dollars. What they are really talking about is inflation and how it impacts ones ability to purchase items.

Obviously, things become more expensive as we get older. We have all heard our parents talk about a Coke costing a nickel or a movie costing a quarter. That a movie costs close to $10 today is because of inflation (though many might call it highway robbery given the quality, or lack thereof, of films today!). The average annual inflation rate over the past 70 years has been approximately 3.1%. This means that approximately every 22 years, things cost twice as much.

Calculating The Impact Of Inflation

The after-tax return that an investment achieves is called the "nominal return." This does not take inflation into account. When you divide the nominal return of an investment over time by the rate of inflation over that same period of time, you get the "real" rate of return, or inflation-adjusted rate of return.

Think back to the mutual fund mentioned earlier—where an 11% pre-tax return meant a take-home 7% after taxes. That 7% return is actually more like a 3.8% REAL return (1.07/1.031 = 1.038), after inflation is factored into the results.

Invest Wisely While Planning For Inflation

If Doctors want to reduce taxes, they should invest in the stock market through tax-managed investment accounts, variable annuities, various types of life insurance policies (variable universal life, equity-indexed universal life or private placement life insurance) or managed accounts if the funds are inside of tax-deferred retirement plans. Within these investment accounts, you can work with the money manager to design a portfolio that will adequately manage inflation risk.

The Diagnosis

When it comes to investing, there is no sure-fire method to avoiding taxes or inflation. However, there are a number of tools that are discussed in this Lesson. The more you know about your options, the easier it will be for you to understand what you are really getting from your investments. Of course, there is no substitute for having a strong team of advisors that includes an investment advisory firm that understands tax management and other advisors who are tax-savvy to help you meet all of your needs. One way to avoid unnecessary taxes on investments is to avoid mutual funds. This is explained in the next chapter.

How Doctors Outgrow Mutual Funds

If you are like most physicians, you likely have over $250,000 in cash or mutual funds. These investments may be inside or outside of your tax-deferred retirement plans. In the previous chapter, we discussed alternatives to taxable mutual fund accounts ideal for your non-retirement plan accounts. Some of these alternatives offer asset protection, tax-deferral and death protection. In this chapter, we will discuss an alternative to mutual funds both inside and outside of retirement plans. Before we compare mutual funds to individually managed accounts, we must first explain what both of them are.

Mutual Funds ("MFs") and Individually Managed Accounts ("IMAs") represent two of the most popular investment programs used by individuals to create wealth. On the surface, at least, one could argue that they are not all that dissimilar. Both offer investors a professionally managed portfolio of securities generally comprised of stocks, bonds or a combination of the two. They are both tailored to provide ample diversification.

When looking beneath the surface, however, two distinctly different approaches emerge. Each offers particular advantages depending upon one's needs. Which is the more prudent choice? Which ones will help you make wise investments? These are questions properly answered only by the individual investor. The information that follows is designed to help you make a wise investment decision, one with which you are comfortable and, we hope, will prove over time to be the "right" choice for you.

Mutual Funds

A MF is a company that invests in stocks, bonds and other securities on behalf of individual investors with similar financial goals. A "no-load" mutual fund is one that is sold directly to investors without an initial sales charge or "load."

Many financial advisors now provide access to no-load funds as part of a comprehensive range of services. However, the charge for the advisor's assistance tends to offset the lack of an initial sales charge, effectively minimizing any cost differences between load and no-load funds. Of course, you get the assistance of an advisor that you would otherwise have to pay anyway.

For purposes of this discussion, therefore, "no-load funds" will refer to funds purchased directly from the company without the help of an advisor.

Both load and no-load MFs are essentially "cooperatives" of investors who pool their money for a common purpose. Investors contribute to the pool by buying shares in the fund. Each share represents an equal percentage of ownership in the fund's assets.

The fund draws from the pool not only to make investments but also to pay for the services of a fund manager (who decides when and if to buy and sell securities for the fund based on its stated objective), marketing and distribution costs, custodian fees and transaction costs. MFs are not limited but generally hold a hundred or more different securities. No matter how many shares of the fund the investor holds, the investor cannot control the buying and selling of these securities inside the fund. You can only buy or sell the basket of securities the fund has by buying or selling your shares of the fund.

Individually Managed Accounts

An IMA is an account that is individually managed by a professional investment manager who decides when to buy and sell securities based on *your* stated investment strategy or individual goals.

Unlike mutual fund investors, managed account investors do not pool their money. Rather, they own the securities in their account directly. They may have many similar holdings with a number of their clients but each portfolio is separate. The investor can direct the manager to buy only certain types of stocks or to avoid certain stocks (perhaps no tobacco stocks for moral reasons or no healthcare stocks because you work as a physician and enough of your income is already tied to healthcare). This obviously gives you greater flexibility and control than you would have with a mutual fund.

There is no doubt that mutual funds are easy. Their forms are easy. Their marketing materials are readily available. The companies are household names with all the advertising they do. These materials and advertising would have you believe that the mutual funds offer better returns with lower fees. Let's see if this is true.

Are Managed Accounts Worth The Money?

One of the most common problems we see with clients is that they are obsessed with the fee associated with any type of planning. If you took this approach to everything you bought, you'd only eat 99-cent Big Macs at every meal. There is truth to the saying "you get what you pay for." You should not be quick to dismiss the advantages of one investment strategy over another based purely on price. The recent popularity of no-load mutual funds is proof that many investors, particularly those who like a no-frills approach to investing, are doing just that.

You invested your time in reading this book in hopes that it would help you. That was time well spent, right? You are considering asset protection, insurance, estate planning and retirement strategies that undoubtedly will cost you something. Why? Because the strategies will offer you something valuable in return. A prudent investor considers differences in:

- The quality of service provided in return for the fee

- How the accounts treat capital gains and losses relative to your situation

- The effect that other investors may have on an investment manager's decisions

- The methods used to report information

- The way in which fees are handled

These are very important factors to consider when comparing investment options because the fee is not important. What you earn net of the fee and taxes is what is most important.

Is Your Tax Situation A Consideration?

With IMAs, you pay taxes only on the capital gains you actually realize. Because you own the securities in your account directly, you can work with your tax advisor to implement planning strategies that mutual fund investors may not be able to duplicate. There are actually IMA firms who will call YOU to ask you how you want them to manage the account at the end of the year. You may want to maximize investment account gains because you have other investment losses to offset the gains. You may want the advisors to generate losses to offset other investment gains you may have. You may just want the investment manager to buy or sell securities to balance your annual tax liability from your portfolio to zero out the tax.

With mutual funds, you pay taxes on your pro rata share of capital gains experienced by the fund, whether you benefit from the sale of the security or not. The following hypothetical example serves to illustrate this point.

Assume that a fund purchases stock at the beginning of the year for $25 per share. Over the next few months, the stock's price rises to $50 per share. Coincidentally, an investor buys shares in the fund just as the stock's price reaches this peak.

Later in the year, the stock's price falls to $40 per share, and the fund sells its position. At the end of the year, the investor is allocated a pro rata share of the fund's gain on the stock (the difference between the purchase price of $25 and the sale price of $40), even though the investor did not fully benefit from the gain; in fact, the stock actually declined in value after the investor purchased shares in the fund at $50.

Over time, investors who own IMAs and mutual funds who hold their investments for the same period and whose portfolio managers follow identical strategies will report little, if any, difference in capital gains taxes on those particular investments. For the mutual fund investor; however, the point at which the gains are realized may be moved forward and that can affect the investor's tax planning strategy. The table on the next page illustrates this point.

Comparing Individually Managed Accounts and Mutual Funds

	Individually Managed Account	Load Mutual Fund	No-Load Mutual Fund
Investment Portfolio	Tailored to meet investor's particular needs	Two-way communication, including in-person discussions with Financial Advisor. Can also call toll-free number.	One-way communication: Call toll-free phone number and talk to sales representative.
Establishing Investor's Goals	Investor benefits from Financial Advisor's help.	Investors benefits from Financial Advisor's help.	Investors determine on their own.
Investment Manager Selection	Chosen by investor with Financial Advisor's help.	Chosen by mutual fund.	Chosen by mutual fund.
Investment Manager Evaluation	Screened and evaluated by investor and Financial Advisor.	Screened and evaluated by investor and Financial Advisor.	Investors must screen and evaluate on their own.
Performance Monitoring	Financial Advisor monitors on investor's behalf.	Financial Advisor monitors on investor's behalf.	Investors must monitor on their own.
Tax Planning	Investors have some control over the timing of capital gains.	Investors have little control over the timing of capital gains.	Investors have little control over the timing of capital gains.
Redemption Requests	Investors are not affected by the actions of others who use the same manager.	Manager may be forced to sell securities at undesirable prices to raise cash to meet redemption requests.	Manager may be forced to sell securities at undesirable prices to raise cash to meet redemption requests.
Reporting	Detailed monthly or quarterly statements; monthly letters; quarterly newsletters; periodic investment literature from manager.	General quarterly statements; semi-annual investment reports; possibly periodic newsletters.	General quarterly statements; semi-annual investment reports; possibly periodic newsletters.
Up-Front Costs	$0	Up to 6% of investment or an additional 1% per year added to the annual cost.	$0
Annual Costs	On average for a stock-based portfolio, between 2.5% and 3% of total investment.	On average for a stock-based portfolio, between 2% and 3% of total investment.	On average for a stock-based portfolio, between 1.5% and 2% of total investment.

The Cost of IMAs

So, what do IMAs really cost? Investors who open IMAs usually do so with a minimum investment of at least $250,000. Some firms have minimums that can be as high as $10,000,000. Depending on the client's particular situation, most firms will make exceptions. As an example, the primary authors' firm (www.ojmgroup.com) invests through their registered investment advisor The O'Dell Group (TOG). TOG has a published account minimum of $500,000. However, they will aggregate family accounts (all IRAs, 401(k)s & other assets of parents and children) to reach that minimum account size. They will also take a smaller account of an investor who has a high income and who is likely to reach that minimum in a few years. This isn't uncommon in the industry.

Fees for IMAs can vary greatly. A common estimate in the industry is about 1% of assets, 0.25% paid quarterly. Now, a smaller account may have higher fees and a larger account always pays lower fees. Some special private placements, private equity and hedge funds can have significantly higher fees. All fees will be disclosed either in the firm ADV (Uniform Application for Investment Adviser Registration) for registered investment advisory firms, a prospectus for a registered security or a private placement memorandum for private placements. You should never invest in anything before receiving an ADV, prospectus or private placement memorandum.

Subsequent transaction costs are paid either by paying commissions on individual trades or by paying an asset-based fee on a quarterly basis. In addition to covering transactions, these fees encompass reporting, custody and the services of a financial advisor as well. For a stock-based portfolio, on average, total fees range annually from 1.3% to 3% of the assets under management. There are no additional charges.

MFs have lower minimum investment requirements, often $1,000 or less. With a no-load MF bought directly from the company, the entire investment is placed in the fund at the time of initial purchase. With a front-end load fund, on the other hand, the investor's money is placed in the fund only after deducting a sales charge. In the case of a 3.5% load fund, the fund would invest $965 of the investor's initial $1,000.

Beyond the initial sales charge, or lack thereof, the difference in fee structure between load and no-load mutual funds virtually disappears. Management fees, transaction costs, custody fees and distribution and marketing costs (known as 12b-1 fees) are deducted automatically from the fund's assets. These fees are usually not seen directly by investors but instead are specified in the fund's prospectus and statements of additional information. MF expenses for stock-based portfolios typically range from 1.5% to 2% per year for no-load funds and from 2% to 3% per year for load funds.

According to Morningstar, a third-party research publication that follows open-end MFs, the average diversified domestic equities fund incurs about 1.63% in annual costs, including a 1.32% expense ratio and 0.31% in transaction costs. Tack on an additional 0.94% annual sales charge on average for load funds, or an estimated 1% annual charge for no-load funds purchased through a financial advisor, and that annual cost figure rises to approximately 2.6% for all funds.

Investment	Investment Minimum	Annual Fees	Tax Treatment of Gains
Mutual Funds (MFs)	$1,000	1.6% to 2.6%	Capital gains or ordinary income tax rates. Varies by fund. No control for investor.
Indiv. Managed Accounts (IMAs)	$500k to millions	0.75%—1.25%	Varies. Look for tax-management in a firm so taxes can be avoided.
Hedge Funds	$1 million	3% or 25% of gain	Primarily ordinary income tax rates (35% to 44% for MDs)

Investors should note that transaction costs tend to vary depending on the type of securities in the fund. Trading foreign securities, for instance, can cost almost twice as much as trading domestic securities.

Doctors should accept the philosophy that "off the rack" mutual funds are not likely to fit into their planning as well as custom-made individually managed accounts.

The Diagnosis

While you may appear to building your fortune by purchasing no-load funds, such savings may not be enough to offset the loss of the value-added services that normally include investment planning, monitoring and communication that only a financial advisor can provide. Beyond perceived cost differences, MFs limit investors' tax planning choices and offer individual investors no control over securities in the fund.

Doctors should use IMAs to build wealth and protect their assets because of the tax benefits and the additional added benefits. They avoid the MF trap of losing 17-44% of their returns to taxes. Another benefit of IMAs is that they offer the ability to add alternative investments to the portfolio. The explanation of these investments and the benefits Doctors look for from these investments are explained in the next chapter.

Alternative Investment Strategies for Doctors

In the last chapter, you learned that IMAs can be more valuable to Doctors than MFs because IMAs are much more flexible. This flexibility offers tax management benefits and customization to better fit the investor's situation. Traditionally, most IMAs purchase stocks and bonds that are readily available to anyone (publicly traded securities). Though IMAs are valuable options, Doctors need to realize that the investment world does not end with stocks and bonds. There are additional classes of investments that cannot be made available to the public because of their complexity or level of risk. These investments can offer greater levels of diversification, inflation hedging and potentially higher returns.

In this chapter, we will discuss who can legally access these alternative strategies, why investors may wish to purchase them and the inherent risks within these investments. Then, we will discuss a few favorite alternative investment strategies. Many successful investors can credit the knowledge and utilization of the material in this chapter as the secret for their significant increase in net worth.

Accredited Investors

Alternative investment strategies can be offered to Doctors who have the financial means to survive the significant losses that can accompany riskier transactions. These investments are only available to a class of investors known as "accredited investors." One definition of this term, can be found on the TIAA-CREF website:

> To qualify as an accredited investor, an investor must either be: a financial institution; an affiliate of the issuer; or an individual with a net worth of at least $1 million or an annual income of at least $200,000, and the investment must not account for more than 20% of the investor's worth.

Why Invest In Alternative Investments?

In Chapter 8-1, we explained that greater risk was generally accompanied by a potential for greater return in financial markets. This increased risk can help investors who are willing to take greater risk to earn higher returns. Alternative investments, by definition, are riskier than traditional investments. As an asset class, the alternative investments traditionally have to offer a significant risk premium (added expected return) to investors to convince them to invest in these riskier investments. Since most Doctors have the financial means to wait out down markets and can survive lost investments, they are ideal candidates for these investments. In addition to the expected returns, there are other reasons to consider alternative investments. A partial list includes:

- *Increased diversification of holdings* by expanding portfolio to include items not within the traditional portfolio

- *Decreased volatility* by investing in strategies not correlated to the stock or bond markets

- *Preserved capital* can also be managed through an alternative allocation

- *Increased access* alternative investments are sometimes called an access class for the reasons mentioned above about accredited investors

The Risks Of Alternative Investments

We mentioned that alternative investments have a higher risk than traditional investments. What are those risks? A partial list includes:

- **Lack of regulation**: Alternative investments are not required to be registered with the SEC. Though many hedge fund managers choose to do so to gain access to institutional investors that require it, many still do not register these securities. This is the old-fashioned *caveat emptor*, ("let the buyer [or investor] beware") situation.

- **Lack of transparency**: Assets held by hedge funds may not have a price quoted each day. Think of your personal residence or car as an example. This also means there is less liquidity so investors may be stuck with these investments for a while even if they want to sell them.

- **Excessive Leverage**: Some managers borrow money and others borrow money against borrowed money, thus exponentially increasing risk.

- **Fraud**: There are people who are not qualified to manage your money but are able to build trust and confidence in an attempt to steal your money.

- **Manager selection risk**: Not all managers are equal. In fact, there is evidence that the difference in manager performance is greater than the benefit of using alternative investments.

Savvy physician investors do not just accept these risks. They work with their investment team to analyze investment alternatives and find investments that fit into the strategy they have developed for their portfolio.

Alternative Investment Strategies

Behind the press reports of big payouts, high returns and bankruptcies, there are sound investment strategies that are grouped together under a category called "hedge funds." One broad-brush term is typically used to paint the picture for over two dozen investment strategies. Instead of using the term "hedge fund," we recommend you view these funds as alternative investment strategies. There are literally hundreds of ways to invest outside of the traditional channels. We will break this down to make it easier to follow. We will begin by giving you a categorical list of investments that traditional managers are often prohibited from offering to clients who are accredited investors:

- **Short-selling securities**: This is selling someone else's shares in return for the promise to replace them later at what you believe will be a lower price. This is a way for an investor who speculates that a stock value will depreciate to benefit from the devaluation of the stock. The risk of short selling is unlimited since every dollar increase to a shorted stock is a dollar the investor loses and there is no theoretical limit to a stock's appreciation. For long investors who buy and hold a stock, they can only lose the original investment since the stock price can't fall below zero.

- **Buying on margin**: This is buying shares with borrowed money. This is a way for someone to leverage someone else's money. If the stock appreciates by more than the interest on the loan, there is a chance to earn money. If the stock price decreases, you may face a 'margin call,' requiring you to invest more of your own money or the lender will sell your stock to cover your debt.

- **Option trading**: These are individual options to buy or sell 1,000 shares of a stock at a particular price. There are options to buy or sell the security at that price and the investor can buy or sell the option.

- **Investing in any unregistered security**: This includes private placements and other worldwide investments that were not registered within the United States.

We have compiled a list of alternative investment strategies that are available to accredited investors. There is not enough space in this book to review them all. If you are interested in learning more about any of them, feel free to contact the authors.

Partial List of Alternative Investment Strategies

- Absolute Return Strategies are designed to achieve a steady rate of return in up or down markets, thereby minimizing volatility. Categories include:
  - Equity Market Neutral
  - Convertible Arbitrage
  - Fixed Income Arbitrage
  - Statistical Arbitrage
  - Risk Arbitrage
  - Multi-Strategy
  - Merger Arbitrage
  - Credit Arbitrage

- Opportunistic Equity Strategies seek to achieve above-market returns by anticipating market inefficiencies before they occur. Categories include:
  - Long / Short Equity
  - Global Macro
  - Short Only
  - Long / Short Specialty
  - Long / Short International

- Enhanced Fixed Income Strategies seek to return income above the market rate of return for a given risk profile. Categories include:
  - Capital Structure Arbitrage
  - Distressed Securities
  - Global / Emerging Market Debt

- Energy and Natural Resource investment strategies direct the purchase of oil, coal, timber and other natural resources. These may have tax benefits as well.

- Real Estate Strategies include direct or leveraged purchases of commercial real estate properties.

- Private Equity includes the purchase of stocks not registered with the Securities and Exchange Commission. This is also called a private placement.

"If You Can't Stand the Heat…"

It is important to point out that not all strategies are successful all the time and not all investors in alternative investments achieve their goals. However, there is a formula that has worked over the years. Ironically, large endowment funds of some of America's premier universities turned to these strategies due to the shortcomings of traditional investing and successfully reduced their risk exposure while preserving the endowment capital in perpetuity.

An endowment is expected to provide a certain level of income, usually at an increasing amount, each and every year. Down years and performance under the required income level will wipe out the corpus of the endowment. Managers of these funds didn't really care what the stock market did. They had to ensure the endowment grew each year. They turned to alternative investments and have not looked back. This is an excellent example of wealth management as opposed to wealth building or accumulation strategies. For the individual investor, the endowment model of multiple alternative strategies would be used for the portion of your portfolio sometimes called the 'stay rich pocket' as opposed to the "get rich pocket."

When Doctors are hiring an asset manager to manage an investment portfolio, the secret to long-term success is to find an investment advisor who can also help find, review and possibly purchase other investment classes to round out the total portfolio. There are countless hedge funds, private placements, options and currency and commodity based investments. To expand your options, you may want to make sure your investment advisor is accustomed to helping successful Doctors with their unique needs. Another way to look at the overall investment portfolio is to review it for Leverage and efficiency. This is discussed in the next chapter.

The Diagnosis

So far, you have learned that diversification is not enough to give you the best possible portfolio. You have learned that attention has to be paid to taxes and inflation and that mutual fund investments may be inappropriate for Doctors with investment accounts of $250,000 or more. You have even learned that the inclusion of alternative investments is an important piece of Doctors' investment planning.

As you learned in Lesson #1, you need to Leverage your team and your investments to achieve wealth. You also need efficiencies to make this work. The best way to do this within your planning is to try to "kill two birds with one stone." By hiring advisors who are experts in multiple areas, you will realize additional benefit. More important, focusing on planning tools and strategies that solve multiple planning problems and are flexible enough to be used in different ways is a great way to gain Leverage and efficiency. In the next few chapters, we will look at investments that do just that.

Life Insurance as an Investment for Doctors

Before you roll your eyes or dismiss this and the next three chapters, oblige us and read the rest of this paragraph for the sake of your own financial success. The authors of this book collectively hold multiple MBAs in Finance, law degrees, CPA designations, and securities licenses, in addition to having managed over $100 million for doctors since 1992 and bringing actuarial experience. We have a very strong working knowledge of financial analysis and don't take such strong positions without proof. The next four chapters will illustrate how life insurance can be used as an investment, how life insurance might benefit high-income taxpayers and how life insurance might compare to other investments.

Life insurance is a contract between you and an insurance company. The most common term of the contract is that the insurance company will pay your named beneficiaries the "face amount" or "death benefit" of the policy when you die. Some life insurance policies accumulate cash over time (permanent policies) and some do not (term policies). For the next few chapters, we will be focusing on all types of life insurance *except* term insurance. To help you better understand some of the different types of insurance, we have put together a brief description of the different categories of life insurance and then discussed the pros and cons of each type. The different categories we will discuss include:

- Term Life Insurance

- Whole Life Insurance (WL)

- Universal Life Insurance

- Variable Life Insurance (VL)

- Variable Universal Life Insurance (VULI)

- A Hybrid: Equity-Indexed Universal Life Insurance (EIUL)

- Private Placement Variable Universal Life Insurance (PPVUL)

Term Life Insurance

Given its affordability, term life insurance is the most common type of life insurance policy. However, because it does not have a cash value (wealth accumulation) component, term insurance can only play a very limited role in your financial plan. It can provide temporary death protection for your family or for business partners as part of a buy-sell agreement.

The premium on a term policy is low compared to other types of life insurance policies because it carries no cash value and provides protection for a limited period of time (referred to as a "term"). This limited time frame is usually 10 to 20 years, though some companies offer a 30-year term product. A term life insurance policy pays a specific lump sum to your designated beneficiary upon your death. The policy protects your family by providing money they can invest to replace your salary and to cover immediate expenses incurred as a result of your death. Term life insurance is best for young, growing families, when the need for death protection of the breadwinner is high and excess cash flow is especially low.

> **Pros:** Affordable coverage that pays only a death benefit. Term life insurance initially tends to cost less than other insurance policies because it has no cash value.

> **Cons:** Term life insurance premiums increase with age because the risk of death increases as people get older. Some term premiums may rise each year, or after 10, 20 or 30 years. Over the age of 65, the cost of a new term insurance policy becomes very expensive, often unaffordable. Term insurance is not available beyond a certain age. It is a terrible tool for estate planning because the coverage cannot be continued at a reasonable price as you approach life expectancy.

Whole Life Insurance (WL)

Whole life insurance pays a death benefit to the beneficiary you name and offers you a cash value account with tax-deferred cash accumulation. The policy remains in force during your entire lifetime and provides permanent protection for your dependents while building a cash value account. The insurance company manages your policy's cash accounts.

> **Pros:** Whole life insurance has a savings element (cash value), which is tax-deferred. You can borrow from this account free of income tax or cash-in the policy during your lifetime. It has a fixed premium which can't increase during your lifetime (as long as you pay the planned amount), and your premium is invested for you long-term. Because it has the cash accumulation component, whole life insurance can offer benefits such as tax reduction, wealth accumulation, asset protection, estate planning and even reduction of the retirement plan tax trap.

> **Cons:** Whole life insurance does not allow you to invest in separate accounts (i.e. money market, stock, and bond funds). Thus, your policy's returns will be tied to the

insurance company's ability to invest its capital. It also does not allow you to split your money among different accounts or to move your money between accounts and does not allow premium flexibility or face amount flexibility.

Universal Life Insurance (UL)

Universal life insurance is a variation of whole life insurance. The insurance part of the policy is separated from the investment portion of the policy. The investment portion is invested by the insurance company—generally, in bonds, mortgages and money market funds. This investment portion grows and is tax-deferred. The cost of the death benefit is paid for out of the investment fund. A guaranteed minimum interest rate is applied to the policy's cash values. This ensures that a certain minimum return on the cash portion of the policy will be paid no matter how badly the investments perform. If the insurance company does well with its investments, the interest return on the cash portion could increase.

Pros: The product is similar to whole life insurance, yet has more flexible premiums. It may be attractive to younger buyers who may have fluctuations in their ability to pay premiums. Because it is so flexible, universal life insurance can offer benefits like tax reduction, wealth accumulation, asset protection, estate planning, and even reduction of the retirement plan tax trap.

Cons: If the insurance company does poorly with its investments, the interest return on the cash portion of the policy could decrease. In this case, less money would be available to pay the cost of the death benefit portion of the policy and future premiums may be necessary in addition to the premiums originally illustrated.

Variable Life Insurance (VL)

Variable life insurance provides permanent protection to your beneficiary upon your death. The term "variable life" is derived from the ability to allocate your dollars to various types of investment accounts (within your insurance company's portfolio), such as an equity fund, a money market fund, a bond fund or some combination of funds. Hence, the value of the death benefit is "variable" and the cash value may fluctuate up or down, depending on the performance of the investment portion of the policy.

Although most variable life insurance policies guarantee that the death benefit will not fall below a specified minimum, a minimum cash value is typically not guaranteed. Variable life insurance is a form of whole life insurance and because of investment risks, it is also considered a securities contract and is regulated as a security under the Federal Securities Laws and must be sold with a prospectus.

Pros: Variable Life allows you to participate in various types of investment options without being taxed on your earnings (until you surrender the policy). You can apply interest earned on these investments toward the premiums, potentially lowering the amount you pay. Because of the ability to invest in more aggressive assets (mutual funds, etc.), variable life insurance is an ideal tool for accumulation and retirement planning, especially if you are looking for growth over a longer term.

Cons: You assume the investment risks. When the investment funds perform poorly, less money is available to pay the premiums, meaning that you may have to pay more than you can afford to keep the policy in force. Poor fund performance also means that the cash and/or death benefit may decline, although never below a defined level if the policy so provides. Also, you cannot withdraw from the cash value during your lifetime.

Variable Universal Life Insurance (VUL)

Variable universal life insurance pays your beneficiary a death benefit. The amount of the benefit is dependent on the success of your investments. If the investments fail, there is a guaranteed minimum death benefit paid to your beneficiary upon your death. Variable universal life insurance gives you more control of the cash value account portion of your policy than any other insurance type. A form of universal life insurance, it has elements of both life insurance and a securities contract. Because the policy owner assumes investment risks, variable universal products are regulated as securities under the Federal Securities Laws and must be sold with a prospectus.

Pros: Variable-universal life enables you to make withdrawals or borrow from the policy during your lifetime, and it offers separate accounts in which to invest. Because it combines the flexibility of universal life with the ability to invest in mutual funds of the variable policy, universal variable can be the ideal tool for tax reduction and retirement wealth accumulation over a long time horizon. It also affords you another opportunity to invest in the equities markets on a tax-deferred basis.

Cons: It requires the policyholder to devote time in managing the policy's accounts. The policy's success is dependent on the investments you make. Premiums must be high enough to cover your insurance and your accounts.

A Hybrid: Equity-Indexed Universal Life Insurance (EIUL)

Equity-indexed universal life insurance (EIUL) pays your beneficiary a death benefit. The amount of the benefit is dependent on the success of the investments of the insurance company. In this case, the investments are contractually obligated to be equal to a market index. If the investments fail, there is a guaranteed minimum death benefit paid to your beneficiary upon your death. EIUL gives you more upside than a traditional UL policy because the insurance company contractually agrees to credit the policy's cash value with the same return as the stock market index the policy holder chooses (typically, the S&P 500 Index, but it can be the Dow Jones or NASDAQ) realizes over the same period of time—subject to a cap. The cap on the upside for two carriers we like, for example, are 12% per annum and 14% per annum, respectively. In return for taking away a piece of your upside, they offer a minimum annual return of 1% or 2% annually.

Pros: EIUL enables you to make withdrawals or borrow from the policy during your lifetime and it offers the investor the upside of the market (with a cap). It also, unlike variable life and variable universal life, offers the investor downside protection so the cash value will always see a positive crediting rate—even in a bad market. Studies have been done by insurance companies showing an investment in a portfolio with the upside cap and downside protection actually outperformed the straight pre-tax S&P 500 Index over every 10 year period in the last 70 years.

Cons: EIUL policies vary from carrier to carrier. Some only allow for 50% or 75% participation (others offer 100%) of the rate of return from the S&P. This means that if the S&P 500 returns 10%, you may only get 5% or 7.5%. The policyholder must pay particular attention to the carrier's contractual obligations. Also, the minimum guaranteed returns are typically 1% to 2%, which is much lower than most traditional insurance products that offer minimum crediting rates of 3% to 4%. EIUL is another instance where you have to give up something to get something. Like all insurance policies, you need to understand what you are getting before you can make an informed decision.

Private Placement Variable Universal Life Insurance (PPVUL)

Private Placement Variable Universal Life insurance (PPVUL) shares most of the characteristics of VUL discussed earlier. However, PPVUL differs from the VUL in a few ways. Some of these differences make it very attractive for wealthy Doctors. These differences are:

1. PPVULs are only available to accredited investors.

2. PPVULs do not generate materials that are available to the public. They must be requested by a bona fide accredited investor.

3. PPVULs have higher minimum premium requirements (differ by company and minimum premiums generally range from $500,000 to $5,000,000 of premium in the first five years).

4. PPVULs have lower fees than traditional insurance products.

5. PPVULs offer more investment flexibility. Policy owners typically choose among hedge funds or can suggest their own investment management firm to manage the funds within PPVUL if premiums are large enough.

Pros: PPVULs allow the client to choose hedge funds or, if the premiums will total $5,000,000 over 5 years, suggest their own independent financial advisor to manage the funds within the insurance contract. Commissions tend to be much lower than traditional insurance policies. PPVUL enables you to make withdrawals or borrow from the policy during your lifetime, and it offers separate accounts in which to invest. Because it combines the flexibility of variable universal life with lower fees, more investment flexibility and investment gains within the sub-accounts are not taxed, PPVUL is the ideal tool for tax reduction and retirement wealth accumulation over a long time horizon for clients who are in high marginal tax brackets. It also affords another opportunity to invest in the equities markets on a tax-deferred basis.

Cons: Very high minimum premium requirements. Limited to accredited investors only. Because this is a private placement, there is very little written marketing material to review. Very few insurance companies do enough of this type of work to be considered efficient. Most insurance agents don't, or won't, sell it. The policy owner bears all the risk of the investments within the investment sub-accounts.

There is an emerging class of insurance policies that offer the lower costs of PPVULs but do not have the same accredited investor requirements and sizable minimum investments. Contact the OJM firm www.ojmgroup.com for more on this developing market trend. At the time of the writing of this book, we were negotiating with two insurance companies to release PPVULs with smaller minimum premium requirements.

The Diagnosis

There are many different types of life insurance policies. All of them have their place in planning for Doctors. What is important to realize is that all policies offer wealth accumulation benefits and tax-free death benefits as well as asset protection in most states. The Leverage opportunities of life insurance are discussed in the next chapter.

Getting More Out of Your Investments = Efficiency & Leverage

If you have read the entire book so far, you have learned the important philosophical keys to wealth accumulation and asset protection—efficiency and Leverage. The reason these two concepts are so important is that there are only 24 hours in a day and everyone wants to work less and build more. As stated in Lesson #1, efficiency and Leverage are the keys to reaching this goal. In this chapter, we will discuss an investment secret that combines Leverage and efficiency better than any others. This much-maligned investment is life insurance.

Why do we call this very popular investment a "secret" when everyone in America has heard of, or even purchased, life insurance at one point or another? The reason is that many Doctors don't think of life insurance as an investment. Rather, they perceive life insurance as a very costly necessity. This is a result of the inappropriate advice that is directed at low income Average Americans but finds its way to Doctors as well. As an example, most financial advisors for Average Americans discourage the use of life insurance while the wealthiest Americans and their advisors maximize their use of life insurance.

In this Lesson, we will discuss why life insurance is a secret investment of successful Doctors. We will also explain why life insurance is so important to the creation and maintenance of wealth. We will then discuss the basics of life insurance and explain how it achieves Leverage as a very efficient and flexible financial planning tool. At the request of many of the readers of our previous books, we have included Chapter 8-8, which shows a comparison of life insurance to mutual funds as an investment. Then, we end the Lesson by discussing creative applications of insurance as retirement planning and college education savings tools.

Investment Efficiency

The concept of investment efficiency is not one you will find in most finance textbooks. In Lesson #2, you learned that Doctors should embrace their affluence. As part of this acceptance, Doctors must also recognize that general information in books, newspapers, articles, websites or on television is likely to be inappropriate for them because it is geared toward Average American's financial planning needs. If you can adopt the philosophy that you are different, you can easily expand your planning opportunities to include investments that can give your family greater flexibility, efficiency and Leverage. A perfect example of this type of investment is life insurance.

The concept of investment efficiency is extremely important in the context of an overall financial plan. In this context, an "efficient" investment is one that:

1. Addresses two or more planning goals at the same time

2. Helps a client reach a planning goal with less effort or with a smaller investment of time or money than other investments

3. Is flexible enough that it can be modified to address different planning needs as the client's personal circumstances change

The Need For Efficient Investments

There are many reasons why efficient investments are such an important key to acquiring and maintaining wealth. First, efficient investments address multiple planning goals simultaneously. As we will see in this Lesson, the efficient investments described here can build wealth while reducing taxes, providing asset protection, allowing for college funding access and providing estate planning benefits. These investments become cornerstones of a Doctor's flexible, multi-disciplinary financial plan.

Second, efficient investments have less tax friction than other investments. As we have discussed repeatedly in this book, Doctors must consider tax ramifications in making their investment decisions. Cash value life insurance has tremendous tax benefits that are unmatched by other investment classes.

Third, efficient investments utilize Leverage. Lesson #1 explained how Leverage is necessary for all wealth accumulation. Efficient investments may allow you to meet a planning need by spending $5,000 instead of having to spend $25,000 or $50,000. By utilizing Leverage with efficient investments, you will have more money left over for living expenses or necessary inefficient investments. Since we all want to achieve our own desired levels of affluence as quickly and safely as possible, it only makes sense to consider using Leverage whenever possible. Without the use of efficient investments to achieve Leverage, you are just like the landscaper who only has so many hours of daylight when he can work. You will never get ahead.

Fourth, efficient investments are your safety net. Perhaps you have heard the phrases "Life is Plan B" or "Life Happens." We speak to thousands of wealthy clients every year at our seminars and in our consulting practices. As our specialty is planning and implementation, we have designed and helped execute hundreds of financial plans for clients. Through all of our experiences, we can tell clients one thing with certainty. The plan we help them create "will never go as planned." We know that life will throw them a series of curveballs. We just don't know what those curveballs will be. So, we have to plan with an expectation that we will have to make many changes to this plan. By using flexible investments that can serve different purposes, we create plans that are more likely to fit the clients' future needs with fewer modifications (and costs) than if we had used inefficient investments in the plan.

Life Insurance Leverage

The basic concept of life insurance was built on the shifting and sharing of risk. The benefits of insurance have always revolved around its Leverage. In this chapter, we will break life insurance Leverage into basic Leverage and advanced Leverage. You can think of the basic Leverage as ways to turn small dollars into big dollars. Advanced Leverage is turning a small amount of someone else's small dollars into your big dollars. Because of this significant Leverage, life insurance is seen as the most efficient way to transfer wealth and protect a family or business. Let's look at some applications of life insurance Leverage, including:

- Part1: Death Benefit

- Part 2: Estate Planning

- Part 3: Tax-Free Accumulation

Part 1: Death Benefit

Lesson #4 is to do no financial harm to yourself or your family. In other words, you have to protect your family from financial disasters. Lesson #9 explains how to preserve your estate. The most efficient tool to address both of these concerns is life insurance. By paying small amounts to an insurance company, you can protect your family from lost income and estate taxes. To illustrate this point, let us consider the story of the Rob W., a hard working, 35-year old who has just started a family.

Case Study: Rob and Ronelle

Rob, 35, has a wife, Ronelle, and two young children, Nigel and Dikembe. Rob is a young dermatologist who is trying to help his family get ahead. He works for a clinic during the week and is a professional dancer who makes extra money during the weekends. Ronelle was a singer before she had the kids. He owns a house and has just started saving for the children's education. He knows that his family relies on his income and that the music would stop altogether for his family if he died. He recently asked us to help him find a life insurance policy that would help to protect his family's financial future.

With the $2,000 per month he was saving from his dancing, we were able to secure a $3,200,000 life insurance policy on Rob. Because Rob doesn't know how long he can dance, he only wanted to look at policy illustrations that assumed premium payments for 10 years. As such, Rob purchased a $3.2 million death benefit insurance policy. He pays $24,000 per year for 10 years to pay for the death benefit and accumulates cash values to pay for future premiums (after the 10 years). If Rob were to die, the death benefit would adequately cover his mortgages, his children's college funds, and leave Ronelle with enough money to raise the children. Now that Rob has insurance, the beat can go on for his family even if it doesn't for him.

What happens if Rob doesn't die? Some people would say that Rob has wasted a lot of money protecting his family when he could have just bought term insurance. However, that couldn't be further from the truth. If Rob's insurance policy earns 8% before fees and expenses (this assumption is realistic here, as Rob's particular policy offers an investment return that is tied to 100% of the S&P Index, an index that has averaged close to 8% over the last 25 years) for 20 years, Rob will have over $248,000 of cash value at the end of 10 years. In other words, at the end of 10 years, it may look like a Christmas club at the bank. $250,000 paid in, $248,000 left, PLUS he had $3.2 million of protection for his family. Not a bad deal. If Rob had bought term insurance, he would have spent valuable money and would have had absolutely nothing to show for after the term ended.

If Rob keeps his coverage for another 10 years, but does not pay another dollar of premium, he could expect the cash values to grow to approximately $460,000 and still maintain the financial protection for his family. That is a 6.5% after tax return (from a pretax, pre-fee return of 8% within an equity indexed life insurance policy) between years 10 and 20 while offering protection to his family. If Rob had invested that $248,000 in stocks and bonds at 8% instead of keeping the insurance policy, he would have paid at least 15% federal tax on his capital gains and up to 9% of the gain to state taxes. In Rob's state, state income taxes are 7%. This means that even if Rob could find an investment manager or mutual fund that didn't charge any fee at all (which is impossible), 22% of the 8% gain would have gone to taxes, giving him a 6.24% gain on his investment. The insurance actually outperformed the market AND it protected his family. Rob looked at this proposal and termed it his "free insurance" plan.

Cash Values in Rob's $3.2 Million Life Insurance Policy after Paying Premiums of $2,000 per Month for 10 Years

Period of Time	Cash Values in Rob's Insurance Policy
After 10 years	$248,000
After 20 years	$460,000
After 30 years	$862,000

Let's assume Rob leaves the policy in place for another 10 years until he is ready to retire. At the end of 30 years, the policy cash value would be approximately $862,000.

That equates to a 6.34% compounded rate of return on an insurance policy with underlying investments yielding 8% gross returns. Another way to say this is that the internal costs of administration, fees, and management of the policy are 1.66%. When you consider that Rob would be lucky to find an investment with total underlying fees of only 1%, his taxes on gains would be no less than 1.54%. This means that the internal rate of return for taxable funds or money management accounts could, at best, be 5.46% when the S&P Index returns 8%. An insurance policy with all of its fees and commissions offers an internal rate of return of 6.34%. Rob gets a better return for his investment in an insurance policy AND he is getting protection for his family.

Impact of Taxes, Fees & Commissions over 30 Years

	Mutual Funds	Cash Value Life Insurance
Gross Return	8.00%	8.00%
Fees & Commissions	1.00%	1.66%
Taxes	1.54%	0.00%
Net	5.46%	6.34%

Part 2: Estate Planning

Let's assume that Rob wins $1,000,000 on the reality show *So You Think You Can Dance* or Ronelle's revived singing career finally hits the big time and they are making more money than they need to support their lifestyle. Because they love their children and want to give them every opportunity they didn't have, they want to put money aside for them. Rob and Ronelle meet with their advisory team who explain a number of options. One of the techniques they chose to implement is the creation of an Irrevocable Life Insurance Trust (ILIT). Under the ILIT, Rob and Ronelle will each make $12,000 of tax-free annual gifts to the trust for the benefit of each of Nigel and Dikembe to remove the funds from their estate. Then, the $48,000 will be used to purchase a 2nd-to-die life insurance policy on Rob and Ronelle. When they finally pass away, their children will receive $10,000,000 tax-free. Even if Rob and Ronelle were to die next year, the children would get $10,000,000.

The ILIT is flexible too. Rob and Ronelle can direct the attorney to draft the language of the ILIT in a way that allows the children to get access to cash values of the policies for certain expenses that Rob and Ronelle find important. If the children need money for college or a wedding or dance lessons, the trust can be drafted to allow the children to access the insurance policy's substantial cash value to do so. For example, one 2nd-to-die policy we reviewed had cash values in excess of $600,000 in year 20; over $1.3 million in year 30; and over $2.5 million in year 40. The family could protect themselves from premature death of both spouses, build an estate for future generations and provide a fund to help pay for college, weddings, first homes and much more if Rob and Ronelle live. Because life insurance withdrawals, policy loans and death benefits can all be income tax-free, this life insurance investment offers amazing Leverage and unmatched flexibility.

Part 3: Tax-Free Accumulation

As established in the beginning of this Lesson, most people don't think of life insurance policies as investments. However, large companies have been purchasing life insurance policies in great numbers over the last five years to protect their assets and accumulate more wealth. In addition, Doctors have used these tax-efficient investment tools for years. We have a number of clients who invest over one million dollars per year into life insurance contracts. We also have many clients who invest hundreds of thousands of dollars every year into life insurance policies. These clients have some interest in the death benefit, but they are primarily interested in the wealth accumulation benefits of life insurance.

Let's look at a healthy 35-year-old male, like Rob in the earlier example. He may look at his equity indexed universal life insurance policy as his unlimited "after tax pension." The big differences between the insurance policy cash values and his pension are that he can take all (or none) of the money from the insurance policy before he is 59½ without penalty; he doesn't have to take any funds out of the policy at age 70½ (like he has to take minimum required distributions out of a pension); he doesn't have to contribute for employees; and the insurance policy appreciates at the time of his death instead of depreciating in value by 70% like his pension does when he dies and leaves it to his children (see Chapter 9-6).

The economics of investing into a life insurance policy look like this:

- Beginning at age 35, Rob invests $2,000 per month for 30 years

- The policy grows at 8% per year (before expenses and fees)

- Cash values in year 30, when Rob retires, are approximately $2.2 million

- He takes tax-free policy withdrawals and policy loans of over $220,000 every year from age 65 until age 90! That is $720,000 of investments yielding over $5,500,000 of tax-free retirement income while offering death protection to the family at the same time.

By leveraging the tax-free accumulation and death benefit features of equity indexed universal life insurance, Rob is able to protect his family from his premature death and provide a very tax-efficient investment return for himself at the same time. He can solve two planning challenges with one investment. That sounds pretty efficient!

The Diagnosis

Life insurance offers more Leverage than any other investment tool—even real estate. First, a very small premium payment can protect a family from a premature death; protect a business in a buy-sell arrangement; accumulate wealth without taxes; or efficiently transfer the wealth from one generation to another. Second, life insurance offers tax Leverage as both a wealth accumulator and as a tax-free death benefit for your family. For more detail on the flexibility and efficiency of life insurance, you should proceed to the next chapter. To see a much more detailed analysis that compares this investment to low cost index funds, you should make sure you read Chapter 8-8.

The Best Investment Option for Doctors

Would you be surprised to read that life insurance is the most important tool in the financial plans of Doctors? If you simply follow the "common sense" advice of the Average American-focused mass media, you certainly would be surprised. On the other hand, if you have been reading the past seven Lessons or if you have advisors who regularly work with high income, high liability or high net worth clients, then you wouldn't be surprised at all. No other financial, tax, insurance or legal tool can play as many roles in a financial plan as life insurance can.

In this chapter, we will discuss the key characteristics of cash value life insurance - that is, permanent (not term) insurance policies whose excess premium is invested in a tax-efficient manner with a cash value account for the benefit of the policy owner. In subsequent chapters, we will share applications that allow you to Leverage these characteristics.

Key Characteristics That Make Life Insurance So Valuable

Life insurance has many characteristics and offers various benefits. Savvy investors take advantage of life insurance as an investment because it can be such a flexible planning tool that will help you address so many planning challenges in an efficient way. The following attributes that make life insurance a valuable investment apply to permanent (cash value) life insurance and should capture your attention:

1. **Amounts in life insurance policies grow tax-deferred**: While investments outside of retirement plans and life insurance policies are taxed on income and realized capital gains, funds growing within a cash value life insurance policy grow completely tax-free. This is why life insurance is so attractive as a wealth accumulation and tax reduction vehicle. It is seen as the "Unlimited After-Tax Retirement Plan" by the most successful business owners in the United States.

2. **Account Balance values in life insurance policies can be accessed tax-free at any-time**: When you take funds out of a retirement plan (pension or IRA), these withdrawals are always subject to income tax and may be subject to a penalty if with-

drawn before age 59½. With a cash value life insurance policy, you can take tax-free loans against the cash value at any time. There is never a tax penalty and there is no tax on the loan so long as you keep the policy in force and the policy is not a modified endowment contract (MEC).

3. **Life insurance is asset-protected:** All 50 states give some measure of asset protection to cash value life insurance policies. Thus, this asset can play a role in your asset protection plan. Working with your advisory team, you can determine how best to Leverage the rules in your state.

4. **Life insurance has beneficial tax valuation:** In dealing with the 70% tax trap facing pensions and IRAs, life insurance can play a very valuable role. The essence of this rule is that life insurance enables the plan owner, who would otherwise <u>lose 70%</u> of his plan holdings to estate and income taxes, to instead pass most, if not all, of those dollars and more to heirs.

As you can see, life insurance can offer so many benefits to policy owners. It can grow tax-free, provide a tax-advantaged death benefit, and is protected from lawsuit creditors. This flexibility is what allows Doctors to use life insurance to meet planning challenges more efficiently.

The Diagnosis

The most important characteristic of life insurance is that it is flexible. You don't have to decide exactly what you want to use the life insurance for before you buy it. You can add more premium later, gift the policy to a person or entity, sell the policy, save it for the death benefit, use the cash values for lifetime needs and return the money you take out or not. The biggest misunderstanding about life insurance is that most people don't see it as an investment tool. The next chapter illustrates how a cash value life insurance policy outperforms mutual funds.

Proof That Life Insurance Outperforms Mutual Funds

If you Google the phrase "buy term and invest the difference" you get 11,500,000 results. This is not an unfamiliar phrase for most Americans. What this "common sense" adage means is that, when considering buying cash value life insurance, you will be better off buying the cheaper term life insurance product and investing the difference into the market. The difference is determined by setting aside money every month equal to the premium that a permanent plan would require, then using a portion of this money for the term premium and placing the rest in an investment vehicle. Though not explicitly stated, this generally means that you should invest the difference in mutual funds.

In this chapter, we will prove that life insurance is a wiser investment for building wealth and protecting assets than buying term and investing the difference. To do so, we will provide two examples that illustrate our argument.

The Debate: Life Insurance vs. Buy Term And Invest The Difference

If you think back to Lesson #2, you may remember our explanation of why the popular press focuses on issues of the Average American. The "life insurance versus buy term and invest the difference" commentary is another example of the financial media perpetuating "common sense" for the common people. These are people who generally do not have significant tax and asset protection concerns because they don't earn much, don't pay very high taxes and aren't able to acquire very much wealth to protect. Doctors should be concerned with after-tax investment returns (i.e., what you take home from the investment after all taxes are paid) and asset protection of those investments. If you want to learn these lessons, you must read this chapter. What you will learn may surprise you—unless, of course, you are already a savvy investor getting the most out of life insurance as an investment!

Basic Assumptions For The Comparison

To compare two investments fairly, you have to develop and use similar assumptions. This is often referred to as "normalizing" the data. In all examples, we will assume a 35-year old healthy male makes investments of $4,000 per month for 30 years and then maximizes his withdrawals for 25 years in retirement. This will cause him to run out of money at 90 years of age. This is well beyond his life expectancy. In both the mutual fund and cash value life insurance policy, there are an infinite number of potential combinations of premium payments and withdrawals. So, we chose a reasonable set of assumptions and applied the same constraints to both the mutual fund and cash value life insurance examples so we would have a fair comparison.

A Crucial Benefit Ignored: Asset Protection

In this analysis, we will look only at pure investment performance. We are simply examining the dollar amounts resulting in either scenario, with the same assumptions. This is fine theoretically. However, as a concrete comparison for any of our clients, we would also factor in other elements—including the costs of achieving a desired level of asset protection for the client.

As you learned in Lesson 6, cash value life insurance policies can enjoy the very highest (+5) level of protection. In many states the entire cash value of an insurance policy is given exempt status—meaning a Doctor can't even lose the cash value in the most extreme situations where a bankruptcy is forced by a creditor. When comparing the financial performance of cash value life insurance to individually-owned (-5) or jointly owned (-3) mutual funds for Doctors who have significant liability risks, it is imperative to factor in the additional costs of asset protection to the mutual fund option.

The goal of any comparison is to "normalize" the data so that you are comparing truly equivalent options. To increase the level of asset protection of the mutual funds (to meet the level of protection offered cash value life insurance), we would have to add significant costs to the mutual fund investment portfolio. While we would not be able to match the protection level exactly (as exempt assets are always preferable for asset protection planning), we could use rather expensive legal tools to give the mutual funds a (+5) level of protection. The creation of an international trust would be one tool that offers a very high level of desired protection. To compare the financial benefits of investing in cash value life insurance in a state where insurance is exempt to the financial benefits of mutual funds, you would have to reduce the total investment into mutual funds by upwards of $25,000 in year one and $10,000 per year on an ongoing basis to account for those additional costs of your desired protection. In a true comparison of the costs and benefits of both investment options, you must realize that the mutual fund projections offered below are unfairly skewed in favor of mutual funds. If asset protection is important to you, please keep in mind that investing in life insurance policies may be even more attractive than investing in mutual funds than the examples below suggest.

The Comparative Analysis =
Stack The Deck In Favor Of Mutual Funds

Notwithstanding the caveat regarding asset protection mentioned above, in this performance-driven comparative analysis, we will offer unrealistic assumptions that will give the mutual funds every opportunity to make a case for being the better investment choice. The purpose of this set of unreasonable comparisons is to emphasize that cash value life insurance is a much better investment than mutual funds even under extreme circumstances that are unrealistically skewed in favor of mutual funds. After we complete this analysis, we will offer a similar analysis with realistic expectations.

In the Mutual Fund Corner...

- We are going to compare an investment in a theoretical no-load mutual fund that has no annual costs or expenses of any kind.

- We are going to assume the S&P 500 Index has an annual return of 8% per year (excluding dividends) for the next 55 years.

- We will assume that every investor lives in a state with no state income tax, even though only 9 states—Alaska, Florida, Nevada, New Hampshire, South Dakota, Tennessee, Texas, Washington and Wyoming—do not have state income taxes. Note: You could remove New Hampshire and Tennessee from this list because they do tax dividend and interest income.

- We will assume that the tax on all gains will be at the lowest possible capital gains tax rate of 15% for the next 55 years, even though we believe rates will increase significantly at some time (and, as you have seen in past chapters, 15% is the lowest the tax rate has ever been on such gains).

- We are going to assume that the cost of the "buy term" portion of "buy term and invest the difference" is $0. In other words, we will completely disregard the buy term portion and just compare mutual funds to life insurance without any accounting for the friction of the term insurance.

In short, these unreasonable assumptions will yield projections that are not reasonable for actual mutual fund investors who will be paying management fees every year and are likely to have to pay state taxes and certainly will have to pay something for their term insurance.

In the Life Insurance Policy Corner...

- We are going to use an insurance policy from one of the nation's top insurance companies. This company has an A+ rating from the rating firm A.M. Best Company (this is the 2nd highest of 15 ratings offered by this rating organization). This insurance company is also rated by Comdex (another ratings firm) as being in the top 8% of U.S. insurance companies, in terms of financially stability.

- To prove that this was not an anomaly, we found a second insurance policy from another A.M. Best A+ rated company that was rated by Comdex to be in the top 12%, in terms of financial stability, of insurance companies in the country. The ultimate income results of this secondary policy were within 3.96% of the first one.

- We are going to attempt to compare investments of equal risk by choosing an equity-indexed universal life insurance product that is readily available to the public in most states. This policy's performance is tied to the S&P 500 Index (excluding dividends). Unlike the mutual fund investment, however, the insurance product has a minimum annual investment return of 1% per year. That is, even if the S&P has a return in a given year that is less than 1%, the insurance company will still credit the policy as if the S&P returned 1%. This actually reduces the risk for the insurance policy vs. the index fund, but we will assume they are the same.

- We will assume the same 8% long-term gross return of the S&P 500 Index (excluding dividends) over 55 years.

- The policy also has a cap of 14%, but that does not come into play here as we are assuming the 8% annual return, as above.

- We will assume a fully commissionable insurance policy that has no term insurance blending to reduce commissions and increase cash values.

In this set of assumptions, we are giving a realistic projection of the S&P 500 equity indexed universal life insurance policy. In both this analysis and the subsequent more realistic comparison, the projection for the equity indexed universal life insurance policy will be the same.

The Comparative Analysis With The Deck Stacked For Mutual Funds

Let's examine how the no-fee, lowest possible tax, mutual fund portfolio and a cash value life insurance policy would perform with 30 years of investments at $4,000 per month, followed by 25 years of withdrawals by referring to the table on the next page:

No Fee Funds with No State Tax Paying Investors vs. Cash Value Life Insurance

Investment in No-Fee, Low Tax Mutual Funds   Investment in Life Insurance

Year	Age	Annual Mutual Fund Investment	6.8% After Tax Growth	Retirement Withdrawal	Year End Balance	Annual Insurance Premium	Withdrawals and Loans	Value at Death	Improvements over Funds at Death
1	35	$48,000	$1,632		$49,632	$48,000	$0	$1,160,944	$1,111,312
10	44	$48,000	$41,723		$679,294	$48,000	$0	$1,832,780	$1,153,486
15	49	$48,000	$76,669		$1,228,158	$48,000	$0	$2,947,312	$1,719,154
20	54	$48,000	$125,227		$1,990,800	$48,000	$0	$4,241,600	$2,250,800
25	59	$48,000	$192,698		$3,050,487	$48,000	$0	$5,815,060	$2,764,573
30	64	$48,000	$286,448		$4,522,913	$48,000	$0	$7,802,940	$3,280,027
31	65		$283,290	$356,879	$4,449,324		$440,000	$7,401,372	$2,952,048
35	69		$261,138	$356,879	$4,101,409		$440,000	$6,828,168	$2,726,759
40	74		$223,848	$356,879	$3,515,733		$440,000	$6,343,556	$2,827,823
45	79		$172,034	$356,879	$2,701,940		$440,000	$5,888,176	$3,186,236
50	84		$100,038	$356,879	$1,571,181		$440,000	$5,597,232	$4,026,051
55	89		($0)	$356,879	($0)		$440,000	$5,660,016	$5,660,016
Total		$1,440,000		$8,921,974		$1,440,000	$11,000,000		

$2,078,027   Increase in Retirement Income

23.3%   % Increase over Mutual Funds

This example is for illustrative purposes only. Contact the authors for a specific example based on your circumstances.

To save space, we compressed the table above to show a sample of the 55 years of data. Even with the deck stacked against the insurance policy - by considering an index fund with NO fees, an investor with NO state income taxes, and with NO costs of term life insurance - the insurance policy still outperformed the mutual fund investment. The mutual fund investment of $48,000 per year in a no fee, low tax environment yields annual after-tax income of $356,879. The investment in the equity indexed life insurance policy offers tax-free withdrawals and policy loans of $440,000 per year. The investment income from the investment insurance policy was over 23% greater than that of the "too good to be true" mutual fund. In addition, the family of the investor who purchased the insurance policy also has death benefit protection. The benefit in the last column is in addition to the increase in retirement income. In short, **the investment in a life insurance policy significantly outperforms the investment in mutual funds, even with ridiculously skewed assumptions.**

The Comparative Analysis With More Realistic Assumptions

Now that we have determined that this type of cash value life insurance policy outperforms a "too good to be true" exaggerated mutual fund, let's conduct a second comparative analysis with realistic assumptions. The differences between this analysis and the previous one are three-fold. First, we assume that the mutual fund has a total of 0.50% in annual expenses. This is quite low for most mutual funds. Second, we assume that the investors live in a state with 5% state income taxes. This is also a very reasonable assumption because 33 states have marginal income tax brackets over 5%. Twenty-four of those states have marginal income tax brackets over 6% and some have rates as high as 9.3%. Third, we assume that the term insurance costs would be approximately $2,000 per year. This is a rough estimate, but it reflects a slight reduction in the investment funds for the "buy term and invest the difference" scenario.

Let's look at how these more reasonable assumptions affect the projections. The table below compares how a low fee, moderate tax, mutual fund portfolio and a cash value life insurance policy would perform with 30 years of investments at $4,000 per month, followed by 25 years of withdrawals.

Low Fee Funds for Low State Tax Paying Investors vs. Cash Value Life Insurance

		Investment in Low-Fee, Moderate Tax Mutual Funds				Investment in Life Insurance			
Year	Age	Annual Mutual Fund Investment	6% After Tax Growth	Retirement Withdrawal	Value at death	Annual Insurance Premium	Withdrawals and Loans	Value at Death	Improvements over Funds at Death
1	35	$46,000	$1,380		$1,160,944	$48,000	$0	$1,160,944	$0
10	44	$46,000	$34,048		$1,832,780	$48,000	$0	$1,832,780	$0
15	49	$46,000	$61,120		$2,947,312	$48,000	$0	$2,947,312	$0
20	54	$46,000	$97,352		$4,241,600	$48,000	$0	$4,241,600	$0
25	59	$46,000	$145,840		$5,815,060	$48,000	$0	$5,815,060	$0
30	64	$46,000	$210,724		$7,802,940	$48,000	$0	$7,802,940	$0
31	65	$0	$208,160	$276,432	$7,401,372	$0	$440,000	$7,401,372	$0
35	69	$0	$190,240	$276,432	$6,828,168	$0	$440,000	$6,828,168	$0
40	74	$0	$161,088	$276,432	$6,343,556	$0	$440,000	$6,343,556	$0
45	79	$0	$122,076	$276,432	$5,888,176	$0	$440,000	$5,888,176	$0
50	84	$0	$69,868	$276,432	$5,597,232	$0	$440,000	$5,597,232	$0
55	89	$0	$0	$276,432	$5,660,016	$0	$440,000	$5,660,016	$0
Total		$1,380,000		$6,910,800		$1,440,000	$11,000,000		

$60,000	Term Insurance Premium	$4,089,200	Increase in Retirement Income
$1,440,000	Total Term + Investment	59.2%	% Increase over Mutual Funds

* This example is for illustrative purposes only. Contact the authors for a specific example based on your circumstances.

With realistic expectations, the annual after tax retirement income of the mutual fund investment is $69,108 per year. The insurance policy offers tax-free withdrawals and policy loans of $110,000 per year. That is a 59% improvement in income over the mutual fund investing. The death benefit is the same with the purchase of the term insurance, but the income suffers dramatically. The reason the insurance policy outperforms the mutual funds is that the actual expenses and the taxes of the funds, combined with the term life insurance costs, are significantly higher than the "supposedly" high internal costs of the cash value life insurance policy. **This is one of the most misunderstood comparisons in financial planning.**

Another Case—The 45-Year Old

Insurance doesn't just work for 35-year old Doctors. We also looked at a recent case from a client of ours. This client was a 45-year old physician who wanted to work full-time for another 15 years, then work part time for 10 years, then take retirement plan distributions from ages 71 through 90 (20 years). We were asked to compare after tax investments of $5,000 per month into mutual funds and cash value life insurance under similar investment return assumptions (8% per year for the S&P 500 Index). This is what we found:

Low Fee Funds for Low State Tax Paying Investors vs. Cash Value Life Insurance

		Low-Fee, Moderate Tax Funds			Cash Value Life Insurance	
Year	Age	Annual Mutual Fund Investment	6% After Tax Growth	Retirement Withdrawal	Annual Insurance Premium	Withdrawals and Loans
1	45	$53,750	$1,613		$60,000	$0
10	54	$53,750	$39,784		$60,000	$0
15	59	$53,750	$71,419		$60,000	$0
20	64	$0	$0	$0	$0	$0
27	71	$0	$0	$201,197	$0	$254,358
35	79	$0	$0	$201,197	$0	$254,358
40	84	$0	$0	$201,197	$0	$254,358
46	90	$0	$0	$201,197	$0	$254,358
Total		$806,250		$4,023,942	$900,000	$5,087,160

$93,750	Term Insurance Premium	$1,063,218	Increase in Retirement Income
$900,000	Total Term + Fund Investment	26.42%	% Increase over Mutual Funds

* This example is for illustrative purposes only. Contact the authors for a specific example based on your circumstances.

In this example, our client would have over $1,000,000 of additional after-tax retirement funds by investing in a life insurance policy instead of into mutual funds or individually managed accounts. Not surprisingly, the client found this to be a much better alternative.

As we explained above, in many states the life insurance option also provides qualitatively better asset protection—(+5) versus (-5) or (-3) for mutual funds. In such states, you do not need to pay additional legal costs for the protection of life insurance cash values but you do have to pay the costs of creating and maintaining asset protection structures when you invest in mutual funds or other investment accounts. In those instances, the cash value life insurance can be a better investment, even for Doctors who are starting this investing at the age of 60 or possibly 70, if in excellent health.

However, in states where life insurance is not an exempt asset, you will have to create asset protection entities to protect both your mutual funds and life insurance policies. In those states, the "Breakeven" analysis basically guides us toward insurance as an investment for Doctors who are under the age of 50 and toward tax-managed investment accounts for clients who are over 50. Of course, if the policy is primarily used for estate planning, life insurance may be a wise tool for clients even in their 70s and 80s.

Possible Explanation

We hope it is clear to you that the common sense adage "cash value life insurance is a poor investment" is generally inaccurate. Before we wrote this book, we believed that the taxes were the biggest factor in the success of cash value life insurance policies as wealth accumulation vehicles. Certainly, for Doctors in the higher combined marginal tax brackets, this is absolutely true. Yet, with the analyses above, we saw that the insurance policy was still a better investment for investors who only pay taxes of 15% on their investment gains. This was surprising, as it indicated to us that the taxes couldn't be the primary reason for the insurance policy's superior performance. It must be the type of insurance policy itself.

Before equity indexed universal life insurance policies were invented, the only practical life insurance investment choices were Whole Life, Universal Life and Variable Universal Life policies. Whole Life insurance policies are very inflexible. Further, Whole Life and Universal Life policies typically have returned 4% to 7% over the last 10 years. Though this return is respectable, it did not keep pace with the appreciation of the S&P 500 Index over the same period. In a strong market, the mutual funds could possibly outperform those policies in states with low taxes. If the people who did the original comparison of "buy term and invest the difference" used whole life policies, those results would perpetuate the aforementioned "common sense" myth.

The Variable Universal Life policies that offer mutual fund choices within the insurance contract could theoretically keep pace with a strong market since their underlying investment are mutual funds. However, these policies have always had the highest internal fees of all insurance products. If you have a variable-type policy with high fees being purchased by an investor in a state that had no state income tax on investment gains, the mutual fund investment may outperform the Variable Universal Life policy. This would also further the "common sense" myth.

With Equity Indexed Universal Life (EIUL) policies, one has access to both the tax benefit and lower costs of certain types for policies and the access to the upside potential of the S&P 500 Index. When you combine these benefits with the results from the direct comparison above, you can see why EIUL policies are able to consistently outperform mutual funds for long term investors who are as young as 30 or possibly as old as 70 years of age.

The Diagnosis

The misconception that "buy term and invest the difference" outperforms an investment in life insurance is common. If you continue to seek financial advice through Average American media channels, you may continue to get this kind of inaccurate and inappropriate information. This chapter gave examples of how cash value life insurance policies significantly outperformed realistic mutual funds. Even when we compared the insurance policy to an unrealistic (and unavailable) mutual fund with no expenses and sold it to a taxpayer in a state with no income taxes and gave that investor the term insurance for free, the cash value insurance policy still outperformed the mutual fund.

Throughout this book, you have learned that life insurance would protect against a premature death, serve as a source of liquidity for estate planning, and provide asset protection for your investment dollars. Now you know that the investment in life insurance can be significantly more attractive than an investment in mutual funds. Doctors maximize their investment in life insurance as a way to accumulate more wealth and protect assets. This is likely to be a significant key to your achieving, and maintaining, your desired level of affluence.

The Ultimate After Tax Pension & College Savings Tool

After reading the chapters within this Lesson, you now understand that life insurance is a wise investment alternative worthy of serious consideration. In addition, you have also learned that life insurance offers asset protection, tax and estate planning benefits. With all of these benefits, and the unmatched flexibility of life insurance policies, you can see why insurance is the cornerstone of the financial planning for Doctors. In this chapter, we will show you how you can use life insurance as a wise investment tool. Doctors can utilize creative applications of insurance, which are:

- Unlimited After-Tax Retirement Plan

- Insured College Savings Fund for Children or Grandchildren

In doing so, you can accomplish more than one goal with one single investment tool and create even more efficiency in your financial plan.

In Chapter 7-2, we explained how Doctors can maximize their use of retirement plans. This is desirable because Doctors want to take advantage of three key elements of a qualified retirement plan:

1. Tax deduction for plan contributions

2. Tax-free growth of plan assets

3. The highest level of available asset protection for plan assets

Doctors can combine the benefits in Chapter 7-2 with the philosophy of "Leverage" from Lesson #1 by involving family members in their businesses so that they can make additional contributions to retirement plans for family members as well. Despite this desired Leverage, there are limits to how much Leverage you can achieve through retirement plans.

To increase the amount of "retirement plan-like" benefits their families can enjoy, Doctors can look to investment vehicles that offer similar benefits to retirement plans. Life insurance is the investment vehicle that has the characteristics that are most similar to those of retirement plans. Cash value life insurance always offers tax-free accumulation and often offers the highest level of asset protection. Though life insurance premiums are not tax deductible, the funds come out of the policy through tax-free policy loans and withdrawals. For those of you who are familiar with Roth IRAs, cash value life insurance can be seen as an unlimited Roth IRA that also offers death benefit protection.

The Roth IRA is a type of individual retirement account in which contributions are made with after tax (nondeductible) dollars. If certain requirements are met, earnings accumulate within the Roth IRA tax-free and no federal income tax is levied when qualifying distributions are taken from the Roth IRA. The major restrictions of the Roth IRA are that only $2,000 per year can be invested into a Roth IRA and funds cannot be accessed before age 59½. When compared to a Roth IRA, the benefits of life insurance are that the annual premiums are practically unlimited and the funds can be accessed before age 59½. These benefits make cash value life insurance a very attractive alternative or complement to retirement plans.

The Ultimate College Savings Tool

When we have children, most of us want to give them every opportunity to succeed and protect them from unnecessary pain. Lesson #4 showed you how to financially protect your family from your premature death, yet protecting children from your death is not enough to ensure their financial success. In Chapter 1-3, we discussed the Leverage of effort and education. Obviously, the more education we receive, the greater opportunity we have to succeed. No one knows this better than a highly trained Doctor.

For this reason, a common dream of American parents is to send their children to college to take advantage of this opportunity. Physicians' families often stress the importance of business school, law school and medical school. Their children do not need to go to work right after college to support themselves, so they have an advantage over students who can't afford to continue their education and must begin working right away.

We all want to help our children pay for college and any additional education we can afford. We can make investments to save for college, but that doesn't ensure that there will be enough to pay for college if we pass away. For that reason, we have to buy some life insurance if it is important to give our children every opportunity to succeed.

Doctors should understand that they have to invest for their children's educational expenses and they have to buy life insurance to guarantee the funds will be there even if they aren't alive to see the child off to college. Doctors should also understand the analysis in the last chapter that explained how life insurance outperforms mutual funds after you factor in tax costs. For this reason, Doctors should make investments in life insurance to protect their children from a premature death and to provide a tax-efficient investment alternative for savings for college. This one tool can handle educational expenses whether you live to see your children off to college or if you die prematurely.

The Diagnosis

You have already learned that life insurance is flexible and efficient. It can offer income protection, asset protection, tax-efficient wealth accumulation and liquidity benefits. The applications of the life insurance can range from the traditional buy-sell, estate planning and income replacement options to more creative applications like retirement enhancing and college savings funding.

So far, you have made it through eight Lessons to Working Less and Building More. Within these lessons, there are dozens of practical applications. It may seem very overwhelming to manage all of this within a financial plan. It is overwhelming! This is why you need to work with an experienced team of advisors who can help you analyze the different options that may help you most efficiently Leverage your assets to meet your planning goals.

Protect Your Family's Wealth from Estate Tax & Fees

For families that want to preserve wealth as it passes from one generation to the next, estate planning is an important part of the comprehensive financial plan. Hard work, the proper use of Leverage, the protection of assets and wise investing can all be undone by estate and inheritance taxes. By making estate planning a priority early on, you can avoid unnecessary taxes and ensure that the wealth you build will benefit your family for generations to come.

It is not just estate and inheritance taxes you can avoid by implementing a comprehensive estate plan. Consider that a proper estate plan can help you avoid:

- **Accidental disinheritance of family members.** Each year, millions of Americans title property in joint ownership without realizing that this form of ownership supersedes their Wills, leaving the property to their joint owner rather than to those they named in their Wills. This "disinheritance risk" might be lurking in your estate plan right now.

- **The costs and delays of probate.** These can be significant if not planned for in advance.

- **Future generations losing funds through irresponsibility, lawsuits or divorce.** All of these can be prevented by savvy estate planning today.

In this Lesson, you will learn about tools you can use to reduce, and even eliminate, estate taxes, avoid disinheritance risk, avoid probate and even deal with "problem assets" such as pensions, IRAs and family businesses. Specifically, you will learn how to preserve your estate by using such tools as Wills and Living Trusts, life insurance policies, Family Limited Partnerships, Limited Liability Companies and charitable planning.

The Truth About the Estate Tax Repeal

It is true, in a limited sense, that Congress passed significant estate tax reform by "repealing" the estate tax as part of the 2001 Economic Growth Tax Relief Reconciliation Act ("EGTRRA"). However, the actual "repeal" only took place in the year 2010 and without subsequent action taken by Congress in late 2010, the estate tax was slated to revert to pre-EGTRRA levels. The action that Congress took came in the form of the 2010 Tax Relief Act which provided a number of key provisions for the estate tax for tax years 2011 and 2012. Below is a brief description of the evolution of the estate tax from EGTRRA to the 2010 Tax Relief Act and the highlights of the 2010 Tax Relief Act.

EGTRRA and the Tax Relief Act of 2010

When EGTRRA was passed in 2001, it was designed to phase out the estate tax during the years of 2001-2009 culminating in complete repeal of the estate tax in 2010. More specifically, EGTRRA over the course of the previous decade gradually phased out the estate tax by increasing estate tax exemption levels ($1 million per person in 2001 to $3.5 million per person in 2009) while decreasing estate tax rates (55% in 2001 to 45% in 2009). EGTRRA repealed the estate tax as well as generation skipping transfer taxes ("GST"- which will be discussed in more detail later in this chapter) in 2010.

While estate tax exemption levels were rising and estate tax rates falling, gift tax (tax paid on transfers of property while still living) exemption levels remained unchanged, which had always been equal or "unified" with estate tax exemption levels, at $1 million. During that same period, gift tax rates mirrored those of the estate tax.

Prior to 2010, whenever property was transferred at death from one generation to the next (i.e. through a will, trust etc.) the basis of the transferred property was increased or "stepped up" to the market value of the property as of the date of death. However, because of lost revenue to the government as a result of the 2010 repeal, EGTRRA attempted to recoup some lost revenue by only allowing a limited (up to $4.3 million) step up of basis on such transferred property. The theory being that more capital gains taxes would be paid when the transferred property was subsequently sold by the next generation.

In late 2010, with the expiration of EGTRRA facing the nation and the very real possibility of returning to pre-EGTRRA exemptions and rates ($1 million exemption and 55% estate tax rate), Congress passed the 2010 Tax Relief Act which provided very favorable exemptions and rates.

You may be wondering why time was spent explaining the nuts and bolts of an expired estate tax law. Why not simply explain current estate, gift and GST tax law? Because the 2010 Tax Relief Act is due to expire after 2012, which means just like in 2010, without subsequent Congressional action, we will be staring down the possibility of pre-EGTRRA estate tax exemptions and rates. While most experts agree that Congress is not likely to allow pre-EGTRRA tax exemptions and rates to be the law of the land, many would agree that there is a very real possibility that legislation could be passed with provisions similar to those during the era of EGTRRA (i.e. 2001–2009).

With that in mind we thought it important to highlight the main points of EGTRRA to give you a better understanding of the key provisions of the 2010 Tax Relief Act. To that end, we have compiled below a brief description of the most important aspects of the 2010 Tax Relief Act:

1. The 2010 Tax Relief Act increases estate, gift and GST exemptions to $5 million (indexed for inflation and rounded to the nearest multiple of $10,000 after 2011) per person (thus reunifying estate and gift tax exemptions) and reducing the rates for such taxes to 35%.

2. The 2010 Tax Relief Act allows estates of decedents dying in 2010 to choose between (1) the new estate tax provisions based on a $5 million exemption and 35% top rate and a full step in basis in property passed to the next generation or (2) no estate tax and the limited (up to $4.3 million) step up in basis on property transferred to the next generation at death.

3. The 2010 Tax Relief Act, allows for the portability of estate and gift tax exemptions between spouses, meaning that if a deceased spouse did not use his or her entire $5 million estate and gift exemption then the surviving spouse may use the unused portion of the deceased spouse's exemption. (GST exemption is not portable). (Note: Only the last deceased spouse's exemption is portable; therefore you can not keep getting married and accruing deceased spouses unused exemptions).

4. Maybe the most important: The 2010 Tax Relief Act is only on the books for 2 years. Therefore, before the end of 2012, Congress will have to pass legislation

addressing how to deal with the estate, gift and GST taxes. Therefore, there may only be a two year window to take advantage of the high exemptions and low rates afforded by the 2010 Tax Relief Act.

State Inheritance and Estate Taxes

Prior to the "repeal" of 2001, the estate of a wealthy family was entitled to a federal estate tax credit for state death taxes paid by the estate. Essentially, while the federal estate tax rate was capped at 55%, the federal government kept 39% of the total tax and gave 16% to the various states (this was called a "sponge tax" because the states soaked up their piece of the total tax). Thus, most states had no need to impose their own estate tax other than the amount they would get from the federal return. This scheme was repealed by EGTRRA in 2001 and effective for individuals dying after 2004.

The estate tax reduction eliminated the states' piece of the estate tax as of 2004. The states no longer receive any of the federal estate tax. The federal government now actually keeps more of the taxes it collects than it did before the repeal.

The states were not happy losing out on tax revenue. To fight this tax loss, many states instituted their own version of estate taxes, sometimes called "state inheritance taxes." These states charge a tax on the assets that are left as an inheritance in their jurisdiction. As of 2008, 23 states (including the District of Columbia) imposed their own state estate (or inheritance) tax, in addition to the federal estate tax. These taxes are currently imposed at rates up to 16% of the value of the estate.

Estate Tax Reform Leaves IRD Alone

In addition to the estate tax, income tax must be paid on certain assets left in a decedent's estate at death, which would have been subject to income tax had the decedent lived. This tax is levied on what is called income in respect of a decedent ("IRD"). The classic examples are amounts left in pensions, profit-sharing plans and individual retirement accounts. Because combined federal and state income taxes—including those characterized as IRD taxes—can be as high as 45%, and estate taxes can reach 35% under the 2010 reform, the combined tax rate can escalate to more than 70% on IRD! This means less than 30% of certain assets could go to your heirs at death unless you make a plan to avoid this serious problem. Because most doctors accumulate the bulk of their wealth in various types of "qualified plans" subject to IRD, special attention should be given to these types of assets during the estate tax planning process.

Beware of and plan for the Generation Skipping Tax (GST)

In addition to estate and gift taxes, The Generation Skipping Tax (GST) is a hefty tax imposed tax if you leave assets (directly or in trust) for the benefit of your grandchildren or later generations. Congress implemented this tax in 1986 so families could not avoid federal estate taxes by leaving wealth to future generations. The goal of the GST is to impose a transfer tax at each generation. For example, if a Doctor and his wife desire to leave assets in their estate plan to their grandchildren, the generation skipping tax could be triggered depending upon the amount of assets left to the Doctor's grandchildren.

As mentioned above, the Tax Relief Act of 2010, provides a $5 million exemption per person for GST transfers and imposes a 35% rate on any generation skipping transfers that exceed that amount. For those estates that were in created in 2010, GST tax rates are 0%, and therefore, effectively, GST taxes do not exist for such estates. Also as mentioned before, there is no portability of the GST exemption meaning that if any portion of the GST exemption that is not used at the time of a pre-deceasing spouses death, then the surviving spouse will not be able to use such unused portion.

The planning necessary to avoid this tax and to leverage your GST exemption is highly technical and can be confusing, but proper planning is extremely powerful. The goal is to utilize your GST exemption so that we *skip the tax* in future generations. A GST-skipping trust can benefit your children, grandchildren, great-grandchildren, etc. and never be subject to estate tax. The goal is not skip your children for purposes of distribution, just to skip them for purposes of estate tax.

As an oversimplified example, assume that your children inherit $1 million from you and that your children and future generations will each be subject to estate tax at 50%. If you leave your $1 million outright to your children instead of in trust, and each generation does the same thing, your $1 million will be eroded to $125,000 in 4 generations simply because each generation paid estate taxes. However, if you planned ahead to properly leverage your GST exemption, the $1 million could stay in trust for your children, then your grandchildren, then your great-grandchildren and NEVER be subject to estate tax.

The bottom line is that the GST is something about which doctors need to be aware when planning their estate because of the potentially high tax rates involved.

The Diagnosis

There has been a lot of talk about the estate tax repeal, yet the tax law change is only temporary. Even if it becomes permanent (which is highly unlikely), new taxes have emerged on the state level and for capital gains that fill the tax void left by a repeal. Thus, if you truly want to see that your estate passes on to your family, you must implement an estate plan for your family's benefit now and not rely on the government to help you. The following chapters in this Lesson will help you do this.

Wills & Living Trusts

A Will and Living Trust are the foundation to any estate plan. Without these two tools, your family's wealth will become public information and the government will decide who gets what assets when you die. In this chapter, we will discuss the importance of Wills and Living Trusts and how to avoid unnecessary pitfalls of Living Trusts that can trap unaware families.

The Government's Will

Are you surprised to know that you already have a Will even if you have never written one or had an attorney draft one? It is true. If you die without a Will, then your property will pass under the scheme that your state government has written for all of its citizens. This is what is known as dying "intestate." While this may seem like a good thing, it probably is not because there is no guarantee that the way the government will split up your estate is the way you would want your property to be divided.

There are various negative consequences of a government's Will. While the precise rules vary among the 50 states, typically the laws are very rigid and formulaic. Usually, all of your nearest relatives get a piece of your property but no one else does—not friends, cousins, charities or anyone else. Furthermore, no one gets more than the state-allotted share, even if it's seemingly unfair. Often, this ends up hurting the surviving spouse. In this all-too-common scenario, the decedent's grown children may get some of the money meant for the surviving spouse, even if it means the surviving spouse then has too little to live on. In larger estates, this could have the very impractical effect of creating an estate tax payable when the first spouse dies if the children's intestate share of the estate exceeds the federal exemption amount.

Moreover, the absence of a Will often leads to expensive and lengthy court battles by family members contesting the division of assets. Sometimes family members produce a questionable Will in court, trying to establish a rightful claim to a portion of the estate. Once again, this can be avoided by having a valid Will in place.

If you have minor children and both parents die without a Will, the courts will decide who becomes the legal guardian of your children. What parents would want to have an unknown judge make the decision of who will care for their children after they pass away? Moreover, your minor children will receive their share of your estate when they turn 18 rather than at some more appropriate later age that you could otherwise specify. For instance, under your Will, you could leave your children's share in trust for their benefit until age 30 or 35. Avoid this tragedy and create a valid Will, including an Appointment of Guardian, sooner rather than later.

The Need For A Will <u>And</u> A Living Trust

Having a Will is certainly better than not having a Will. However, your entire estate will be stuck in the probate process if you only have a Will. Probate is the process by which the state administers your Will. Probate is time-consuming, a matter of public record and quite costly in many states. In most states, knowledgeable advisors combine a Living Trust with a short Will called a "pour-over Will" when planning for Doctors. This combination ensures the vast majority of the estate will avoid probate and keeps the estate plan private. Before we examine how a Living Trust works, we must first see why it is so important to avoid probate.

The Pitfalls of Probate

Delays. Probate often takes between one to two years to complete. During that time, your beneficiaries must wait for their inheritance. Perhaps worse, the representatives of your estate may have to petition the court for permission to conduct any transactions involving your estate's assets during this time. This can make it difficult to sell estate property or invest estate assets during the probate process.

Costs. Probate can be very costly and is an expense that can be avoided. These costs pay for additional legal fees, executor's commissions and the costs associated with marshalling assets. In some states, these probate fees are assessed on your gross estate—not taking into account any mortgages on your assets! In these states, if you die owning $1 million worth of assets that have mortgages of $800,000, your estate will pay probate fees based on the $1 million fair market value, or approximately $50,000 (i.e. $23,000 as the statutory fee for each of the attorney and the personal representative, for a total of $46,000—not including the filing fees for the probate petition!). In other states, the probate fees are fixed costs, but tied into the value of your gross estate. This is money that could have gone to your beneficiaries rather than to the courts and lawyers!

Privacy. Probate is a public process in all states. Anyone interested in your estate can find out who inherits under your Will; how much he or she inherits; the beneficiaries' addresses; and more. While you may not be famous or worry about the newspapers exploiting this information, you should think of your beneficiaries—your surviving family members. They certainly will not appreciate the many financial advisors calling them with "hot tips" on investments or welcome less scrupulous individuals who try to take advantage of recent inheritance recipients. These people find beneficiaries by examining probate records. They know who they are and how much "found money" they have to invest.

What seems fair to some may seem completely unfair to others. This is definitely the case with privacy and probate. Probate is designed to make sure that all potential beneficiaries are given an opportunity to review the Will and make objections. For this reason, the Will has to be public. When you die, it could take a very long time just to track down all potential beneficiaries (even if they live abroad) to give them notice. Not only will your intended heirs have to wait a very long time, but they may also lose a significant part of an inheritance to people you haven't spoken to in decades. Even if the probate process does distribute your assets to the people you intended, they still have to pay the costs of administering this process.

Control. In probate, the court controls the timing and final say-so on whether or not your Will—and the wishes expressed in your Will—are followed. Your family must follow the court orders and pay for the process as well. This can be extremely frustrating.

Double Probate. If you own real estate outside your state of residence, your Will must be probated <u>again</u> (in an ancillary proceeding) in each state where real property is located. This becomes very time consuming and expensive.

You are probably thinking, "Why would anyone choose to use a Will as the estate planning document of choice when probate is this unappealing?" It is hard to believe. We are continually astonished by how many families endure the time and expense of probate when it is completely avoidable by simply having a Living Trust.

The Problem-Solver: A Living Trust

As mentioned earlier, a Living Trust is a legal document that provides direction for the use of your assets both while you are alive and at the time of your death. A Living Trust is ordinarily revocable, meaning you can change it at any time before your death. During your life, the assets transferred to the Trust are managed and controlled by you, as the Trustee, just as if you owned them in your own name. When you die, these Trust assets pass to whomever you designated in the Trust, automatically, outside of the probate process. Other benefits of the Living Trust include:

- Avoiding the unintentional disinheritance caused by joint tenancy or joint owner-ship (this happens in most 2nd marriages)

- Preventing court control of assets if you become incapacitated

- Protecting beneficiaries with special needs

- Providing for guardians of children if you are incapacitated (but are still alive) or when you pass

"Funding the Trust"

The transfer of assets to the Living Trust is also known as "funding the Trust." If you create a Trust and don't fund the Trust with assets, it is just a useless piece of paper. This is like building a car and not putting an engine in it. If you want to get any benefit from your Trust, you must fund it!

"Funding the Trust" is a step you can't forget to take. When you transfer your assets to your Living Trust while you are alive, you maintain 100% control over these assets as though you still own them in your own name. For your car, stocks, bonds, bank accounts, home and any other assets, the process of transferring an asset to your Living Trust is the same. If the asset has a registration or deed, change the name on such a document. If the asset is jewelry or art-work that has no official ownership record, use an assignment document to officially transfer ownership to your Living Trust.

These ownership changes will transfer the name of the registration or deed to the "John Doe Revocable Living Trust" or "John Doe, Trustee of John Doe Revocable Living Trust," rather than "John Doe" as it now reads. As sole Trustee of the Trust, you have the same power to buy, sell, mortgage or invest as you did before. Further, because the Trust is revocable, you can always change beneficiaries, remove or add assets, or even revoke your Trust entirely.

It must be remembered that the transfer of assets to the Living Trust is a necessary activity. While it has no income tax ramifications at all (you are still treated as the owner for income tax purposes), it is crucial to gain the probate-saving benefits afforded to you at the time of your death. Below is a list of some of the valuable benefits of a Trust that allow you to achieve important estate planning goals without sacrificing your quality of life. The benefits of a Trust are:

You may name yourself or someone else as Trustee.
You need not name yourself as the Trustee of your Living Trust, although most people do. You could name an adult child, another relative or close friend or even a corporate Trustee, like a local bank or Trust company. However, if you do not like the way the outside Trustee is handling the Trust, you always have the power to remove him.

When you die or become disabled, your successor Trustee will take over.
If you are the Trustee while you are alive, you will name, in your Living Trust, an individual (or possibly a corporate Trustee) as the successor Trustee. That person or entity will take over the Trustee duties when you die or become disabled. If you

have a co-Trustee while you are alive, that person will have complete Trustee duties after you have died. These duties involve collecting income or benefits due your estate, paying your remaining debts, making sure the proper tax returns are filed and distributing your assets according to the Trust instructions. This person or entity acts like an executor for a Will. However, unlike a Will, actions under a Living Trust's directions are not generally subject to court interference or supervision.

You decide when your beneficiaries receive their inheritances.
Another significant advantage of a Living Trust over a Will is that you, rather than the court, decide when and how your beneficiaries get their inheritance. Because the court is not involved, the successor Trustee can distribute assets right after your final affairs are concluded.

If you choose, assets need not be distributed right away.
Instead, you may direct that they stay in your Trust, managed by your individual or corporate Trustee, until your beneficiaries reach the age(s) at which you want them to inherit. One of the advantages to distributing assets in this manner is that while the assets remain in the Trust prior to distribution, they are protected from creditors—a feature that may interest you if you have concerns about your heir's creditors or potential future divorce.

The successor Trustee must follow your Trust instructions.
Your successor Trustee (as well as your primary Trustee if it is not you) is a fiduciary—a legal term meaning that there is a legal duty to follow the Living Trust instructions and to act in a reasonably prudent manner. The Trustee must treat the Living Trust as a binding legal contract, and must use their "best efforts" to live up to the obligations of the contract. If your successor Trustee mismanages the Trust by ignoring the instructions in your Living Trust, they could be legally liable.

Tax Benefits Of The Living Trust

For many physician (and other wealthy) families, there is a financial blunder hidden in their estate plans. Many couples plan to provide for the surviving spouse by having the first spouse simply leave everything to the surviving spouse. Most Americans, in fact, don't know any other way to leave money to support the survivor. *This mistake may cause your family to pay hundreds of thousands of dollars in unnecessary estate taxes!* Advisors to affluent clients (like Doctors) always suggest the use of a tool that helps Doctors preserve their estate. This tool is the Living Trust. Because of reasons you will learn later in this chapter, the Living Trust is also referred to as an A-B Trust or A-B Living Trust. Those terms will be used interchangeably from here forward.

We will now discuss how you can take advantage of tax breaks afforded those who properly utilize the A-B Living Trust. The tax breaks are the Unified Tax Credit (UTC) and the Unlimited Marital Deduction (UMD).

UTC And UMD

To understand why you should not simply leave everything to your surviving spouse, you must first realize the two fundamental creatures of our estate tax system: the unified estate tax credit and the unlimited marital deduction.

The Unified Estate Tax Credit (UTC)

The UTC translates into a dollar amount which can be left by a decedent estate tax free (commonly called the "estate tax exemption"). As explained in the opening chapter of this Lesson, after the 2001 changes, this exemption grew to $1.5 million in 2004 and 2005, $2 million in years 2006 through 2008 and will rise to $3.5 million in 2009.

We often explain the UTC as a "get-out-of-estate-taxes-free" card, like in the board game Monopoly. Every one of us gets one of these cards to use either during our lives or at the time of our death. However, the card is non-transferable and, if not used at death, it is lost forever.

The unlimited marital deduction (UMD)

The UMD rule means that a decedent can leave an unlimited amount to a surviving spouse without any estate tax—provided both spouses are US citizens.

Unfortunately, when thinking about their estate plan, too many married couples look at the UMD as their solution. They simply leave everything to their spouse, using the UMD to avoid all estate taxes. While this effectively eliminates all estate taxes at the first death, it is a "penny-wise" and "pound-foolish" mistake. That's because the first spouse did not use his UTC, or "get-out-of-estate-taxes-free" card. Because he didn't use it, it is gone forever.

While this seems innocuous when the first spouse dies, the IRS gets you back when the second spouse dies. At that point, the surviving spouse's estate can only make use of one exemption. That means everything over the exemption amount will be subject to estate taxes—at a rate of up to 45%.

To illustrate this point, let's take a look at the case study of Tina and Ike.

Case Study: Tina & Ike

Tina and Ike owned a home with $500,000 of equity, have life insurance policies with combined death benefits of $2,000,000, had another $500,000 in a retirement plan, a business worth $500,000 and general investments totaling $500,000. They might not think of themselves as "wealthy," but to the federal estate tax authorities they are "estate taxable."

When Ike died in 2007 and left everything to Tina, there was no federal estate tax, because of the UMD. Tina inherited the entire estate and lived off of the earnings until she died the next year in 2008.

As per Tina's will, the entire estate went to her children when she died. In 2008, the children were not taxed on the first $2,000,000 worth of property they inherited from their mother because of the UTC. The children do, however, pay federal estate taxes on the amount in excess of $2,000,000, or in our example, $2,000,000. The tax rate maxes out in 2008 at 45%. This means the children will be paying almost $900,000 in federal estate taxes!

The terrible fact about the case of Tina and Ike's children is that the entire $900,000 of taxes could have been avoided easily. Moreover, Tina still would have been able to live on the earnings of what Ike left her during her last year. This could this have been achieved by implementing an A-B Living Trust.

Why Is It Called An A-B Living Trust?

The A-B Living Trust is a revocable, testamentary Trust that may also be referred to as a "loving" Trust, "family" Trust, "A-B" Trust or "Living Trust." The A-B Living Trust is the building block of estate planning as it helps maximize the exemptions and provide other benefits. When using an A-B Living Trust, the property is divided into two "buckets"—bucket "A" (or Trust A) and bucket "B" (or Trust B)—at the death of the first spouse. Most people transfer assets that are the equivalent of the UTC amount into bucket "B"—which ultimately passes to the heirs. The balance of the property is then transferred to "Trust A," which becomes the Trust for the surviving spouse. During his or her lifetime, the surviving spouse can be the full legal owner of Trust A. As Trustee, the surviving spouse can do virtually anything with the assets of the Trust. This Trust can be made completely revocable during the lifetime of the surviving spouse.

The concept of Trust B is different. The surviving spouse does not own Trust "B" technically. But he or she will have an ability to draw income or interest from the Trust; may be able to use the property (for example, live in the home); use the principal for health, education, maintenance and support; and typically use up to either 5% of the principal or $5,000 a year, whichever is greater, for any reason whatsoever.

After the death of the second (surviving) spouse, the Trust B assets directly pass to the heirs without any estate taxes. This is true even if the value of the assets has grown to equal more than the UTC amount.

Trust A, which belonged to the surviving spouse, will also be distributed to the named beneficiaries. First, all the debts and liabilities will be paid. Then depending on the year of the death, the wealth that is equivalent to the UTC amount will be transferred estate tax-free to the beneficiaries. If the value of the Trust A assets exceed the UTC amount, then that portion of the estate will be subject to estate taxes. After paying the federal and state estate taxes, the assets will be transferred to the heirs.

Case Study Revisited: Tina & Ike

Let's now assume that, during their lives, Tina and Ike hired an attorney to create a joint A-B Living Trust and they funded it properly. When Ike died, the Trust created the B Trust and funded it with the UTC amount in 2007, which was $2 million. During the rest of her life, Tina had access to the income and principal for her health, education, maintenance and support—nearly anything she needed. The remainder of the property—$2 million—funded the A Trust, which Tina could access and spend for whatever reason she wants. She could live in the home as well.

When Tina died in 2008, the B Trust paid out directly to the beneficiaries of that Trust—their kids. Because the B Trust qualified for Ike's UTC when it was funded, there is no estate tax on what is left in the Trust; regardless of whether it has grown past $2 million or been spent down to less than $2 million.

Any property left in the A Trust will qualify for Tina's UTC. Thus, if there is less than $2 million in this Trust when she died (and likely there is because she has been living on the interest and a portion of the principal of the $2 million), there would be no estate tax on this portion either. In this way, the A-B Living Trust would have saved Ike and Tina's family $900,000 in estate taxes.

The Diagnosis

Under our estate tax rules, any married couple whose total assets might put them above the estate tax exemption amount by the time they pass away (in 10, 20 or 30 years) should consider at a minimum an A-B Living Trust. Without such a Trust, one spouse is forfeiting his "get-out-of-estate-taxes-free" card for no good reason. The next chapter is going to explain a very common and significant mistake that many couples make. You will learn why a couple should **never** own any assets in their own names or jointly.

Joint Ownership & Disinheritance Risk

The most common way for married couples to own property is to own it jointly. Though this is very typical, it is very inappropriate for Doctors and their families. Not only does this form of titling assets leave your assets unprotected from lawsuits, but it also creates estate planning problems. By owning assets jointly, you can negate all of the work you may have done with your Living Trust. This is a serious problem to avoid if you want to build and preserve wealth. In this chapter, we will discuss the dangers of joint ownership.

The Dangers Of Joint Ownership

Joint ownership is the most popular form of ownership for Average Americans' real estate and bank accounts. This is not so for Doctors who know the risks and understand their options. With joint property, when one joint owner dies, property owned in joint ownership automatically passes to the surviving joint owner(s). In this way, jointly owned property passes outside of a Will and avoids the expense of probate. Though avoiding probate is important, joint ownership of assets can create additional problems.

Using joint ownership as an ownership form is almost always a big mistake. This is because joint ownership "overrides" Living Trusts and other estate planning. This ownership structure can render your hard work useless and ruin your estate plan. Let's examine how joint ownership can be harmful.

Joint ownership threatens your estate plan because any property you own jointly will pass automatically by right of survivorship to the surviving joint owner(s). In the eyes of the law, this automatic transfer takes effect the instant you die, before any Will or Living Trust can dispose of your property. In this way, your Will or Living Trust will have no effect on jointly held property. If you designated certain beneficiaries in a Will or Trust to receive your share of jointly held property, they will be "disinherited" and the surviving joint owner(s) will take title to the property. This avoidable tragedy occurs everyday because people do not realize the dangers of joint ownership and because their advisors are not giving them adequate information.

The Negative Side Effects Of Joint Ownership

To fully understand the negative consequences of joint ownership, consider these stories:

1. William, a man in his late 60s, marries for the second time. Shortly after the wedding, he puts all of his significant property—his home, his winter vacation condominium and his stock portfolio—into joint ownership with his new wife. Within six months, William dies. The home, the condo and the stocks all go to William's new wife. His three children and eight grandchildren inherit virtually nothing, even though William had made ample provisions for them in his Will.

2. Susan's Will bequeathed her property equally to her son and daughter. Because her son lives near her and he pays her bills, Susan put her house, her safe deposit box and her bank account in joint ownership with him. When she dies, Susan's son will get all of the money in the bank account and deposit box, as well as the house, regardless of the Will provisions. Unless the son is extremely generous, the daughter will get nothing. Do you want to rely on your children's generosity to carry out your estate plan?

3. Assume the same situation as in #2, but add to the facts that the son has serious creditor problems. Overdue on $15,000 in credit card debts and a defaulted loan, the son's creditors can come after the bank account, the safe deposit box contents and, likely, the house the moment Susan dies. The only real beneficiaries of Susan's estate may be banks and finance companies.

4. Becky, a single mother in her thirties, is trying to build a college fund for her ten-year old son, Dylan. Becky has invested some of her excess income to buy old residential multi-family homes, which she and her partner fix-up and rent to owners. While her relationship with her partner has been strained at times, Becky nevertheless takes title to the investment properties in joint ownership with her partner without realizing that, if she dies before they resell the properties, her partner will take them all and leave nothing for Dylan.

Many well-intentioned people get stuck in these predicaments because they do not know any better and their advisors are not doing their jobs. Sometimes, owners may not even realize what type of ownership they have chosen. In other cases, people consciously decide to use joint ownership because they know it will avoid probate. Avoidance of probate is never a reason to use joint ownership. If your goal is to avoid probate, use a Living Trust rather than joint ownership. You will get many more benefits without any of joint ownership's pitfalls.

The Diagnosis

Joint ownership is the most common way to title assets and it does offer a way to avoid probate. However, joint ownership can create significant asset protection and estate planning problems. After reading this chapter, you should now know the dangers of joint ownership and should see the value of using a Living Trust as an alternative. The next most common estate planning mistake results in the unnecessary wasting of 50% of life insurance proceeds. This problem, and various solutions to it, are explained in the next chapter.

Estate Planning
with Life Insurance Policies

Every Doctor's financial plan should include cash value life insurance because of its ability to leverage, tax-free growth and ability to access cash values tax-free. This was discussed in Lessons #6, #7 and #8.

This chapter is not going to discuss how the cash value of life insurance can be a tax-efficient wealth accumulation vehicle; as that was covered in Lesson #8. Rather, this chapter focuses on the death benefit proceeds of life insurance. Many Doctors maximize their investments in cash value insurance policies for tax-efficient wealth accumulation. For other Doctor clients, who are usually older, they often purchase second-to-die (or survivorship) insurance policies for the pure death benefit. That will be the focus of this chapter. We will call such policies "estate planning life policies" or "EPLPs".

Avoiding EPLP Pitfalls

Estate planning life policies (EPLPs) are life insurance policies that are purchased for the primary purpose of transferring wealth and creating liquidity for future generations. This is in sharp contrast to the purpose of the insurance policies that were discussed in Lessons #6, #7 and #8. The life insurance policies discussed in those chapters were created primarily for wealth accumulation, not estate planning, reasons.

For estate planning purposes, it is important to remove the EPLP proceeds from your taxable estate. The following are two popular "strategies" for removing the EPLP proceeds. Both have distinct drawbacks and pitfalls.

- **Having the spouse own the policy or be its beneficiary.** One popular method of sheltering EPLP proceeds from estate tax is to name your spouse as owner or beneficiary of the policy. This works so long as you purchased the policy with your separate property proceeds and the surviving spouse will spend down the policy proceeds before he or she dies. As you learned previously, the IRS is happy to see you pass everything to the surviving spouse so that you forfeit your "get-out-of estate-taxes-free" card (unified tax credit). This is because when the surviving spouse dies, the IRS gets a piece of everything above only one exemption amount rather than only the amount above two combined exemptions.

A second pitfall of this approach is that you lose all control of the proceeds when you die. The assets will pass to your surviving spouse outright. If he or she spends them down, gets re-married and divorced or gets sued, then your planning just benefited someone other than your family members. As you'll see below, you can control the funds, even after you're dead, and keep them in the family for generations by using a special life insurance Trust which dictates exactly how the funds can be used.

- **Having the children own the policy.** A different approach of removing EPLP proceeds is to have your children own your EPLP and indicate that they will receive the proceeds at your death. They can apply for the policy, pay the premiums (with money you may gift to them) and receive the proceeds at your death. If the policy and the proceeds are outside your estate, no estate tax will be due.

  However, there are some drawbacks with this strategy, such as:

  - If the EPLP proceeds are paid to children, your surviving spouse may run short of funds to pay bills and support himself or herself. This can be a very big problem in the situation of second or third marriages, as children may not agree to support a step-parent.

  - If the EPLP policy is a cash-value policy (typical in estate-planning situations because it is permanent insurance), your kids may be tempted to borrow against the policy, thus reducing the future death benefit.

  - If any of your children get divorced, the EPLP policy may be considered a marital or community property asset of your children. Some of the cash value could end up going to an ex-son-in-law or ex-daughter-in-law.

  - If your children are still minors, the policy would have to be owned by a custodian or a guardian.

The Irrevocable Life Insurance Trust

The wealthiest American families know that they can avoid many of the pitfalls discussed above by creating an Irrevocable Life Insurance Trust (ILIT) to be the owner and beneficiary of life insurance policies. As mentioned earlier, an ILIT is an Irrevocable Trust designed to purchase life insurance for the benefit of your children and grandchildren.

There are many benefits of having an ILIT. First, if the ILIT owns the policy, the policy is out of your taxable estate. Moreover, a properly structured ILIT can keep the proceeds from irresponsible children or their disgruntled spouses or creditors. The funds can then be used to pay estate taxes, provide an income stream, pay off debts, mortgages or notes and keep other valuable and needed assets intact for the family.

In many cases, the ILIT will use the insurance proceeds to buy illiquid assets, such as shares of a closely held business, real estate or other assets from your estate to keep them in the family. A purchase of this type is considered a tax-neutral exchange, so no tax will be due on the asset itself. Alternatively, the Trust can lend money to your estate, with the loan secured by the estate's assets. This is sometimes done to use the money to pay the estate taxes that are due on the other assets. Because estate taxes are due nine months after the date of death, this ability to have liquid cash available is crucial to avoid selling assets in a "fire" sale where the family may not get a reasonable price.

In either case, the estate will receive cash that can be used in a variety of ways. Later, the Trustee can distribute the assets to the Trust beneficiaries, the surviving spouse and children. This can be done in a lump sum or, if desirable, the assets can be maintained in Trust for their later benefit and use. If kept in Trust, these funds can be structured so that creditors of the surviving spouse, children, and even grandchildren will have no access to them—even in the case of potential lawsuits, bankruptcies and divorces. In this way, the ILIT can be an asset-protecting tool for many generations.

The bottom line is that all the insurance proceeds are available to help pay estate taxes and provide cash for whatever need might arise. Your family keeps control over the assets. No distress sale is necessary to raise money to meet the estate tax obligations.

Accessing Irrevocable Gifts: A Valuable Secret

Quite often a client will ask us if there is a way to use an ILIT to own life insurance and still have access to the policy's cash values during retirement. Though many advisors unfamiliar with planning for Doctors would say "No," our estate planning attorney colleagues around the country do this on a regular basis for clients.

Essentially, the only persons who could access the cash values during your life would be the ILIT beneficiaries. However, if the policy insures your life, then you cannot be the Trustee—or the beneficiary—of the ILIT. Thus, you personally could not have access to the cash values. However, if the policy insures only your life, then your spouse could have access to the cash values if she were a Trust beneficiary. Further, if the policy was on your joint lives (often called a "survivorship" or "2nd-to-die" policy), then your children or grandchildren could access the cash values to the extent they were Trust beneficiaries, or the Trustee could utilize cash values to benefit them. This could include paying their college tuition. There are also more advanced combinations of legal entities and insurance policies that combine trusts, irrevocable gifts, LLCs, loans and life insurance policies to allow Doctors to protect assets, manage estate planning challenges and offer access in retirement should the Doctor need it. Advanced strategies like these are outside the scope of this book, but can be included in your comprehensive financial plan.

The Diagnosis

Life insurance is a very important piece of any financial plan. How you own life insurance can have a very different impact on how that insurance will benefit you, your family or your business. It is very important that you work with your team of advisors to determine how to utilize an ILIT in your planning. Another way to own life insurance, and other assets, is in either an FLP or LLC. These tools will be discussed in the next chapter.

FLPs and LLCs as Estate Planning Tools

In Chapter 6-7, we explained how Doctors can use Family Limited Partnerships (FLPs) and Limited Liability Companies (LLCs) to shield assets from risks. In this chapter, you will learn how FLPs and LLCs—in addition to being excellent asset protectors and income tax reducers—are also superior estate planning tools. In this chapter, we will discuss the estate planning benefits and offer a couple of case studies to help illustrate the power of these tools within a Doctor's estate plan.

3 Estate Planning Benefits

A Family Limited Partnership or Limited Liability Company has at least three major benefits for estate planning. Let us examine each one separately:

- **LLC Assets Avoid Probate and Allow the Business to Continue.**
  Assets owned by your FLP/LLC do not go through probate. Only your interest in the FLP/LLC will. However, if you structure your LLC so your intended beneficiaries eventually own most of the FLP/LLC shares when you die, these beneficiaries will control the FLP/LLC and its assets before you die. Your beneficiaries can effectively control the FLP/LLC assets or business while the probate process continues its deliberation over distribution of your remaining membership interests. Because probate can last several years, this continued control can be crucial for operating a business or real estate interests.

- **FLPs/LLCs allow you to get property out of your estate WITHOUT giving up control.**
  Because your estate only pays taxes on property you own at death, a common tax-saving strategy is to gift your property away during your lifetime. The property passes to people you wish to inherit your assets at the time of your death and the government gets a smaller share. The main objection you might have to this type of planning is that you will have to give up control of the property while you are still alive. That's where the FLP/LLC adds additional value.

If the FLP/LLC owns the asset(s), and you are made the FLP general partner or LLC managing member, you get the best of both worlds. You can gift FLP/LLC interests to intended beneficiaries and remove the value of those interests from your estate, yet you still control the FLP/LLC and all if its assets while you are alive. Let's see how this works by referring to the case study of Stewart's Mutual Funds.

Case Study: Stewart's Mutual Funds

Stewart, a 63-year-old psychotherapist, owned almost $1.1 million in mutual funds. He set up an FLP to own the mutual funds, naming himself as the sole general partner. At the outset, he owned 2% of the FLP as general partner and 93% as limited partner, gifting 1% each to his five grandchildren. Since this 1% was worth approximately $11,000, the gifts to each grandchild were tax-free.

Stewart can continue to gift each grandchild $11,000 in FLP interests each year, completely tax-free. If Stewart lives to age 75, he will have given $660,000 worth of FLP interests to his grandchildren ($132,000 each), tax-free. This equates to 60% of the FLP.

This $660,000 will no longer be in his estate and not subject to estate tax. Moreover, any future growth of the gifted portion of the FLP will also be out of his estate.

Because Stewart's other assets put him in the 48% state and federal estate tax bracket, his tax savings using the FLP will be $316,800 (48% x $660,000). Because he is the FLP's sole general partner, Stewart retains control over the mutual fund investments while alive and can determine the amount of distributions. In this way, Stewart maintains significant control of his assets for his lifetime, pays less estate tax, and also provides more for his grandchildren.

Note that the FLP agreement and the gift structuring must be carefully crafted or Stewart's retained control could be grounds for the gifted FLP interests being brought back into his estate for tax purposes.

- FLPs/LLCs Lower Estate Taxes on Assets They Hold:
  You may not want to gift your entire FLP/LLC interests during your lifetime or you may start such a gifting program too late to "give away" much of your wealth. In either case, you will die owning FLP/LLC interests, which are then subject to the estate tax. The issue thus becomes what valuation the IRS will attach to your remaining FLP/LLC interests. It may not be:

  your % ownership of the FLP/LLC x fair market value of the FLP/LLC assets

This is because of powerful tax rules applying to FLPs and LLCs regarding valuation discounting.

Valuation Discounts With FLPs/LLCs

An important estate tax benefit of the FLP/LLC is that FLP/LLC interests often enjoy discounted values by the IRS. The IRS recognizes that owning a percentage ownership of an FLP/LLC that owns an asset, is generally worth less than owning the asset outright. If you own a $20 bill and hold it at death, then the IRS would assign an estate taxable value of that bill of $20. However, if you died owning a 20% interest in an LLC with four other family members, all with equal management rights, and the LLC owned $100, the IRS would allow a valuation of your 20% interest at a number well below $20! In case it is not obvious, let's explain why.

The IRS would first allow a *lack of marketability* discount to that interest, recognizing that your LLC interest is not really marketable so its value should be reduced for tax purposes. There is likely not much of a market for your 20% LLC interest when the other LLC members are all family members. Who would want to own part of an LLC worth $100 when the other owners are members of one family? What would an outsider pay for such an interest? This discount is available even if you retain all the management rights in the LLC.

Second, because you own less than 50% of the LLC, the IRS will also apply the *minority ownership* discount to your interest unless you have retained most or all of the management rights. Again, the IRS recognizes that there is very little market interest for shares of an LLC controlled by others.

Both of the aforementioned tax valuation discounts can be maximized by the proper drafting of the FLP/LLC agreement. Any provisions that restrict the transferability of any FLP/LLC interests will weigh toward a higher *lack of marketability* discount. Likewise, clauses that limit the control of minority interest-holders will substantiate greater *minority ownership* discounts. In this way, with proper drafting, FLPs and LLCs can often enjoy valuation discounts of *20% to 35% or more*. This can translate into an estate tax savings of millions of dollars for larger estates.

Case Study Revisited: Stewart's Mutual Funds

Assume that when Stewart dies, he still owns 40% of his FLP interests—having gifted 60% to his grandchildren during his lifetime. This 40% partnership interest, as part of his estate, is subject to estate taxes. Assume also that the mutual funds in his FLP have a value of $2 million when Stewart dies. His 40% interest in the FLP is then economically worth $800,000 (40% x $2 million).

For estate tax valuation purposes, however, the IRS may agree that Stewart's FLP interest is worth only around $500,000. The IRS will allow both the lack of marketability discount and the minority ownership discount. The lack of marketability discount exists because Stewart's five grandchildren own the other FLP interests, so non-family members would not be interested in buying his interest. Also, under the FLP agreement, the FLP interests are not freely transferable. The minority ownership discount may be applied because Stewart owns only 40% of the FLP when he dies, if he has gifted a majority of general as well as limited partnership interests. Even in this situation, he will retain de facto control if the other general partnership interests are split 12% to each grandchild—only one needs to side with him in a vote for him to control a majority!

These valuation discounts translate into an estate tax savings of about $144,000 ($300,000 x 48%). More important, he retains significant control over his funds while he is alive.

The Diagnosis

The FLP and LLC are tremendous planning tools. Earlier in the book, you learned how they can help Doctors reduce income taxes and protect valuable assets from lawsuits. In this chapter, you learned how they can afford you valuation gift Leverage and valuation discounts. After speaking to thousands of Doctors in our careers, it is hard for us to imagine how any Doctor's plan could be complete without at least one FLP or LLC. In most cases, multiple LLCs are used. If you review Lessons #6 and #7, you will see the other benefits that these tools offer.

Avoiding the 70% Tax Trap of Pensions and IRAs

In Chapter 7-7, we highlighted the fact that there is one type of asset that can generate a tax that can be as high as 70%—your tax qualified retirement plan. This results from a combination of income and estate taxes being applied to retirement plan balances at death. By leaving less than 30% of your retirement plan assets to your heirs, it will be very hard to achieve a high level of affluence for the future generations.

One of the "common sense" lessons you will hear repeated in the financial media is that you should contribute as much as you can to your qualified retirement plans (pensions, profit-sharing plans, IRAs, 401(k) plans, etc.). The conventional wisdom is that because you get an income tax deduction and tax-deferred growth, these plans are a huge tax win for the client. Generally speaking, this isn't bad advice as we have an entire Chapter (7-2) devoted to this topic.

However, for the most successful Doctors, this "conventional wisdom" could be terrible advice. Retirement plans are a potentially dangerous tax trap for three reasons:

1. It is likely that you will ultimately pay income taxes at the same or higher rates after using a retirement plan.

2. You may not need most (or all) of the funds in retirement.

3. Perhaps most damaging, any funds left in these plans at death will be decimated by taxes. Quite literally, these plans act as "traps," capturing huge sums of money that is eaten up at tax rates of 70% to 80% before your heirs get to enjoy any of it.

If you can accumulate more in your pension, profit-sharing plan, IRA, or other qualified plan than you will need during retirement (because you have other assets, an inheritance or die early), this chapter is a crucial one for your overall estate planning. In this chapter we will discuss how both unaware and very aware taxpayers can get caught in this tax trap as a result of circumstances that are both in and out of their control. This is what makes this trap so dangerous. Let's examine the three dangerous traps of retirement plans stated above.

Trap #1: You May Pay Tax At The Same— Or Higher—Tax Rates

A common misconception among Doctors and their families is that when they retire, they will be in a lower income tax bracket. Though this may be true for some, there are myriad reasons why this may not be true for you. One reason is that you may become accustomed to a certain quality of life that you don't wish to "scale back" when you retire. You didn't work hard in your career and as a parent so you could be put out to pasture and live on tomato soup and grilled cheese sandwiches. In fact, many retirees will increase their expenses and do the things they didn't have time to do when they were working 50, 60 or 70 hours per week. Most notably, the thing most Doctors will do is travel. Nonetheless, even if you do scale back your quality of life, you still may have to pay MORE in living and entertainment expenses because of inflation.

For example, just 15 years ago we used to go to the movies for $3-$5 and we could go see Red Sox play at Fenway Park for $34 (2 tickets at $17 per). Last week, we paid $12 per ticket to see a movie and the same Red Sox tickets in the Green Monster seats or on the right field roof are over $100...each!

Not only might your lifestyle, which you can control, increase your expenses (and taxes) in retirement but your plan itself might also contribute to increased taxes. The Internal Revenue Service has rules requiring what are called Required Minimum Distributions (RMDs) from retirement plan assets. This means you MUST start taking money out of your retirement plans at the age of 70½, whether you need the money or not. Of course, if you take the money out of the plan, you must pay income taxes on those withdrawals.

These RMDs can be quite high—bringing a higher tax burden with them as well. Typically, you invest your funds inside the retirement plan and those assets grow on a tax-deferred basis. This means you get greater accumulation than in a taxable account. A larger accumulation forces even higher RMDs. This can affect your tax bracket in retirement as well.

You may have other income producing assets like rental real estate, another business, limited partnerships, dividend-paying stocks, bonds and money market accounts. Each of these income-producing assets adds to your income, and increases your income tax bracket further.

Given the amount of invested assets inside and outside of retirement plans, and the continued long-term growth of the securities markets, many Doctors will enjoy retirement incomes which put them in the same tax bracket as they are in now. For example, we have a client named Frank, a 50-year old dermatologist with $500,000 in his profit-sharing plan. By the time he is in his late sixties and begins his planned retirement, assuming 9%-10% annual growth, the plan funds will likely grow to $3 million. If Frank withdraws only the interest from the plan from then on, without using any principal or other sources of income (like Social Security), then Frank and his wife will likely still be in the top tax bracket for the rest of their lives.

What this means is that, for the majority of Doctors, the value of the tax deduction and deferral are not as great as "conventional wisdom" would espouse. Clients like this have no tax arbitrage—that is, they simply get the deduction at one tax rate and then pay the tax in the future at the same rate. In fact, the plan may actually cause "reverse arbitrage" if future income tax rates in place when you take distributions exceed the rates in place when you deducted the original contribution. Recalling the chart we shared earlier with you in the Lesson on taxes, you will remember that tax rates now are at their 2nd lowest in the history of the U.S. income tax. Thus, such a "reverse arbitrage" is not unlikely. A *Wall Street Journal* columnist reviewed this comparison a few years ago, concluding that for many taxpayers qualified plans were a "fool's game" (April 15, 1999).

Trap #2: You May Not Need The Funds In Retirement

The second dangerous trap of retirement plans is that some people may not need the funds while they are in retirement. Because the amounts contributed to retirement plans are relatively small for high income Doctors, most will accumulate significant non-plan assets over their careers. If plan contributions are capped at $45,000 or less (in most cases), what happens to the rest of the after-tax earnings? Over a career, they end up in non-retirement plan brokerage accounts, ownership interests in closely-held businesses, rental real estate, precious metals or any number of other investments.

Given the compounded interest on your investments in the securities and real estate markets over 10-30 years, these non-plan investments can throw off significant income in retirement—so much so that the retirement plan assets are hardly needed. Though this is a problem we should all hope to have, it is a problem nevertheless and it needs to be addressed.

We see this problem with many of our Doctor clients, including, by way of example, our client Charlie, a 58 year-old plastic surgeon. Charlie contributed $20,000 to his pension for each of the last 25 years. Meanwhile, he and wife Margie have also amassed $1.2 million in other investment accounts. By the time Charlie retires, and he plans to do so at age 65, he should have enough in his brokerage accounts for a very comfortable retirement.

Charlie & Margie Won't Need Pension Funds to Retire

Clients:	Charlie & Margie
Ages:	Charlie 58; Margie 57
Average Pension Contribution:	$20,000 for 25 years
Non-Pension Investing:	$20,000 for 20 years
Present Pension Balance:	$2.2 million
Outside Investments:	$1.2 million
Planned Retirement Age:	65
Forecasted Pension Balance, Age 65:	$4.4 million (10% gross/year)
Forecasted Outside Investments, Age 65:	$2.3 million (8% post-tax/ year)
Post-Tax Earnings, Outside Investments, Age 65:	$184,000/year ($15,000+/mo.)
Post-Tax Amount Needed For Retirement:	$10,000 post-tax per month

As you can see from the above list, Charlie, who earned about $275,000 per year over the first 25 years of his practice, did not even maximize his pension contributions over that time ($30,000 per year was allowed). Instead, he chose to control some of his investments himself (about $20,000 per year) in a separate investment account. By the time he retires at age 65, Charlie will clearly have enough to fund his retirement (he and Margie need about $10,000 per month post-tax) just from his non-pension plan investments.

To be extremely conservative, let's advise Charlie and Margie to keep another $1.4 million of the pension funds secured for emergencies. That still leaves $3 million of the pension at age 65 that will continue to grow. Charlie and Margie think that this $3 million, plus most of this growth, will benefit their children and grandchildren as designated in their will and Trust. As you'll see below, they are really benefiting the IRS and state tax agencies-because over 70% of the funds will be eaten by taxes if they don't change their plan!

Trap #3: Most Remaining Funds Go To Taxes

The third trap of retirement plans is that any funds in the plan will be decimated by taxes if they are not used by the taxpayer and spouse during their lifetimes. Most Doctors are surprised that the vast majority of these funds end up with state and federal tax agencies. They are shocked to learn that after paying taxes for a lifetime of work, their "tax qualified" plan would be taxed at rates between 70% and 80%! Upon hearing these facts, most clients are shocked, appalled and want to learn how to do something about it. Let's take a look at how these taxes are levied and what you can do. The first thing you must learn is what "IRD" means.

Basics Of IRD

IRD means "income in respect of a decedent" (a deceased person). IRD is income which would have been taxable to the decedent had the decedent lived long enough to receive it. Whoever receives these items of IRD must report them as taxable income and pay any resulting income taxes in the year in which the items are actually received—generally, the year of death (spouses are entitled to defer IRD until payments are actually withdrawn).

The IRD is treated as ordinary income and is subject to income tax in addition to any federal estate taxes and state estate or inheritance taxes. Because federal and state income taxes (including those characterized as IRD) can reach up to 45% in many states, and estate tax is assessed between 45% and 55% (we will assume 46.5% here), assuming no additional state estate tax (an increasingly unlikely assumption). When you combine both taxes, you can see how quickly the combined tax rate escalates. Although the rules provide for a partial income tax deduction for estate taxes paid, the total tax on assets characterized as IRD assets can be over 70% in some cases.

What types of assets qualify for the dreaded IRD treatment? Income earned by a decedent but not yet paid, like bonuses or commissions, qualify as IRD. Once they are paid to the estate, they'll be hit with income taxes and estate taxes under the IRD rules. The most important asset hit by IRD? Retirement plans, such as pensions, 401(k)s and IRAs (to the extent contributions were originally tax deductible).

To see how IRD eats up a Retirement Plan, let's consider the case study of Jim.

Case Study: Jim

Jim is a widowed professor of medicine whose other assets exceed the current estate tax exemption. His IRA is fully taxable as it was funded entirely with tax-deductible contributions. (The same illustration could be made for a married couple but the estate tax wouldn't be due until the second spouse dies if he/she were the plan beneficiary due to the unlimited marital deduction).

Assuming Jim's fully-taxable IRA has a value of $1,000,000 at his death, Jim's estate (or heirs) would first pay $460,000 in estate taxes upon Jim's death, and then pay another $251,212 in state and federal income taxes (i.e., 45% of the remaining amount after giving a deduction for federal estate taxes paid). Thus, only $283,788 is left out of the IRA for Jim's beneficiaries—less than 29%! Over 70% of the funds—built over a lifetime of working and paying income taxes—were taken by the IRD tax system. Let's see how that happened (assuming Jim lived in a state with only a "sponge" estate tax prior to the state enacting its own estate tax):

Jim's IRA: IRD Eats Up Over 70%!!

IRA Value—IRD Item			$1,000,000
Less:			
Federal Estate Taxes (95% of 46.5%)	($441,750)		
State Estate Taxes (5% of 46.5%)	($23,250)		
Total Estate Taxes		($465,000)	
Balance in Estate			$535,000
Income in Respect to a Decedent	$1,000,000		
IRD Deduction	($441,750)		
Taxable IRD	$558,250		
Income Tax (45%)		($251,213)	
Amount for Beneficiaries		$283,787	
Total Taxes			$716,213
			(71.6%)

NOTE: In this example, we used a 46.5% total tax rate and assumed that the "sponge" state tax rules were in place. In some states, under 2008-2009 rules, the 46.5% would actually be too low, as would be the total 71.6% tax rate used here. To determine what the tax rate would be for you, feel free to contact us.

How To Avoid The Tax Trap

Judge Learned Hand observed that "Anyone may so arrange his affairs that his taxes shall be as low as possible; he is not bound to choose that pattern that will best pay the Treasury; there is not even a patriotic duty to increase one's taxes." For this reason, we all look for ways to reduce our taxes. So what can you do about the pension situation? The answer to that question depends on where you are in your retirement plan funding.

For all Average Americans and some Doctors, it still makes sense to maximize participation in qualified retirement plans, as they are excellent (+5) asset protection tools. In fact, this may be 100% true for your plan at this point. It may also make sense for you to fund some type of "after tax pension" as well.

The analysis depends on an accurate financial analysis of what your plan balance is and what you will need to spend in retirement. If, after such a financial analysis, it looks like you now have more in your retirement plans than you will need in retirement, then you should consider ending participation as soon as possible. Ideally, you want to amass just enough in retirement plans to cover retirement expenses and a "safety buffer."

What if you have already built up a large balance in a pension or IRA—and now realize that you won't need some or all of the funds in retirement—like our example of Charlie and Margie earlier? Unless you want 70% or more of these funds to go to state and federal taxes, you must do something… and the earlier you act, the better chance you have of avoiding this trap.

Essentially, you have three potential strategies for attempting to reduce the heavy tax burden on qualified plans:

- Stretch IRAs

- Liquidate and Leverage strategy

- Pension Insurance Purchase strategy

Strategy Option #1: Stretch IRAs

Recently, Stretch IRAs have been discussed as a viable tax-reduction option. Stretch IRAs lengthen the time over which distributions must be taken from retirement plans or rollover IRAs. They also allow you to leave the IRA to your heirs, who can then stretch out the distributions over their lifetimes and pay income taxes as they receive the funds. The common belief underlying this strategy is that "tax-deferred growth" is always a great idea. However, when you crunch the numbers, you will realize that the stretch IRA is generally a bad idea for anyone who will have an estate tax liability and it may be only a minor benefit to everyone else. There are at least two reasons why the Stretch IRAs is not beneficial:

1. Stretch IRAs completely ignore the estate tax problem

2. Stretch IRAs may create additional unnecessary taxes for your heirs

Let's consider both problems briefly.

Stretch IRAs Ignore The Estate Tax Problem

The Stretch IRA gives your heirs the benefit of deferring their withdrawals and deferring their income tax liabilities. It ignores estate taxes entirely. The IRS doesn't care that the children or grandchildren have not received the money. The total value of the IRA will still be included in the estate at the time of your death. This will force your heirs to pay estate taxes right away. To illustrate this point, let's look at the case study of Jeff.

Case Study: Jeff Leaves A Business And A Stretch IRA

Jeff listened to his advisor, who told him to create a Stretch IRA so he would avoid the 70% IRD problem at death. When Jeff passed away, his three children received his family restaurant and a Stretch IRA worth $800,000. The total estate tax bill was $700,000. His children didn't want to sell the restaurant, so they took the $700,000 out of the stretch IRA to pay the estate tax bill. The kids should be happy because they now have the business and an additional $100,000, right?

Wrong! The kids now owe income taxes on the $700,000 withdrawal (income taxes are never waived or avoided with a Stretch IRA). Their average state and federal income tax rates were 40%. Therefore, they owed $280,000 in income taxes because of their $700,000 withdrawal the year before. They used the last $100,000 from the IRA and took out a $180,000 loan against the business to pay the $280,000 tax bill. Then, they owed income taxes on the $100,000 withdrawal—another $40,000 to the IRS—and they owed another $15,000 of interest on the loan. This put them in the hole on another $55,000. Eventually the children had to sell the business to pay off their debts. Jeff's plan failed because he received bad advice from his financial advisor.

Stretch IRAs Could Cost Your Heirs More Taxes

The stretch IRA may generate more taxes to your heirs for three reasons:

1. **Your heirs may be in the same or higher tax bracket than you are by the time you die.** If you die in your seventies, eighties or nineties, your heirs will be in their prime earning years and will likely have another income to put them in that higher marginal tax bracket. You may be deferring 27% taxable income in lieu of 35% taxable income later.

2. **All withdrawals will be taxed as ordinary income when withdrawn from the plan by you or by your heirs.** The long-term capital gains rate of 15% doesn't apply to IRAs. If you'd taken the funds from the plan and paid the taxes earlier, you would have had the opportunity to invest in long-term investments, and you or

your heirs could possibly realize 15% tax on your gains—or no taxes at all if you received a step-up in basis at your death!

3. **You have no flexibility for intergenerational planning.** You can only invest in securities inside a Stretch IRA. You cannot buy life insurance. If you left the Stretch IRA to your children and they didn't need it and wanted to leave it for their children, they would have to let the income-taxable IRA appreciate. It would continue to be income and estate taxable until their children receive the money. If you paid the taxes and left the children after-tax dollars, the children could have invested in tax-free life insurance or a tax-free 529 plan for your grandchildren. You wouldn't be handcuffing them with a Stretch IRA.

In our opinion the Stretch IRA can be both shortsighted and penny-wise and pound-foolish. Of course, if you or your spouse is completely uninsurable, if your IRA is your only asset and if your estate definitely will not be worth over $1 million when you pass away, then the stretch IRA may make sense for you. If you don't meet all those conditions, you should seriously consider another alternative.

Strategy Option #2: Liquidate & Leverage

The "Liquidate and Leverage" ("L&L") strategy is much superior to the Stretch IRA. In fact, you can think of this strategy as allowing you to Leverage your IRA, 401(k) or pension, five to twenty-five times!

Assume that you and your spouse are 60 years old and have $1 million in your qualified plan. We will also assume that your financial advisory team analyzed your financial situation and found that you could support your quality of life in retirement (and allow for a substantial safety-net) by allocating your after tax investments and $400,000 of your qualified plan funds to this cause. This means that you won't need $600,000 of the funds, or the interest on those funds, in your retirement plan to support your retirement. In this case, more than 70 cents of every dollar in your plan will go to the government if you don't take action. Below, we will discuss a strategy that is very popular with high net worth clients and practically absent from most Doctors' financial plans. A technique known as Liquidate and Leverage can maximize lifetime income from a pension, minimize total taxes, Leverage the gift tax exclusions and maximize the total estate to junior generations.

The L&L Method: One Time Gift

The L&L strategy will ensure that your heirs not only get the full $600,000, but also an additional $2.9 million as well. Best of all, they will receive the $3.5 million tax-free! The L&L steps are as follows:

1. Take $600,000 out of the plan and pay the $240,000 in income taxes (assuming a tax rate of 40%). As we learned from Jim's case, this liquidation eliminates IRD and saves at least 6% of the $600,000, or $36,000.

2. Use a portion of your estate tax exemption amount and gift the remaining $360,000 to a properly drafted irrevocable life insurance Trust (ILIT).

3. The ILIT then purchases a second-to-die life insurance policy on you and your spouse. Depending on your age, health, net worth and other factors, that policy might be worth from $1.5 million to $3.5 million.

4. When you die, the insurance company pays up to $3.5 million, income tax free, to the ILIT. Then, all $3.5 million will be available to your heirs estate tax free as well.

If you consider that the $600,000 in your plan would have been worth less than $80,000 to your children and grandchildren (if you lived to age 80 and the funds grew at 8%), the L&L strategy left your heirs more than four times that amount—over $2.7 million more to your heirs after-taxes!

8% growth for 20 years = 4.66

4.66 x $600,000 = $2,796,000

After 72% tax, your heirs receive approximately $783,000

Wouldn't you rather leave your heirs $3.5 million than $783,000?

Alternative L&L Method: Guaranteed Income/Annual Gifts

Many Doctors don't like paying for insurance in one lump sum. Others already have life insurance policies that require annual premiums. Still others aren't sure how much of their retirement plans they need. They only know how much they need each month to pay their bills. For these people, the guaranteed income/annual gifts method of L&L is ideal. The guaranteed income/annual gifts method is a combination of three techniques. First, the retirement plan assets are used to purchase a life annuity. A life annuity will pay a monthly, quarterly or annual payment to the annuitant (you or your parents if you chose to purchase a life annuity on your parents) for as long as you live. This way, you never run out of money. Second, the annuitant will gift the after-tax proceeds from the life annuity to an ILIT for the benefit of the second or third generation. Third, the Trust will purchase a life insurance policy on the annuitants (usually you and your spouse—or your parents in that application). To illustrate this point, let's consider the case study of Marian.

Case Study: Marian's Guaranteed Income Allows Gifting

Marian, a 78-year old woman, has $800,000 in retirement plan assets. By purchasing a life annuity with the $800,000, she receives a guaranteed monthly income of $8,600. After-taxes, Marian still has $5,400 per month. Because she has some income from her municipal bonds—which are outside her retirement plan—and additional income from Social Security—she only needs $2,000 of the retirement plan income to pay her family's bills and to fund the college savings plans she created for her grandchildren. This leaves Marian with $3,400 per month of excess income. She gives this $3,400 per month to an ILIT, which pays for a $1 million life insurance policy that is guaranteed to Marian's 115th birthday!

By using the steps, Marian took $800,000 of potentially 70% taxable money and turned it into guaranteed supplemental income for her and a $1 million inheritance for her son and grandchildren.

Strategy Option #3: Pension Insurance Purchase

The IRS and ERISA allow for certain types of retirement plans to purchase life insurance within the plan with pretax dollars. Typically, we use profit-sharing plans here because the rules are most generous for these types of plans. Thus, for clients with roll-over IRAs, they will have to roll the IRA back into a properly-drafted profit-sharing plan (PSP) before being able to take advantage of this strategy.

From this point forward, let's consider that you have a retirement plan that you don't expect to completely empty before you die. What can you do? You can purchase life insurance on yourself inside your retirement plan. When you die, the insurance company will pay a death benefit to your retirement plan.

While some Doctors will argue that life insurance is not a good investment in their plan—consider two factors: (1) as noted elsewhere in the book, the policies can reflect almost any underlying investment you want—tied to a money manager you select (PPLI), mutual funds you choose (variable policy) or even a market index (S&P 500); (2) you MUST consider the tax consequences of the investment. Here, when considering IRD, life insurance will almost always outperform mutual funds.

Mutual Funds vs. Life Insurance— Another Surprise Upset Winner

Let's assume that you could invest $500,000 into mutual funds inside your retirement plan. After 20 years, assuming a 7% return on your mutual funds, you would have approximately $2,000,000 in your retirement plan. If you died at that point, your spouse would have access to the funds—but would have to pay income taxes on any withdrawals. If you assume a combined state and federal tax rate of 40%, the $2,000,000 pension is worth $1,200,000 to your spouse. Then, if you children wanted the funds, there might be estate taxes to pay.

If you invested the same $500,000 into a $1.8 million life insurance policy, you might think you would be at a disadvantage for investing in the mutual funds. You would be wrong! At the end of 20 years, after paying for mortality costs and administrative expense of the life insurance policy, your policy would have $600,000 of cash value at the time of your passing. When the $1,800,000 death benefit paid to the pension, only $600,000 of the benefit was income taxable to the spouse. $240,000 was due to the IRS and the remaining $1,560,000 went to the spouse tax-free! That is 30% more money to the survivor from the life insurance policy (as compared to mutual funds). The same estate tax rates would apply, but 30% more money escaped the pension...and the taxes associated with it. This is not an aggressive strategy any more than buying a home for the tax-deductible mortgage interest is. It is a benefit that is clearly spelled out in the Internal Revenue Code. It is simple, but very few people take advantage of it.

The Diagnosis

Retirement plans certainly have their appropriate place in planning for Doctors and their employees. Chapter 7-2 explains many of these. However, if you have a sizeable pension balance, you should be concerned that your heirs may unnecessarily have to pay the 70% tax on IRD. What you can do is work with your advisory team members who are familiar with pension law, life insurance and estate taxes and ask them to help you with your planning. There is one other significant threat to your retirement assets. Unlike IRD, this threat raises its ugly head while you are still alive. It is the increasing cost of long-term care. This is addressed in the next chapter.

Protection From Rising Medical Costs

It may seem like medical costs are a lifetime issue and estate planning is a death issue. Doctors should be familiar with the soaring costs of medical procedures and nursing home care and how they may wipe out retirement funds AND decimate an inheritance for a future generation. This is why there is a chapter on long-term care in the estate planning section. Doctors need to realize the folly of relying on the government to provide for their medical coverage and their comfortable retirement. Doctors need to recognize the role that Long-term Care Insurance ("LTCI") must play in their financial and estate plan.

Long-term care is considered a type of health insurance because it pays for a variety of health costs that may or may not be covered by Social Security, Medicare or your state plan. The details of long-term care insurance and our recommendations on what to look for in an LTCI contract are covered in Chapter 4-3. Chapter 7-4 offers a discussion of the income tax benefits of LTCI planning. The purpose of this brief chapter is to explain why LTCI is an important part of any estate plan. By reading *For Doctors Only*, you will gain a full understanding of how LTCI will help you and your family in many areas—including protecting an inheritance from rising medical costs.

If you met with your advisors to discuss your estate plan under EGTRRA, you probably didn't count on having to pay $100-$300 per day for nursing home or in-home care. You also probably didn't factor in medical expense inflation rates of 5%-10% per year that could make a very mediocre $100/day nursing home in year 2000 dollars cost over $500 per day in 2020. If you need long-term care for just one year, it could use up $182,500 of funds that you had hoped would go to your children, grandchildren, or other beneficiaries.

Do You Need LTCI?

According to the Center for Long-Term Care Financing, Americans face approximately a one-in-ten chance of spending at least five or more years in a nursing home after age 65. 48.6% of people age 65 and older may spend time in a nursing home. More startling is that 71.8% of people over age 65 may use some form of *home-health care!* Do you think the developments in medicine will help or hurt this situation?

The longer people live (as a result of medical advancements) the greater the likelihood that people will eventually need some significant medical assistance on a long-term basis. We may find treatments for cancer or osteoporosis, but that just increases the likelihood of eventually having Alzheimer's or some other debilitating disease that forces us to require significant, and very costly, care.

The table below lists some costs, by city, for nursing home care as compiled by the MetLife Assisted Living Market Survey 2007:

The Average Annual Cost of Nursing Home Care

Anchorage, AK	$186,150	Omaha, NE	$73,000
Phoenix, AZ	$71,905	Las Vegas, NV	$73,000
Los Angeles, CA	$78,475	New York, NY	$128,480
San Diego, CA	$86,870	Cleveland, OH	$74,825
San Francisco, CA	$135,415	Portland, OR	$78,110
Stamford, CT	$135,780	Philadelphia, PA	$85,045
Miami, FL	$77,015	Providence, RI	$84,315
Honolulu, HI	$98,915	Nashville, TN	$70,810
Boise, ID	$73,000	Dallas, TX	$60,955
Chicago, IL	$57,305	Houston, TX	$61,685
Boston, MA	$108,405	Alexandria, VA	$94,900
Baltimore, MD	$78,840	Rutland, VT	$86,140
Detroit, MI	$60,955	Seattle, WA	$93,805
St. Paul, MN	$76,650	Milwaukee, WI	$85,410
St. Louis, MO	$57,305		

Source: Met Life Website

Nursing home care costs in most cities in the table above fall between $5,000 and $8,000 per month. Some are as inexpensive as $4,000 per month and some can be over $10,000 per month. Is there any reason to believe that nursing home care will become less expensive? Are you wiling to risk losing this much of your estate to nursing home costs or would you like to plan ahead?

The important point to take from this chapter is that you will most likely eventually pay for long-term care coverage. The question is: "Will it be paid for in advance or will it be paid for from your intended inheritance or retirement funds?"

You may wonder "Doesn't the state or Medicare pay these expenses?" The answer is "Yes... *and* No." The State of California for instance will not pay for a senior's medical bills until that individual has depleted all but $2,000 of his or her net worth. That means that if a retirement plan or any investments are titled in an individual's name, or have been titled in the individual's name in the last 30 months, the state will require those assets to be sold to pay for medical costs. In addition, income units may disqualify you from receiving any benefit. And if your income is below the limit, they will then take all but $30 per month of your income to pay them for your long-term care coverage.

It isn't hard to see how this could deplete someone's assets immediately. You are likely willing to buy insurance, create a Living Trust and consider other estate planning strategies. Ignoring long-term care planning could be a potentially devastating mistake. Let's plan not to make that mistake.

If you intend to leave an inheritance, then you may wish to purchase long-term care insurance now, while you have the money. You can purchase an LTCI policy in one year, over 10 years, over 20 years or make payments every year for the rest of your life. You also have options to have all of your premiums go to your heirs at death even if you collect on the policy during your life. In fact, there are policies on the market today which combine a universal life insurance guaranteed death benefit for your heirs with a guaranteed daily benefit for long-term care costs. This can be an ideal tool to achieve two planning goals.

Do Pride and Dignity Matter To You?

One of the most difficult emotional challenges for any family involves the caring for older relatives who are not able to take care of themselves. We know many of you have already seen your parents deal with this with your grandparents and many of you have already dealt with this concern with your own parents and in-laws. By purchasing long-term care insurance, you are shifting the financial risk to someone outside your family—the insurance company.

When someone else is paying the bills for this home health coverage, there is never a financial reason to have to send a relative to a nursing home. Further, the insurance could pay for in-home care for the rest of your life. This way, the family avoids horrible fights and you won't ever be put into a nursing home or have to ask your children or grandchildren for financial assistance to stay out of a nursing home. For many Doctors, this is reason enough to purchase long-term care insurance.

The Diagnosis

Rising medical costs can be a significant cost for any retiree. If planning is not implemented in advance, these costs can wipe out retirement funds and any inheritance that would have otherwise gone to your heirs. This devastating financial situation can also force you (or other relatives) into a nursing home unnecessarily. By purchasing LTCI, you are making sure that soaring medical costs don't take away the head start you wanted to leave your children or grandchildren or destroy the legacy you wanted to leave behind. LTCI can also support you so you never have to be "put" into a nursing home. For these reasons, LTCI should be an important part of the multi-disciplinary financial plan for every Doctor.

Of course, if you aren't interested in leaving an inheritance to your heirs, you need not sit back and let medical costs and taxes take your money. You can implement charitable planning that will leave your estate to a deserving cause and give you tax benefits while you are alive. This is the focus of the next chapter.

Charitable Estate Planning

Doctors spend their entire careers contributing to others. Many Doctors continue their altruistic ways later in life and want to give back to the world that provided them with their success. What many Doctors don't know is how to take this charitable intent and use it to create as much benefit to their family while benefiting a charity at the same time. In this chapter, we will briefly examine only one tool often used in charitable estate planning—the Charitable Remainder Trust (CRT). Because charitable planning is such a vast topic, we can only hope to give you a tiny hint of the types of planning we implement for our clients.

> "To give away money is an easy matter and in any man's power, but to decide
> to whom to give it, and how large and when, and for what purpose and how,
> is neither in every man's power nor an easy matter"—*Aristotle*

Rather than ramble on about a series of planning options, we think it best to be succinct and show the power of charitable planning through the story of Steve and Martha.

Steve, a 56-year old man, is an orthopedic surgeon and his wife Martha, age 48, is an OB/GYN. They have two boys in college. As a result of prudent investing, good luck and great investments in some start-up businesses, Steve is considering early retirement so he can travel and enjoy his hobbies of flying and sailing.

In addition to his significant retirement plan account, Steve has $3 million in essentially zero basis stock in his friend's company (that he helped finance in return for stock) that recently went public. He is in line with qualified stock options to acquire an additional $5 million over the next three years. Faced with planning for the disposition of an estate of $10 million (almost all of it in an undiversified portfolio), Steve and Martha decided that they'd like part of their financial plan to include a plan to eliminate estate taxes, if possible. In short, they're willing to give to charity those assets that would otherwise default to the IRS in the form of estate and capital gains taxes.

As a part of this strategy, they will also make aggressive gifts of stock to their two sons and other family heirs over the next few years, through family limited partnerships. By freezing estate growth and squeezing the value of the assets, we hope to be able to eliminate all unnecessary estate taxes. Additionally, our plan will provide an excellent retirement income stream through the use of a CRT.

Examine the following carefully as we compare selling a highly appreciated asset, paying taxes and living off the interest versus contributing the asset to a CRT, selling the asset and living off the annuity from the CRT. We will refer to this chart throughout the chapter to illustrate a number of points.

Steve and Martha Use a CRT to Benefit Charity & Their Family

	Sell	CRT
NNet fair market value (FMV)	$3,000,000	$3,000,000
Taxable gain on sale	$3,000,000	
Capital gains tax (20%) at federal level	$600,000	
Net amount invested	$2,400,000	$3,000,000
Annual return of reinvested portfolio	10%	10%
Reinvested for 10% annual income produces annual retirement income of	$240,000	
Trust payout of 5% (averaged with 10% returns over Trust term of 40 years)		$452,999
Annual average after-tax income (@ 39% tax and 20% capital gains rate for CRT payout)	$146,400	$321,622
Years—projected joint life expectancy	40	40
Taxes saved w/ $616,290 deduction @ 39%		$240,358
Tax savings and cash flow over 40 years	$5,856,000	$13,105,233
Total increase in cash flow	$5,856,000	$13,105,233
Total value of asset in estate in 40 years	$2,400,000	$0
Estate taxes on this asset at 48%	$1,152,000	
Net value to family	$1,080,000	
Total insurance expense—wealth replacement	$0	($530,000)
Insurance benefit in wealth replacement Trust	$0	$3,000,000
CRT remainder value to family charity	$0	$20,415,967

What is happening here? The stock that Steve owns is publicly traded, so its value is readily ascertained and is easily transferable to the Family Charitable Trust. This CRT will take the highly appreciated stock and sell it without being taxed on its sale. It will then reposition the proceeds into a more balanced portfolio of equities designed for both growth and security.

The CRT, with Steve as co-Trustee, will buy and hold stocks and mutual fund shares so that most of the portfolio will continue to appreciate while Steve and Martha, as income beneficiaries, receive quarterly payments of 5% of the Trust's value every year. They've made the decision that leaving each son with a $5 million inheritance is part of their family's financial goals, so with some stock and life insurance held in an ILIT, the two boys will be well protected for the future.

Everything else in their estate will either be spent during retirement or left to their favorite charity when they pass away. After examining the numbers, Steve and Martha felt that it made great sense to re-exert control over their social capital and follow through with their plan. Because Steve felt a need to sell in order to diversify his unbalanced portfolio, the only comparison to be made was between: (1) selling, paying tax, and reinvesting the net proceeds; and (2) contributing the stock and reinvesting inside the CRT. We have made such a comparison in the "Sell" and "CRT" columns.

You can see that the benefit to their family of the CRT is significant. Steve and Martha will enjoy $118,000 in additional annual retirement income in the CRT scenario ($264,000 post-tax versus $146,000 post-tax). Over their joint life expectancy, this difference will amount to over $5 million!

Furthermore, because of the use of life insurance in an ILIT (also known as a "wealth re-placement Trust"), their kids will get more out of that asset than in the "sale" scenario ($3 million of insurance proceeds income and estate tax-free vs. a $2.4 million asset netting $1.08 million to the family after estate taxes).

By combining a charitable remainder Trust with a wealth replacement Trust for their heirs, Steve and Martha were able to enjoy a greater retirement income than they had anticipated and leave a substantial legacy to their children (of which they have to pay no estate taxes). As if that were not enough, they were able to leave over $21 million to charity. This is quite an accomplishment, yet is feasible with the right financial planning and advisors.

The Diagnosis

Although you may not have the wealth of a famous American family like the Rockefellers or Kennedys, you may still be able to benefit from charitable planning. Once you have protected your family wealth from lawsuits, taxes and estate taxes, you have put your family in a better position. Now, the most important thing to do is to analyze your situation with the help of your advisory team. Work with your team of advisors to see how this tool may help you. The last Lesson of the book—Take the Prescribed Medicine—will help you outline the necessary steps for you to start addressing your issues and realizing the benefits that can be achieved from implementing the strategies in *For Doctors Only*.

Take the Prescribed Medicine

Everyone wants to be rich, but only a very small minority of Doctors will become Super-Affluent (defined as having a net worth of $10 million+). Why is this? There are countless ways to fail, but only one way to achieve financial success—that is to efficiently leverage your assets, effort, and time while avoiding financial catastrophes. In this book, we sought to provide the financial secrets Doctors need to know so they can work less and build more in this very difficult time of increased risk and reduced reimbursements. *For Doctors Only* shares the steps to success, explains how to work with advisors and points out how to address most financial planning needs. Despite this guidance, most readers still won't follow them. Do not be one of them!

Every year, thousands of Doctors spend hard-earned money and valuable time attending our seminars, hoping to learn important financial and legal lessons. Over 90% of the response forms we receive from attendees acknowledge that the information is valuable and that the attendees plan to take immediate action to improve their financial situation. However, when we check in with attendees months, or years, later, we find out that fewer than 10% actually make a serious improvement.

We'll assume that you will be a member of the 10% who will actually take the necessary actions to reach your financial goals. Since you want to achieve desired levels of wealth and we want to help you do so, we would like to show you what you have to do to start the process and successfully continue it throughout your life. If you follow these steps, you can be sure to build your fortune and protect your assets. The steps are:

Step 1—Accept That You Have A Problem You Can't Handle Alone

Step 2—Hire the Right Team

Step 3—Pay Advisors to Help You Develop the Plan

Step 4—Implement the Plan

Step 5—Monitor the Plan

Step 6—Review the Plan (At Least) Annually

Step 7—Question Advisors and Planning Decisions

Step 8—Be Willing to Make Changes to the Plan or the Advisory Team.

There is an old saying, **"Plan to Succeed or Prepare to Fail."** We can't stress this strongly enough. If you follow these eight steps, you will be on your way to building a fortune and protecting assets just like the Savvy Affluent do.

Step #1: Accept That You Have A Problem You Can't Handle Alone

With apologies to all 12-step participants, we can't think of better way to make this point without borrowing a familiar philosophy. The building of wealth and protection of assets is a complicated process that requires expertise in the areas of:

- Accounting

- Asset protection

- Benefits planning

- Business structuring

- Buy-out planning

- Estate planning

- Insurance planning

- Investments

- Tax planning

- And others

You can't continue to be an expert in your career and become an expert in all the areas where you need financial planning assistance. To expect to do all of this alone is akin to expecting a pediatrician to become in expert in other fields of medicine as a patient ages and develops new medical concerns. This leads to the next step.

Step #2: Hire The Right Team

Once you realize that you need help with your financial planning, you have to find the professionals who have the expertise and experience to help you. Don't let the brevity of the description of this step fool you. This is a very important step in your quest for financial success. The choice of members for your team of advisors is as important to your long-term financial success as the choice of a spouse is to your emotional security. Some might say the advisory team is even more important because many financial mistakes are irreversible.

Step #3: Pay Advisors To Help You Develop The Plan

A scalpel in the hands of a physician is a tool that can save a life. The same scalpel in the hands of a mugger can take a life. How you utilize your advisors can be the difference between the life and death of your financial stability. Once you have the right team of advisors to help you, you have to make sure you utilize their skills and talents properly. The best way to get the most out of your relationship with your advisors is to pay them to give you their unbiased analysis and recommendations.

Even if your advisors also provide other services or can be paid from the sale of products, they can still be valuable members of your team. By offering to pay them what their time is worth to work with you, they will be able to give you honest advice without an ulterior motive to sell you anything. Doctors should pay advisors to create a plan and then pay these advisors to meet as a group at least once each year to review the situation and provide additional recommendations.

Step #4: Implement The Plan

Implementing the financial plan may seem like a silly step, but you would be surprised how many people pay for plans to be created only to put the plan on the shelf and let it collect dust. Like an X-ray, MRI or any diagnostic medical analysis, the financial plan is a document which analyzes the present state of affairs. Like a Doctor's diagnosis and treatment plan, the financial plan also serves as a series of recommendations and action items. It seems foolish to go through the cost and effort of getting a plan done, only to ignore the analysis and recommendations. Yet, we see this lack of implementation from numerous clients each year.

Another common mistake in implementing the financial plan is something we call "the unanimous position dilemma." Some clients won't implement a piece of the plan until they run it by every member of the team and get 100% agreement. Other clients need more—including approval from family, friends, the guy at the health club, the butcher and whoever else will listen. Doctors must hire the right team to work together for them. If there is a discrepancy among the team on a certain plan element, the advisors should get as educated as possible and attempt to evaluate the merits of each side. The client may choose to move forward on that element or not, but Doctors need not ask non-expert friends and family for their input, especially when these people are in completely different financial situations. Also, Doctors should not let disagreement among team members on one action item prevent them from implementing other items. Typically, there will be at least 5 to 10 action items within the financial plan so a stalemate on one item shouldn't cause a slow down with the other elements of the plan.

Step #5: Monitor The Plan

Step #5 could also be called "communication and monitoring of the plan." Just as the client's active involvement is important in the initial plan creation and implementation, so too is it for the plan monitoring. The crucial role here for the client is communication, especially with the advisor "quarterback" firm—who typically drafted the plan in the first place.

The advisors on your team can't do their jobs if they don't know what everyone else is doing. Doctors also need to realize that they are too busy to keep everyone abreast of each nuance of the plan. If advisors have to track down data from you or from the other advisors, there is going to be a significant cost for all of this duplication of effort. That is why the quarterback advisor is so helpful in monitoring the plan. The quarterback can coordinate the other advisors and get them the information they need to properly play their roles.

Technology Can Help

Modern software products can be helpful. Two years ago, in fact, a new client of ours showed us an online tool that tracked all investments daily, kept secure online-accessible scanned copies of every legal document and insurance policy statement, and had tools for the advisors to use to run scenarios for the client under different circumstances and leave them online for every advisor to see. It was such an impressive tool that we went out and bought a license to use it ourselves. Every client of ours who has used this service always has the same reply after it has been in place for a few months—"How did we ever manage without this?" We call this the "ATM" or "cell phone" response!

Step #6: Review the Plan

Doctors rely on peer review as an important element of the practice of medicine. This same philosophy can, and should, apply to financial planning for physicians. Doctors need to have at least one full-day meeting or multiple day retreat with their advisors each year. During these meetings the advisors will review the plan. The reason for the meetings is to force the advisors to be in the same room where they don't have the distractions of their offices. By paying the advisors to be there for you, they will focus solely on your needs and concerns and have time to brainstorm with you on future planning. This is a benefit you would never get from any number of conference calls.

Although you may not be able to attend multi-day retreats to Hawaii or fly fishing in Wyoming, as many of our clients do, you can certainly afford a 3-4 hour meeting with all of your advisors each year. This meeting should be distraction free and should be guided by an agenda developed in advance by the quarterback advisor and you.

Step #7: Question Advisors And Planning Suggestions

Doctors should understand that they can trust their advisors and still ask questions about the existing and suggested planning. Most advisors who work with affluent clients respect the intelligence of their clients and want their input. This is not a universal feeling, but we prefer working with clients who take the time to understand as much of the planning as possible. You should also encourage your other advisors to question the other members of the group. You don't want a fight over every issue, but you do want your team to discuss pros and cons of every possible alternative in an effort to find the best decisions for you. This is especially important on elements of the plan where there are significant arguments on both sides of the proposed action step.

To review the planning process that Jason, Chris and David's firm has created, please visit www.ojmgroup.com.

Step #8: Don't Be Afraid To Make Changes To The Plan Or To The Advisory Team

Over time, a family's circumstances change. Often these changes can be very significant. These changing circumstances may dictate significant changes to the plan and its implementation. Of course, if there is an open line of communication between the client and quarterback advisor and the team of advisors who participate in periodic plan reviews, these changes will not take anyone by surprise. Nonetheless, it is important to be flexible enough to re-examine the plan assumptions when there are significant changes like a divorce, the closing of a practice or others and be open to making changes to the implementation strategy as well.

As for the advisors on your team, they are not life appointees. Earlier in the book, we emphasized the importance of getting second opinions. This is particularly important when you have been with certain advisors for a long time and haven't looked for additional input from outside experts. We also explained why the "if it ain't broke, don't fix it" mentality can be very costly to your planning.

Sometimes, your team requires advisors with different fields of expertise. Other times the interaction of a group is hurt by certain persons or personalities. In these instances, it may be best for you to ask an advisor to leave the team. Actually, since it is your money, you can think of it as "firing" the advisor because you don't need the advisor to agree with your decision. Just because someone has worked with you for a while is not a sufficient reason to keep that advisor on your team if you are not getting good advice or if you might be better served by a new advisor whose expertise or personality may be a better fit under your new circumstances.

Next Steps

We admit to making the planning process seem pretty easy in the last few pages. Practically speaking, there will always be roadblocks. The biggest one you will face is "Time." There will never seem to be enough hours in the day to do what you want to do and there will always be other things that appear to need to be done right away. The only way that you will ever overcome this roadblock will be to make the planning process a priority for you, your family, your business partners and your advisors. Once you make your planning a priority, you can start to approach the steps to implement the proper planning.

Of course, planning for your long term, sustained financial success requires a great deal of effort and commitment of your time. This process will cost you money. This process will not be without a certain amount of frustration and aggravation. This is normal. You are trying to change the way you have behaved for years. As such, the most important Lesson to help you achieve your desired level of wealth is to understand that anything worth having is worth the effort.

Once you find the right team, get it up and running and work through the initial bugs in developing your team process, your financial life will get easier every year. This is another little "secret" that has helped many Doctors maintain their wealth and protect their assets through multiple generations.

The Final Diagnosis—Words of Encouragement

Changing your philosophy and planning process to incorporate the lessons in *For Doctors Only* may seem overwhelming. There are many different steps to be taken within each of the ten Lessons. On top of that, this book includes only a partial list of the potential strategies that you could utilize to achieve your desired level of wealth. Practically speaking, there is no way one person could handle the challenge of planning alone. There is no way to do all of this planning without the help of a team of advisors. This is why the most important thing you can do is find the right team to work with you.

Once you hire the team, you have to make the time and devote the effort to work through the steps in this chapter. If it seems like a lot to do, you should understand that every wealthy family began as an average family until one person saw greater opportunities to leverage the family's wealth. If you dedicate yourself to the process in this Lesson, you can be that person for your family.

We wish you the success and affluence you desire. If you are having a tough time getting started or need a little help bringing your plan to the next level, please feel free to contact OJM via email at odell@ojmgroup.com or mandell@ojmgroup.com or via phone at 1-877-656-4362. We always enjoy hearing from our readers and we would be honored to help you achieve your goal of working less and building more wealth so you can achieve your ultimate goal of leading a more enjoyable life. We can set up a meeting with one of the authors who has offices that are most convenient to you.

Appendices

OTHER BOOKS BY THE AUTHORS OF FOR DOCTORS ONLY
Please visit www.ojmgroup.com to order or download your copy

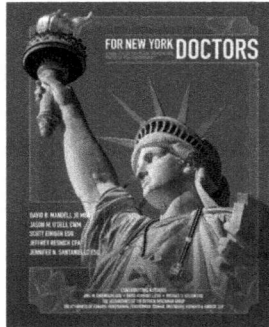

For New York Doctors: A Guide to Asset Protection, Tax Reduction, Practice & Wealth Management teaches doctors the important lessons they never learned in medical school, residency or fellowship. Doctors will learn how to efficiently leverage their time, money and effort so they can get more out of a medical practice. More specifically, doctors learn how to protect their personal and practice assets from lawsuits, state-specific taxes and bad investments in addition to learning the secrets to building wealth and avoiding catastrophic financial disasters so they get the most out of their practice and leave the most for their heirs. *For New York Doctors* is a MUST HAVE for any New York doctor wishing to achieve financial success.

For Georgia Doctors: Fresh Ideas on Asset Protection, Practice Planning, Wealth Accumulation and Estate Planning teaches doctors how to handle the unique challenges of practicing medicine in Georgia so they will get more out of their medical practice and personal finances. Reduced reimbursements, higher taxes, and significant liability risk make it imperative that Georgia doctors work "on their practice" not just "in their practice" if they want to achieve any reasonable level of financial security. *For Georgia Doctors* is a MUST HAVE for any Georgia doctor wishing to achieve financial success.

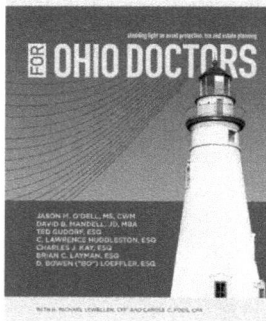

For Ohio Doctors: Shedding Light on Asset Protection, Tax and Estate Planning teaches doctors how to handle the unique challenges of practicing medicine in Ohio so they will get more out of their medical practice and personal finances. Reduced reimbursements, higher axes, and significant liability risk make it imperative that Ohio doctors work "on their practice" not just "in their practice" if they want to achieve any reasonable level of financial security. *For Ohio Doctors* is a MUST HAVE for any Ohio doctor wishing to achieve financial success.

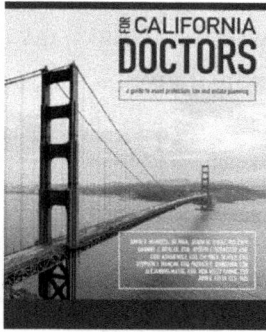

For California Doctors: A Guide to Asset Protection, Tax and Estate Planning teaches doctors how to efficiently practice so they can get more out of a medical practice. More specifically, *For California Doctors* will help doctors protect their personal and practice assets from lawsuits, taxes and bad investments while showing them the secrets to building wealth through the leverage of people, assets and effort. *For California Doctors* is a MUST HAVE for any California doctor wishing to achieve financial success. Get a copy now!

Written by OJM principals and well-known Orthopaedic surgeon Dr. Peter J. Millett, of the Steadman Clinic in Vail, CO and formerly of the Harvard Medical School, *Wealth Protection Planning for Orthopaedic Surgeons and Sports Medicine Specialists* focuses on four concise lessons that may have a significant impact on your practice efficiency and long- term financial well-being. Featuring strategies for practice structure, tax and cost reduction, asset protection and building wealth in up, down and sideways markets, the book is structured in a Challenge-Solution format that allows you to focus on the areas you find most valuable.

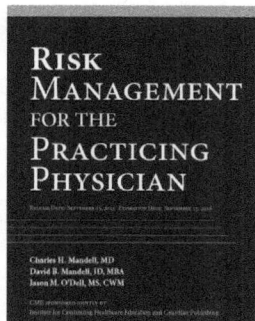

Risk Management for the Practicing Physician is nationally accredited for 5.5 hours of Category I continuing medical education (CME). Co-written by a practicing physician and an attorney and financial advisor, this 104-page monograph includes chapters on: providing care in today's malpractice environment, liability and the doctor-patient relationship, managing diagnosis-related liability, minimizing risks of miscommunication, managing high risk communication areas, managing the dangers of drug therapy, non-medical liability risks for the practicing physician, HIPAA risks, telemedicine liability and more.

Leaders in the world of wealth management reveal how affluent families build and maintain wealth in any economy. *Wealth Secrets of the Affluent* is the first book designed to help affluent families and their advisors take practical steps to build and preserve wealth. Filled with in-depth insights and expert advice, the goal of Wealth Secrets of the Affluent is to allow readers to make more informed financial decisions for building and preserving their various assets.

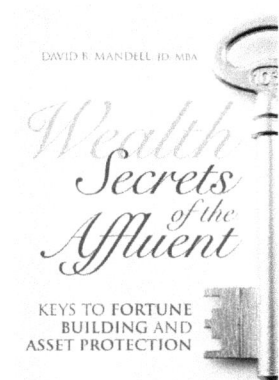

SCHEDULE A **CME** SEMINAR

Guardian Publishing's education experts have delivered seminars on asset protection, tax and estate planning that range from one to four hours for over 200 medical groups, associations, hospitals and organizations.

Guardian can provide the Category I CME enduring material Risk Management for the Practicing Physician to attendees, to provide a CME component. In some instances, seminars can be created to generate revenue for an association. In other situations, seminars can be arranged for only the costs of travel and materials.

Please complete the form and someone from our offices will contact you to go over the logistics of arranging this important seminar for you.

Name: _____

Specialty: _____

Address: _____

_____

City/State/Zip: _____

Phone: _____

Email: _____

____ Association   (name: _____)

____ Society   (name: _____)

____ Group   (name: _____)

____ Hospital   (name: _____)

____ Organization   (name: _____)

____ Other   (name: _____)

Tentative   Date   of   Presentation:

Location   of   Presentation:

Approximate Number of Attendees: _____

FAX to (866) 913-4911

REQUEST AUTHORS' ARTICLES
FOR YOUR PUBLICATION

The authors of Guardian Publishing have written eight books for physicians and have written articles for over 100 periodicals, newsletters and websites. The authors have also appeared on hundreds of radio shows and on Bloomberg and Fox television.

Guardian can provide the content to educational publications at no cost, provided the articles include by-lines that instruct readers how to reach the authors if they have questions or require some consulting assistance.

If you are interested in publishing articles by the authors on asset protection, practice management, retirement, insurance, tax and estate planning, please complete this page and fax it back to (866) 913-4911 and someone will contact you.

Name: _____

Specialty: _____

Address: _____

_____

City/State/Zip: _____

Phone: _____

Email: _____

I am interested in (check all that apply):

____ Articles   (magazine: _____)

____ Book Review   (title: _____)

____ Interview   (media: _____)

Target Audience: _____

FAX to (866) 913-4911